The Diaries of Me...
A Traveller

— ANDY FOSKER —

An environmentally friendly book printed and bound in England by
www.printondemand-worldwide.com

Mixed Sources
Product group from well-managed
forests, and other controlled sources
www.fsc.org Cert no. TT-COC-002641
© 1996 Forest Stewardship Council

PEFC Certified

This product is
from sustainably
managed forests
and controlled
sources

www.pefc.org

This book is made entirely of chain-of-custody materials

www.fast-print.net/store.php

The Diaries of Me... A Traveller
Copyright © Andy Fosker 2012

ISBN 978-178035-444-6

First published 2012 by
FASTPRINT PUBLISHING
Peterborough, England.
Printed by Printondemand-Worldwide

Acknowledgements

With sincere thanks:

To my niece Kat for all her help with typing, visuals and all things computer related.

To my niece Nicole and Sister June for their help in typing.

To my Sister Sandra for her expertise and guidance with the proof reading.

To my great friend Jonesy for allowing me to stay with him in Australia and allowing me to finish the manuscript in peace.

To Simon for planting the seed in my mind to travel in the first place.

And to Mum and Dad who supported me all my life. God bless you, I miss you.

Contents

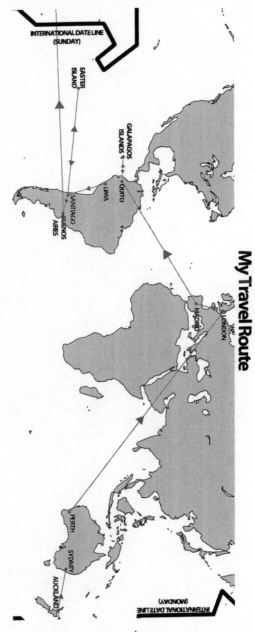

My Travel Route

INTERNATIONAL DATE LINE (SUNDAY)

EASTER ISLAND

GALAPAGOS ISLANDS

QUITO

LIMA

SANTIAGO

BUENOS AIRES

MADRID

LONDON

PERTH

SYDNEY

AUCKLAND

INTERNATIONAL DATE LINE (MONDAY)

And in the beginning...

It was a beautiful summer's afternoon, and what nicer way to spend it than with a good friend, sipping a few beers at a riverside pub? That was exactly what I was doing with my friend Simon, at the Swan Public House, Ash Vale on the Surrey/Hampshire border.

Simon had just sold his house, after splitting with his girlfriend, and had made a handsome profit on the original purchase price. He told me that he was considering taking a working break and travelling around the world, and asked me why I didn't join him?

Why? Well for one thing, I was a house owner with a mortgage, had a good full-time job that I enjoyed for the most part and well, at 41 years of age didn't have the advantage of Simon's younger years. Whilst it sounded a great adventure, my more cautious side told me to not get too carried away.

Anyway, as the afternoon progressed and over a few more beers, we began to discuss where we might travel, and what indeed we might get up to! We both worked in the travel industry, which is how we had met, when Simon worked for me whilst living in Ipswich. Our understanding of the travel business was obviously an advantage in this 'pipe-dream' and both of us had been watching the adventures of Michael Palin on television, as he re-enacted the famous 'Around the World in 80 Days' trip.

Back home in Ipswich and back to work, I couldn't help but keep thinking about the concept of such a journey. I was single, with no dependants, and after so many years of helping other people realise their travel dreams, why couldn't I maybe realise my own?

Money would be the first stumbling block to my dreams, but I did own a house, or rather, the Building Society who advanced my mortgage actually did. I calculated that if I was able to sell my house for a modest profit and cash in the endowment insurance policy I had linked with it, I might be able to afford to undertake such a trip.

That was obviously a key factor, but perhaps a bigger dilemma was my employment prospects after any such trip. I doubted whether my current employers would grant me a working break, as some companies were beginning to do, and at my age, it might be difficult to find a suitable job on my return.

I wrestled with these thoughts for a number of weeks and in the meantime, Simon had been offered a new job that he felt compelled to accept. The more I thought about things, the more I began to convince myself that if I was going to undertake such a career break, then now was as good a time as any. Small matters such as my health were conveniently brushed aside for the time being, and I instigated the first step of putting my house on the market.

My father had recently been diagnosed with prostate cancer and the prognosis for a full recovery was not good. I did not wish to add any stress to his condition, and in agreement with my mother and family, decided not to tell him my plans. Somehow, despite often walking past my house on his way to and from a social club that he frequented on Sunday lunchtimes, he seemed not to notice the 'For Sale' board on the edge of my property.

Nothing much happened in the way of offers despite an initial couple of views (I'm sure estate agents send their friends round to encourage you to stay with them) and the months slipped by, as did the Millennium celebrations. Dad eventually lost his battle with the cancer and died on 27th August 2000 (RIP), and still I had received no firm offers on the house sale.

I had been steadily using my travel experience to plot and research a route and had sought advice and help from a specialist travel agency based in London, whom I visited on a couple of occasions. With my knowledge and their help I was able to get a quote for the best airfares and for internal travel overseas.

Then out of the blue the estate agent (my third) called to advise me that they had received an offer from an interested party that exceeded my reserve price. It was now 15 months since I had first placed the house on the property market and at last it looked as if I could begin to finalise my plans. The sale was completed and the handover date was agreed.

My brother Pete had agreed that I could move into his house until I was ready to depart and fortunately, I didn't have too much in the way of posh, modern furniture (well, none actually) to store, so it was more a case of crockery, glasses and personal effects to put into storage at various places. Pete's and my best friend Carlton's lofts were kindly utilised. It's surprising how much 'stuff' you can accumulate in a relatively short space of time and that was just for me. It must be a nightmare for a family when moving home.

My employers were disappointed to lose me, but at the same time wished me luck and whilst being unable to hold my position open, encouraged me to contact them upon my return to see if anything was available. One of my colleagues, Anne, who was based in Scotland, was particularly interested in my trip and asked if she could accompany me on part of it during her annual leave. This would be great and we met to discuss dates and destinations. Anne would join me at the outset of my travels in Ecuador and stay with me through the Galapagos Islands and to the Inca Trail in Peru. This would mean that one of my big fears, namely how I would cope on my own in a foreign land with little or no Spanish language, the common language of many South America countries, would initially be shared.

The airfare was agreed and paid for and then began the task of sorting out the many, and in some cases painful, inoculations mandatory for travel to certain countries. These included Polio, Malaria, Hepatitis and Yellow Fever certification and the more common but equally important, Tetanus.

With these things underway, I then had to turn my attention to clothing and equipment. So many things to think about, and time beginning to run out until my departure date of 9th December 2001.

Planes, trains and oh... backpacks, etc.

I had been planning and researching my journey for over a year before I actually confirmed the flights. My many years of travel industry experience were used to good effect in reaching decisions; which places and attractions did I want to visit, and which friends and relatives? Using the answers to these questions, I was able to plot them onto a blank world map and begin to put together a route.

Climatic conditions should be taken into consideration, as seasonal weather can cause the closure of both natural and man-made attractions or, necessitate the use of special equipment and precautions.

There are a number of ways open to travellers for checking airfares. Newspapers have regular travel features, but undoubtedly the most popular methods are the internet and travel agents. Airline and travel websites have been continuously developed and improved, and quotes can be obtained either instantly or within a few hours. Travel agents have access to vast banks of data to help prospective customers, but not all have the expertise to be able to quote for a complex itinerary.

There are a number of 'specialist' agents, whose staff are experienced and knowledgeable in arranging independent travel arrangements such as mine. My intention was to travel for a year, commencing in Quito, Ecuador, and completing my journey in Mumbai, India.

An around-the-world (r-t-w) ticket allows you to travel from country to country, but is limited in the number of stops that you may make in total. The greater the number of stops, the greater the price of your ticket. Usually, such a ticket will also stipulate that you must only travel in one direction, i.e. easterly or westerly. This means that you cannot back-track or take side trips unless you purchase separate tickets. Fares, rules and routings are far too complex to discuss here, so an experienced travel agent would be able to advise you on the best fit for your needs, and probably save you some money at the same time.

The agent entrusted with my itinerary planning not only gave me excellent advice on fares, but also on land arrangements. These included travel, must-see attractions and accommodation. Perhaps the most useful for me was an approximation of the travelling times and distances between destinations. These are really important factors to be taken into consideration, as it is easy to seriously underestimate these when studying a map. This agent also handles visa applications and advice, as well as having an on-site medical centre able to ensure that the traveller has all of the necessary inoculations for travel to foreign climes.

Having taken care of the travel arrangements, well, for the time being, it was time to start thinking about other items on my list. Unlike a normal two-week holiday, where you pack enough clothes for a month, I would need to be very careful about what I packed and indeed, into what I packed it.

Whilst I wasn't going on a hiking holiday, there would be times when I would be doing just that. One of my foremost plans was to tackle the Inca Trail to Machu Picchu in Peru. A backpack therefore seemed like the most practical form of luggage to take. Remember, that whatever you put into your backpack, you must be able to carry comfortably. I found a number of websites with practical information about what to pack for a long trip, but one tip I was given by a seasoned traveller, is to take a change of underwear for each day of the week, plus one extra set. Hopefully you will be able to do your laundry at least once weekly! What have I let myself in for?

It was time to visit an outdoor specialist, so in the company of my sister Sandra and my mother, I did just that. This particular specialist was family-owned and the young chap who was helping me was one of the sons. He had travelled fairly extensively himself, and was most helpful with suggestions and advice.

It soon became evident that there is a plethora of equipment one could purchase, at varying costs, and it has to be said, quality. I did my best to tell him my itinerary and plans so that he could make suggestions suited to my perceived requirements.

As previously mentioned, I was not intending to do much camping, and I was given to understand that hostels provided bed linen. However, there would be occasions when I would need some form of bedding, so he suggested I try a sleeping bag. Many of the bags appeared to taper in towards the foot and I was going to need a large bag to fit my stout, (alright, overweight), body.

He provided the largest bag that they stocked and assured me that it folded into a relatively neat rolled package for carrying. Unzipped, I slid into the bag and then started to draw the zips upwards. As I reached level with my shoulders I began to have difficulty, especially not being double-jointed, and Sandra tugged the zips up and past my shoulders.

There I was a rather large caterpillar in my cocoon, unable to move my arms or turn in the bag. I also couldn't reach the zips and, as the assistant was helping another customer and Sandra had wandered off elsewhere in the store, I was rather helpless.

A surprised lady nearly fell over me, then smiled down at my by now very red, chubby face staring up at her. Not wishing to disturb me, she carefully stepped over me, and continued her browsing.

By now, as the temperature inside the bag was approaching critical level, a mild panic began to envelop me and I started wriggling, in the hope of moving myself into an area where I might be seen and rescued.

Fortunately, Sandra returned to release me and the assistant suggested an alternative, a thermal fleece blanket. This was lighter, more compact and could be zipped up like a conventional sleeping bag. 'Ching, Ching', a sale, and before I left, I had also purchased a medical kit complete with sterile needles, a micro-towel (about the size of a face flannel, that dries incredibly quickly and would suffice in place of a bath towel!), a folding cutlery set, a water bottle and a universal door lock. This last item is a small piece of metal that fits against the doorframe and ratchets shut to create a lock for any door. It's very handy for toilets - I'll have to start using it at service stations in the UK!

This left me with a backpack to purchase and this again proved to be more difficult than I anticipated. Having settled on a size deemed suitable for the task, the straps needed adjusting to be able to do up around my tummy. In fact I had to have an additional strap attached to allow this to happen!

This particular backpack had a detachable daypack that you were advised to carry your valuables in, and which you would carry in front, so that you could keep an eye on it and its contents. Good security advice I thought.

The bag felt heavy enough empty to me, so a number of items were added to give me an idea of what it would be like loaded. I could see a smile spreading across Sandra's face, and it did seem comical at the time, but seriously, this was going to take me completely out of my comfort zone.

I thought that this was it for the backpack, but not quite. What was now suggested was a waterproof backpack cover. I remembered now a book by Bill Bryson, where he was in a similar situation, and couldn't believe that backpack manufactures wouldn't make the actual backpack waterproof.

I couldn't either; let's face it, who uses a backpack indoors? Anyway, I ended up with an enormous poncho that covered both me and the backpack when carried. This sight was too much for Sandra and with tears running down her face, we left, with me kitted out and considerably poorer.

The remaining major item of essential equipment needed was a pair of sturdy boots. Because of a lymph gland problem in my left ankle that left with me with a permanently swollen left lower leg, I needed to purchase a size larger than normal with footwear.

I found a pair of boots with 3 removable inner-soles that would allow me to compensate for any slackness in the right foot. They came quite high up the calf and gave good support to the ankles. These were waterproof and could well be needed, as I anticipated that the Inca Trail in January would potentially be slippery and muddy and I would need to cross small streams at times.

They felt reasonably comfortable while padding around the shop, but they would need 'breaking in' properly for sure before my departure. Normally, you would be able to take boots back after a home trial, but as these were in a sale, there would be no such compromise.

My opportunity to road test these boots came sooner than I had expected. My friend George and my godson, Adam, were taking part in a charity walk called 'The Orwell 25', and I was invited to join them. We were going to attempt 12.5 miles, half the distance, although this was about 11.5 miles further than I had walked for some time.

The Orwell 25 follows the course of the River Orwell in Suffolk and finishes at Felixstowe on the coast. It is a combination of tarmac roads, public footpaths and the actual shore of the river, so potentially a good test of both boots and person.

Being late October, the weather had been pretty foul leading up to the day, but this could be a good simulation of conditions on the Inca Trail, well, except for the heat and altitude! I resisted the temptation to burden myself with a backpack - all in good time, eh!

Things went well for a while, but then my general lack of fitness began to tell, as did the chafing of my new boots on my calves in particular. I was just not used to wearing footwear that came so high up my legs.

The beginning of the end for me was when I needed to make a call of nature whilst using a footpath alongside a field. A handy hedgerow presented itself and for modesty, I ducked behind it to attend to matters at hand. Regrettably, I didn't allow for the wind direction and….yep, the strong gusts left me embarrassed! My also new khaki coloured zip-off trousers failed to hide what had happened, much to the great hilarity of George and Adam.

Now sore and soggy, I decided to call it a day at the next checkpoint, having completed 8.5 miles. I had until December 9th to rediscover the sort of fitness that the previous 25 years or so had ruined.

It's time to go.

The last few weeks preceding my departure were hectic. I never realised that I was so popular or was it that people just wanted to make sure that I actually left? Whatever, I was genuinely touched by the numbers of folk who wanted to wish me well and remind me what a lucky so and so I was to be able to take a year out to travel.

The final packing of my backpack caused me endless consternation. What to take and what not? What to put inside the pack and what to dangle from the outside? Eventually, at the 11th hour, and I do mean the 11th hour, I closed the zips and hefted the pack onto my shoulders.

My God, I fell backwards onto the bed like a helpless tortoise, with my arms and legs flailing. How on earth was I going to manage this journey when I couldn't even leave the sanctuary of my bedroom?

Peter, my big brother, had been kindly letting me stay at his home after the sale of my little house. The sale was necessitated by the need to have funds for the next 12 months' travelling.

Peter was going to take me to London Heathrow Airport for my departure, and sisters Sandra and June came along to provide some company on the return journey to Ipswich.

I was scheduled to fly first to Madrid on the national Spanish Airline, Iberia. Here I would spend a couple of days before starting my journey in earnest and flying onwards to Quito, the capital city of Ecuador.

Goodbyes said, I struggled to the Iberia check-in desks and deposited my backpack onto the scales. Boing! 42 lbs read the display. Just inside the 44lbs free luggage limit applied to my ticket. Good job my daypack was now slung over my shoulders, as this alone must have been a further 8lbs or so!

Everything seemed to be in order and I was able to proceed to the passport control area and go airside. This brings you directly into the duty free area first. Guess what the airport wants you do? That's right, spend lots of lovely money. I was carrying enough already and didn't need to be further hindered by the addition of booze, cigarettes or perfume.

My flight would be shown on the giant screen when boarding was due to commence, so I took a seat and waited. Airports are fantastic places for people watching, one of my favourite pastimes. The young and old, big and small, timid and loud were all on display. My favourite game was to guess the nationality of individuals. This was in the main an inexact science as I could hardly walk up to someone and question them as to their ethnic background. However, I did employ a form of stereotyping to a degree and this helped me to while away the time.

My departure gate was shown and I shuffled off for what turned out to be a long walk before reaching the correct area. Showing my ticket and passport I was then ushered into yet another seating area with a considerably large number of passengers. The business people were conspicuous by their briefcases and laptop computers, whilst the others were a mixture of returning Spaniards and tourists such as me.

Boarding commenced by row order with First and Business passengers in the vanguard and then passengers with small children and then, by allocated row. I was in no hurry to board and didn't bother to join the scrum that inevitably occurs at such times.

Being a large chap, I needed to ask for a seat belt extension to ensure I was safely strapped into my seat. I have always found this hugely embarrassing but in fairness to the cabin crew, they handled my request quietly and efficiently. (Got a big belt for this fat b*****d!).

The flight to Madrid was on the Spanish National Airline, Iberia. They were amongst a number of airlines that my 'One World' RTW ticket allowed me to use. This type of ticket had been recommended by my travel specialist and would allow me travel to three continents; South America, Australasia and Asia. Further, I would be allowed four flights within each continent, excluding the arrival and departure flight to that continent. Confused? You should be, but it worked out to be the best deal for my particular needs and intended itinerary

I arrived into Barajas Airport, Madrid on time and was soon through immigration control and waiting for my backpack to appear on the baggage carousel. This would be the first test of my 'extra' items attached to the backpack, namely a rolled up sleeping mat and my hiking boots. (I'm a real backpacker now!). As the backpack came into view the sleeping mat seemed to be missing. Lost an item already, I thought, but a few items later the missing mat appeared, still rolled and tied up. This was going to be something to ponder before boarding my next flight to Quito in Ecuador.

With all my gear reunited with me, I manfully and painfully hoisted the backpack onto my shoulders, attached the belts and staggered out through the 'Nothing to Declare (except perhaps 'I'm knackered!') Gate' into the Arrivals terminal.

I had discovered that there was an airport transfer bus into the city centre and looked for signs to that effect, and I was soon in a small queue of travellers waiting for the bus. I departed the bus at Plaza de Colon that seemed to be close to my pre-booked hotel, The Euro Madrid. However, as I yet again struggled into my backpack using a handy wall to rest it upon, I couldn't get my bearings and opted for flagging down a passing taxi.

He was perplexed, I think, as the hotel was indeed close by, but in the tradition of taxi drivers worldwide, he proceeded to take me on a longer route than was necessary as if to justify his time. I was just thankful to be there and waddled into the Reception, very nearly taking out the doors with my bag as I entered.

Safely ensconced in my room and free of the backpack, I slumped onto the bed and realised that I was sweating from the effort of carrying the bag. 9th December in Madrid wasn't boiling by any means, so how was I going to cope in warmer climes and with the prospect of high altitude conditions?

Madrid, as I am sure you are aware, is the capital city of Spain and not 'S' as in the capital letter of Spain! It has a population of 3 million plus and sits at 646 metres above sea level.

My hotel had been carefully selected for its location (as well as being very affordable) and after a rest I went for a short orientation of the immediate area. I was just off Calle Gran Via, a major through road in Madrid, and close to Puerta del Sol (Gateway of the Sun) and Plaza Major, both important and historic landmarks in the centre of the city.

Puerta del Sol was one of the gates around the walls of the city in the 15th century and is the starting point (0km) for all Spanish roads. Found within the square is the famous Bell Tower, whose tolling sees in the New Year and the tradition of the eating of The Twelve Grapes. A grape is eaten at every toll of the bell at midnight and is supposed to bring good luck and prosperity and ward off evil spirits. This is broadcast live on Spanish television every year. Most of my friends have twelve bottles of grapes every New Year!!

Plaza Major, a short walk from Puerta del Sol, dates from 1576 and is surrounded by three-storey buildings with some 237 balconies facing out onto the square. It has seen bullfights, soccer matches, and executions and is dominated at its centre by a statue of King Philip III. The festival celebrating Madrid's patron saint, Saint Isidro is held here annually.

One of the best ways to see a city is, in my opinion, to take a guided bus tour. This is what I did and in Madrid there are two routes that take in the main city sights. I always stay on for the entire route first and then when better orientated, decide where I want to hop on and off for longer visits.

It was a gloriously bright and sunny day but, being December, it was also somewhat chilly. I was on the open top deck of the bus, which afforded better photographic opportunities and at the same time put some colour into my cheeks! It was a good test of the new fleece jacket that would be my mainstay against any cold weather I would encounter on my travels. The tour also accounted for my first loss of the trip after just one day - my gloves, that I left on the bus, having taken them off to use the video camera.

The Palacio Real (Royal Palace) seemed a good place to start. This Palace has 3,000 rooms and yet is rarely used by the Spanish Royal family. When I think about it, our own Buckingham Palace is also rarely inhabited by the British Royal family.

Completed in 1764 on the instructions of Philip V, this impressive building is built almost entirely of granite and white Colmenar stone and surrounded by majestic gardens. Although there are various tours of the Palace throughout the day, it is subject in frequency to numbers, and a sign at the entrance advised that today's tour would be at 2.00pm. I decided to view other attractions and, if time permitted, to return for the Royal tour.

The world famous Prado Museum of Art was next on my list as I got off the bus at the wrong stop and had to walk a few blocks in the pleasant sunshine. This is Madrid's most famous attraction and home to works by amongst others, Diego de Velázquez and Francisco de Goya. These court painters' masterpieces dominate the first floor, which is considered to be the 'Principal' floor of the entire collection.

Let me be the first to admit that I am no art devotee and my knowledge is limited. Nonetheless, I felt it incumbent upon me to at least show some interest, having the opportunity to visit such an eminent venue. However, at the Puerta Alta de Goya entrance I was told that the Velazquez Rooms, considered the Prado's greatest attraction, were closed, and asked if it made any difference to my paying the entrance fee?

Well, of course it did! To an art connoisseur such as me, no visit to the Prado would be worthwhile without seeing the Velázquez Rooms. I thanked the attendant and refused a chance to purchase a book with prints of the famous works, as I had seen a similar book at a newsstand down the road at a cheaper cost.

The cold was beginning to get to me and so I found a café and ordered a 'café con leche' and a 'tortilla de patata' in my best Spanish. The waiter looked a little surprised, but smiled and went off. Must have been my excellent pronunciation, I thought. The coffee with milk was what I was expecting however, an entire potato omelette was not.

So that was what he had been smiling about? I had only wanted a slice, and my lack of passable Spanish was to be something that would continue to haunt me as the months in South America passed. To be fair, he did get me a slice, and then in near perfect English asked me if I would like some salad with it. Oh, how inadequate I felt. I had never had the opportunity to study Spanish at my school, only French, and this was no better, I can assure you.

That evening I read up on Ecuador and Quito, in particular, as I would be departing for that city the next day and the real start of my world tour. Excitement, trepidation and yes, the first feelings of homesickness were upon me as I settled back to watch Barcelona and Celta Vigo do battle in a live match on Spanish television before falling asleep.

Quito, Ecuador.

The flight from Madrid to Quito takes just under eleven hours and covers 5,434 miles (8,745kilometres). I spent this long journey in the company of a young Dutch girl by the name of Mikia. She was travelling to stay with her Ecuadorian friends and would be met at the Mariscal Sucre Airport in Quito.

The flight departure was delayed for two and a half hours and Iberia's economy legroom left me feeling slightly cramped by the time we touched down in Quito at 7.15pm local time, which is minus five hours GMT.

The flight had been very busy with lots of Ecuadorian families returning home for the Christmas holidays, as was evidenced by the large parcels and gift-wrapped items being carried off the aircraft.

I was aware that Quito is the second highest capital city in South America at 2,850m above sea level and had been warned that I might experience oxygen deprivation (or altitude sickness to you and me).

Collecting my backpack from the luggage carousel, all I experienced was muscle failure at lifting it onto my back! I saw quite a few other backpackers who didn't appear to be struggling with their loads. I couldn't help noticing that their packs didn't look as large as mine and certainly looked more used than my new and rather stiff backpack. The other noticeable feature of these folk was that they were also somewhat younger than me!

I had pre-booked a hotel in Quito, the Hostal Plaza International, for three nights initially and decided that a taxi would be the best means of getting me there. The airport is about five kilometres north of the city but I had not been able to establish relative costs of taxi fares in advance.

As I emerged into the arrivals hall, more like a large shed, I was assaulted by a frenzied mob of small, swarthy local men trying to interest me in everything from a taxi to the purchase of locally made tourist tat.

Fortunately, my new friend Mikia and her local friends came to my rescue. They advised me to go to a desk in the arrivals hall that had the sign, 'Cooperatives Taxi'. Here you could book a registered taxi to your destination, pay them and receive a voucher to give to your driver. In this way no monies were exchanged with the driver who would only get his fare if and when he returned the signed docket.

This I did, and the fare was quoted as $4.00. Since 2000, the US dollar is the official currency of Ecuador. I was at least familiar with dollars, so was more able to convert prices back to sterling. A five kilometre taxi journey for about £1.50 seemed like a good deal to me.

I arrived at the Plaza International, a modest hotel, and my booking was retrieved without any problems. It was by now nearly 9pm and the receptionist, resplendent in stained off-white vest (what else!) advised me in faltering English that the restaurant was closed. Looking at his vest I could almost tell what the menu had been! Just as well that I wasn't feeling hungry I guess, and besides, I was feeling rather light-headed and sick. Perhaps the first effects of the high altitude had struck?

He showed me personally to my room although he did stop short of carrying my backpack. To be fair, it was almost as big as him and besides, I had started to become accustomed to it. (No, not really!).

The room was quoted as a standard en suite single. It had a bed, bedside cabinet, chair, toilet, washbasin and shower, and a large old looking television with what looked like a coat hanger as an aerial.

Thanking my host, I closed the door and collapsed onto the bed, at which point I realised I was still wearing my backpack. Falling sideways onto the floor and shrugging the pack off my shoulders, I felt incredibly dizzy and found my breathing becoming laboured. Wow, this altitude thingy was really strange, and I lay on the floor for some minutes before getting back to my feet somewhat unsteadily. The last time I had felt like this was the night of my farewell party and that had nothing to do with altitude.

I switched on the television and turned a dial that seemed to be the channel finder. Basically all channels seemed to be the same, a grainy, black and white picture with Spanish dialogue. Perhaps the television was also suffering from altitude sickness, or perhaps it was just my eyes.

I conceded defeat, cleaned my teeth with my precious bottled water (don't drink the local water) and retired to bed feeling wretched. Despite the feeling of nausea and breathlessness, I fell asleep fairly quickly.

My odyssey had begun in earnest. What would the future bring?

First Tentative Steps.

Waking and gasping for breath frequently, my first night's sleep hadn't been good. It was a most unpleasant sensation and I was actually glad when I felt that it was a reasonable hour to get up properly.

After a shave and a shower, and despite not feeling at all hungry, I went in search of some breakfast. Breakfast was included in the room rate and the breakfast room was situated at the rear of the reception area.

I found one other guest there at this time, yet another Dutch lady, here with her two small children to meet her husband who was working in Quito. I was by now feeling quite dizzy and nauseous, but forced down some incredibly strong black coffee and a slice of bread and some jam. The selection of cereals, fresh fruit, cold meats and boiled eggs would normally have been attacked with gusto, but not today.

A former work colleague of mine, Anne had been envious of my planned journey and asked if she might join me for a few weeks in South America. I was delighted to have some company, especially at the beginning of my journey. Anne's flight was due in today, but before I had a chance to check on her arrival and meet her at the airport as planned, she had arrived. Anne was a Training Advisor with TTC Training, as I had been, but based in Scotland. We had become friends and met a few times to plan the time that she would be here.

One of the destinations that we had both wanted to visit was the Galapagos Islands, lying on the Equator, 970 km west of the Ecuadorean coast. We had found a tour company called Angermeyer's Enchanted Expeditions, based in Quito, and had made a reservation with them for a five-day cruise commencing on 14th December.

Having paid a deposit, we had to find their office, pay the balance and collect our travel documents. It didn't look too far on the map so with plenty of water, we set out to find it. It was probably about a thirty-minute walk, but combating the effects of the altitude added probably a further twenty minutes to this time. It wasn't a cheap excursion by any means, but a once in a lifetime opportunity to see these unique islands and their equally unique wildlife.

Both feeling decidedly dodgy, we took a taxi back to the hotel and slept from 3pm until 8pm, before having a light meal at the hotel and retiring for the night.

The next morning we both felt somewhat better and after breakfast had arranged a tour of the city with a local taxi driver called Edwin, who Anne had met on her journey from the airport and who spoke good English. We agreed a price with Edwin in advance and he would not only drive us, but act as our guide.

We undoubtedly paid more than had we booked on an official sightseeing tour, but we also had the comfort and the one-to-one (or two) attention of our guide. Edwin seemed to know his history and we enjoyed a tour that took in the Cerro Panecillo, an area 183m above the city and with a giant statue of the Virgin de Quito. These huge statues are common in South America. The most famous is probably the statue of Christ the Redeemer above Rio de Janeiro in Brazil, which I hope to visit later in my odyssey.

Quito is set in a hollow at the foot of the volcano Pichincha at 4,794m and as I have previously stated, the city itself sits at 2,850m. This makes it the second highest capital in Latin America after La Paz in Bolivia at 3,558m, which is incidentally the highest capital city in the world.

Looking down at the old city of Quito, Edwin explained that it is a UNESCO World Heritage Trust site and is centred on the old Spanish colonial-styled Plaza de la Independencia. The new city is situated to the North and it is here that the majority of tourist hotels are to be found, together with restaurants. We could quite clearly see the wider avenues of the new city as opposed to the winding, cobbled streets of the old city that we traversed on our journey to the Panecillo.

Edwin took us down into the old city and we walked through Plaza de la Independencia. The Cathedral that dominates the square has plaques on its outer walls listing the names of Quito's founding fathers. Everywhere were street traders and locals just either sitting talking or promenading.

One block's walk took us to the Jesuit Church of La Compania. Its interior is one of the most ornate and richly decorated of any church in Latin America. Once inside past the armed guards, you can see the ten-sided altars and the gold-plated high altar and beautifully gilded balconies. Many of its most precious treasures are kept in a vault at the Banco Central de Ecuador and only see the light of day on festivals and special occasions. Now I understood the armed guards' presence.

Finally, we were taken to view the Museo de Arte Colonial, a 17th-century mansion, where Edwin explained that the small collection of paintings and sculptures here were all Ecuadorean. As on my visit to the Prado in Madrid, they looked impressive and old but were somewhat beyond my real interest. I am not a cultural moron, I promise! I can appreciate their beauty or otherwise without going into raptures, that's just me.

On the way back to the hotel, Edwin was trying to persuade us to let his cousin drive us to Banos, our next intended destination after our side trip to the Galapagos Islands. Easier and more comfortable, he enthused, but we quibbled at the cost and the fact that his cousin did not speak such good English, and finally that he wanted money up front for petrol and other costs.

We agreed to let him know our decision after sleeping on it and arranged that his cousin would take us to the airport in the morning for our early departure to the airport and the Galapagos Islands.

In Darwin's Footsteps.

Our flight from Quito's Mariscal Sucre Airport to Guayaquil and then onwards to Baltra Island, departed at 7.30am. We had arranged with Edwin to have us collected at 5.15am from The Hostal Plaza International so that we would be in plenty of time to check-in.

It was as well that we had allowed extra time for this transfer, as by 5.30am no taxi had arrived and calls to Edwin's mobile phone went unanswered. Whether he had decided that he was not going to get any more money out of us we didn't know, but we needed to get to the airport, so asked the hotel to call us another taxi. That made up our minds, and we decided there and then to make our own way to Banos and we never heard from Edwin again. Perhaps it was a good thing that we hadn't parted with any cash up front as he had been keen for us to do.

We checked in for our flight and found four other girls, three Dutch and one French girl, who were also travelling to the Galapagos Islands and were on the same tour as Anne and me. The flight aboard TAME (Transpores Aereos Militares Equatorianos), the national airline of Ecuador, was rather cramped, but also thankfully short.

We arrived in Baltra at 9.45am where a strict immigration service and inspection takes place. You can even have your passport stamped with the official Galapagos Islands stamp even though the islands are part of Ecuador. This was a must as far as most visitors were concerned, and a nice memento.

It was then a short bus ride to the dock and then the equally short ferry ride to Isla Santa Cruz, before a bumpy, sweaty and dusty drive to Puerto Ayora. On route we stopped off to have our first views of one of the Galapagos's most famous inhabitants, the giant tortoises. I had seen a couple of these lumbering beasts whilst in the Seychelles Islands some years before, but here they were dotted about all over the place as opposed to being in a caged run. They actually move faster than you would give them credit for, as anyone who has had a tortoise for a pet will testify.

On arrival in Puerto Ayora we were met by our naturalist guide, a guy called Juan.   He was very good looking (I suppose) and Anne hoped that he might be a naturist guide and not a naturalist guide! He took us first to the Charles Darwin Research Station and the Galapagos National Park Headquarters. Here we were able to see the conservation work that is undertaken by a dedicated team made up primarily of volunteers.

Charles Darwin arrived on the Galapagos in September 1835 aboard HMS Beagle during the English Navy's struggles with the Spanish Armada. He spent 5 weeks on the islands visiting San Cristobal, Floreana, Isabela and Santiago, collecting samples and studying the creatures that roam, swim and fly around the islands. It was from these studies and particularly those of the finches, who had adapted perfectly to their individual environments that he presented his 'Origin of the Species', the work that so dramatically challenged and changed Western thoughts on nature's development.

One of the rarest animals in the world resides at the Research Station. 'Lonesome George' is the last surviving giant Pinta Island tortoise and is estimated to be 90 years old. Despite the addition of two 'foxy' female tortoises to his pen and the production of eggs, as yet none have hatched. The staff still hopes that he can become a dad, however, so go on George, show them that there's life in a 90 year old yet!

A large 3-D map display showed us clearly the islands that we would be visiting during our 5 day cruise and the wildlife that we could expect to see. It is from these buildings that all tours of the islands are controlled and monitored. To ensure that the islands' delicate ecological balance is not interrupted and that breeding seasons are strictly observed, all cruise ships are given routes that they must follow. In this way controlled landings are made on the individual islands to the benefit of both the wildlife and the visitors. Nothing worse than taking photos of unique species in their natural environment, only to have them spoilt by the legs or worse, of a gaggle of tourists. This would appear to be a problem that is occurring all too often on African Safari holidays, and is one of the downsides of mass tourism.

We used a small tender to transfer to our vessel for the cruise, the 'Sulidae'. The 'Sulidae' was a small, gaff-rigged motor/sailed ketch and Anne and I had chosen this particular vessel for its traditional look. With a maximum capacity of 12 passengers in six air-conditioned double berth cabins, five of which were en suite, it gave us a feeling of intimacy that we felt might be lacking on some of the larger vessels available. As it transpired, there would be just the 6 of us plus Juan, a captain, a cook and one sailor.

All meals were included in the cruise cost but our first meal was ashore at a delightful local restaurant overlooking the bay. This was definitely one of the advantages of being on such a small vessel. As we ate and became better acquainted, the crew made ready to sail overnight to our first island, Floreana.

The cabins may have been advertised as being air-conditioned, but mine certainly wasn't, and I just had to get out on deck as we sailed through the night to Isla Floreana. This was fantastic for some time, with a cooling breeze, the stars for a blanket and the gentle creaking of the boat and the lapping of the waves against the hull. (This is beginning to sound like Mills & Boon novel!). As the 'Sulidae' was using its sails to take advantage of the breeze, there wasn't even the throb of the diesel engines to disturb my thoughts. I was soon asleep and having sweet dreams, but was rudely awoken and then driven inside by the whining of mosquitoes.

Breakfast was served aboard whilst we were at anchor off Floreana and was a combination of cereals, fresh fruit, bread and jam. I was feeling particularly hungry that morning and ate well. An onboard safety talk was given by the captain, translated by Juan, and we were shown the scuba and snorkelling equipment that we would be free to use during the cruise.

We used the outboard dingy to be ferried ashore, as the landing at Floreana was off the beach. My weight was a consideration in the loading of this small craft from the deck of the 'Sulidae', and my fellow passengers showed some trepidation as I clambered aboard as delicately as possible and tried not to literally rock the boat. First drama averted...phew!

Floreana is most famous for being the first island in the archipelago to be settled in 1807 by an Irishman Patrick Watkins. He had been marooned at sea and survived for two years by growing vegetables and trading them with passing whaling ships that had been using the islands as way stations on their long voyages that lasted many years. He eventually stole a boat and together with some other deserters, set sail for the Ecuadorian coast some 600 miles (1000 kilometres) away. Apparently he was the sole survivor to reach Quayaquil on the coast.

At Post Office Bay there is a wooden barrel mailbox where you may leave postcards and letters. The whalers left a wooden barrel as an unofficial post office with their mail in it and other passing seafarers would sort through it and take them with them for delivery at some distant point in time.

This tradition still exists today and visitors can leave their stamped mail here for others to take and post as appropriate. I left a card for home in the barrel and took another addressed to people in Coventry, England to post when back on the mainland. I hope that theirs arrived safely, as mine did to my family in Ipswich, England.

We had time to snorkel off the beach in the presence of inquisitive sea-lions and a myriad of colourful tropical fish. Juan took us on a walk and we came across a pair of mating turtles. This act takes place in the ocean and can last for several hours as the male mounts his partner and basically hangs on for dear life. I don't know if this particular couple were having a lovers' tiff, but she was constantly rolling back and forth in the surf as if trying to unsaddle her mate. Further along the beach, a beached turtle lay seemingly exhausted in the surf. Must have been one hell of a session, we thought!

Later we saw the infamous and quite unique 'Blue Footed Booby'. These large birds display their feet during the mating ritual and the bluer the feet, the more attractive they are to prospective partners. It gives a whole new meaning to 'watching a blue movie' I suppose!

Back on the 'Sulidae', the cook had made us a marvellous chicken curry meal. I did wonder about the Boobies, but less of my perversions! As we set sail for another overnight sailing to Isla Espanola, we sat on deck and chatted and watched the Frigate birds, so populous here, following the ship to see if they could glean any food scraps. I guess they are the equivalent of our more common seagull in the United Kingdom. We even had the company of a pelican who sat quietly on the deck rail beside a large (very) hand of green bananas.

We awoke to a murky and misty morning off the Isla Espanola. It soon improved however and we were able to use the larger tender to ferry ourselves to the island and a small concrete pier.

We had landed at Suarez Point and the pier had been taken over by sea lions that didn't have the least care about our presence in their world. Stepping over these creatures, they literally posed for our camera shots. We saw any number of albatross gliding around, but as Juan explained, these were Waved Albatross, not Common Albatross. (Like we had a clue!)

The island is only 23 sq. miles and its highest point is only a modest 675ft. From Suarez Point we were taken on a gentle hike and the humidity had now increased as the sun burnt off the mist. We spotted the number one predator on the islands, a Galapagos Hawk, which was calmly tearing apart and devouring its prey. Top of the food chain here, Juan remarked, with no other natural enemies. We came to a place up on the cliffs from where we would be able to see a blow hole spraying water in large plumes, and providing some spectacular photo opportunities.

After lunch on board 'Sulidae' we had an opportunity to snorkel off the dinghy. It was one thing getting into the water but quite another getting back out again. I really struggled to heave myself back onto the dinghy without capsizing it. Juan hauled me over the side eventually, and

I lay exhausted like a hooked fish on the floor in a puddle of water.

It had now become very hot and we were taken to the other side of the island to Gardner Bay to swim and relax on the beach alongside the sea lions. Small furry sea lion pups were so adorable and made almost mewing sounds as they awaited the return of their mothers who were out fishing for their youngsters.

The next morning we were at Isla Santa Fe after yet another overnight cruise. We still hadn't seen any other boats and yet Juan assured us that there were many being directed carefully around the archipelago from The National Park Headquarters on Santa Cruz. This really confirmed the care with which tourism is controlled here.

Here we saw our first Land Iguanas, large lizard-like creatures with fearsome-looking claws, but with absolutely no fear of human beings. Unlike the sea lion pups however, you wouldn't want to pick these up and cuddle them. The Marine Iguana is unique to The Galapagos and this reptile has developed the ability to survive and forage for food at sea and is distinct from the Land Iguana by its red colouring (and the goggles and snorkel it wears!).

In the shallows of the bay we saw a number of white tipped reef sharks. Not surprisingly, none of us took up Juan's offer to do some snorkelling, despite his assurances that we would be perfectly safe with them.

A hike to the cliff top presented us with some stunning views and I was enthralled by watching and videoing a sea lion trying to land on the rocks below despite the heavy surf it was encountering. Time and time again it seemed to be defeated by the crashing waves, but eventually it succeeded and I found myself whooping and encouraging it, so caught up was I by the experience.

We day cruised to Islas Plaza, or South Plaza to be precise, a journey of about two and a half hours. This small island lies off the East coast of Isla Santa Cruz and like the others in the archipelago, was formed by volcanic eruptions. The island is covered with Opuntia cacti, and it is from these that the Land Iguanas get their water. It also has one of the largest colonies of sea lions of any of the islands. I passed on the opportunity to snorkel off the dinghy, instead helping Juan to haul the girls aboard. (Good job if you can get it!).

Talking to Juan as we floated around, I realised how much knowledge this guy actually had to have on all of the fauna and flora of the Galapagos and as a local, how proud he was of these enchanting islands.

As it was our last night aboard 'Sulidae', our chef had prepared a gala dinner for us and we enjoyed a sumptuous feast, with wine, beer and even an island-shaped cake. (Well it looked like an island to me). We sang along to some Beatles music and recalled the individual highlights of our Galapagos experience.

We were up at 5.30am to see in a beautiful dawn and a dinghy ride through mangrove islands to a spot where Golden Rays swam around us in the still, clear waters. After breakfast we said our goodbyes to the crew and Juan, and our Galapagos Island trip was over.

We arrived back at Quito at about 3pm and checked in again to the Hostal Plaza International for one more night. We met our new friends from our cruise for dinner before an early night and the next leg of our Ecuadorian journey.

Quito, Banos and Cuenca.

In trying to formulate a route to take in as much of Ecuador and Peru as possible whilst Anne was with me, we had spent time studying a couple of guidebooks on South America prior to leaving the U.K.

There was nothing particularly scientific about our research methods. We started off by trying to list our respective must see destinations and attractions and then mapping these to see the feasibility of actually being able to visit them.

We had identified the Galapagos Islands and had succeeded in marking that one off. Another must see/do for both of us was the Inca Trail and the lost city of Machu Picchu in Peru.

Just by looking at a map it became clear that we were going to be undertaking a considerable distance and that timing would be tight as Anne had to catch her return flight to the U.K. from Lima, Peru on 8th January.

After the Galapagos, that left us nineteen days to achieve our objectives. Anne also had a desire to spend a few days in the Amazon rainforest of Peru before flying home, so again this needed to be taken into consideration.

We could have flown but this would increase our costs and deny us the experience of overland travel and seeing other points on the way. We had worked out a rough route that would take us to the small town of Banos in Ecuador, then onto Cuenca also in Ecuador, before crossing the border into Peru.

It sounded feasible and so with that rough plan in place, here we were. Since I had left the U.K. on the 9th December, Anne had made a booking with a local travel agency in Cusco, Peru, for a two-day Inca Trail hike commencing on the 2nd January. We therefore had a deadline to work to, so now it was a case of adding detail to the rough plan.

As our 'friendly' taxi driver, Edwin, had obviously decided we were not for ripping off and had made no further contact, we found out that there was a bus from Quito to Banos via Ambato, which left from the main bus station daily.

We were advised that it took about three hours give or take to Ambato, where we would easily connect to Banos. The way in which they had said 'easily' should have maybe aroused suspicion, but at the time it didn't.

The bus was scheduled, a word not commonly used with South American transportation, to leave at 8.45am and we arrived in plenty of time to buy our tickets. This was again easier said than done and we were grateful to a student behind us in the queue for his translation services.

The bus departure was relatively punctual and we boarded with our backpacks as there didn't seem to be any viable option, besides it soon became obvious that anything, and I mean anything, goes on Ecuadorian buses.

As the bus headed out of Quito, the temperature was beginning to rise, and as the bus filled up at successive stops the air inside the bus began to become more fetid. Not only was overcrowding tolerated by the driver, so was the carrying of livestock. I have seen this depicted in films but here it was happening for real. A lady boarded with a large sack over her back that was wriggling and moving of its own volition. Whatever was inside was very definitely alive, possibly a child, I couldn't guess.

Various vendors boarded and squeezed their way down the bus offering food items and drinks to the gasping passengers only to disembark some miles further down the road when they had sold all their supplies.

Another temporary visitor to the crowded bus was some form of Christian or Political commentator who, with a captive audience, proceeded to preach his message to anyone who cared to listen. He handed out some leaflets and eventually also disembarked in the middle of nowhere!

The air quality was getting worse and I was adding to this by sweating profusely. Suddenly, all hell broke loose on the bus. People began shouting and screaming and climbing over other people onto the seats. What was happening? That sack apparently had been full of live guinea pigs, either bound for or coming from market. The lady owner was now in a desperate search to recapture her escaped cargo. Guinea pigs are a much sought after delicacy in Ecuador and Peru so there was probably a fair amount of money running loose in that bus. I just couldn't help but laugh and thought that perhaps they were little 'piggy banks'!

The panic eventually subsided and gradually the passenger numbers dwindled and we could feel some air coming in through the windows. I had read somewhere that Latin American buses were 'delightfully decrepit' and this one lived up to this description, as it creaked and shook its way to Ambato.

Ambato is known as the city of fruit and flowers, situated as it is in the heart of fertile orchard country. The driver ushered us out of the bus at a point some way from Ambato's centre as he had told us that this would be where the Banos bus would pick up from.

It was now past midday, hot and dusty, and there didn't seem to be anyone about to ask for further directions. Ambato had been almost completely destroyed by an earthquake in 1949 and certainly this part of it looked to me as if it hadn't been rebuilt since then.

Just as we were thinking that we had been dumped in the wrong place, a bus came into view with the legend, 'Banos' upon its front. We showed the driver our tickets and he gestured us aboard. Grateful to be out of the sun we slumped down for the supposedly short one hour journey to Banos.

We were travelling through the area of Ecuador known as the Central Highlands and there are numerous national parks and hiking trails into the mountains to be found here. The scenery was certainly more pleasant and Banos promised a great setting.

We checked into our pre-booked accommodation, the Hostal Culture, with a stunning view towards the Manto de la Virgen waterfall. This waterfall at the south-eastern end of Banos has become a symbol of the town.

Whilst at the Plaza International in Quito we had befriended a Canadian brother and sister duo called Jason and Pam, and established that they would be in Banos at the same time as ourselves. We had arranged to meet them and that evening had a pleasant dinner together at one of the many restaurants in Banos.

Banos sits between the Rio Pastaza and the Tungurahua volcano and is famous for its thermal baths. These have helped give Banos a spa town feel and much needed tourist income. It is also popular with hikers and climbers and also attracts a number of pilgrims visiting the Basilica, where they can view the paintings of miracles performed by Nuestra Senora del Agua Santa (who?). The miracle is being able to pronounce her name!

We took a walk across the river and up a steep and fairly narrow track that was frequented by locals and their donkeys hauling goods to their homes beyond the town. We were rewarded with some fabulous views across the ravine to the town below but I was completely knackered and glad to return to the hostel for a shower and a rest before dinner.

The next day we were travelling onwards to Cuenca, Ecuador's third largest city and reputedly one of the most splendid. The journey involved a return trip to Ambato and then an onward long journey to Cuenca. Our bus left Ambato at 1.30pm and eventually rolled into Cuenca's bus terminal at 8.30pm. What a long time to be trapped on an Ecuadorian bus!

We took a taxi to our pre-arranged hostel but neither of us liked the look of it from the outside and walked around a bit until we found a nicer looking hotel on a main street called the Chordeleg. They only had a twin room available but at this stage we were too tired to be bothered and agreed to the $12 per person fee. This did include breakfast however, so not too bad.

The room was huge and so we had our privacy anyway. We were both so tired that neither of us could be bothered to go in search of food even though we had last eaten at 7am that morning.

Early the next morning we were awoken by the sound of traffic and looking out of the windows we realised we were overlooking one of Cuenca's main thoroughfares and traffic was heavy. Virtually every vehicle appeared to be a large yellow taxi and the use of the horn was obviously a favourite, even though nothing was moving!

There was no point in trying to sleep any longer, and besides I for one was ready to eat a rabid horse, so breakfast won out over sleep. After refuelling, we took an exploratory walk and found a travel agency where we enquired about the possibility of flights to take us to Trujillo in Peru.

We had identified this town as a good spot to spend Christmas and had also found accommodation run by an English chap married to a Peruvian lady. Unfortunately, being the Christmas holiday period, all flights were full and so we were left with the prospect of two very long bus journeys and with having to negotiate the Ecuadorian/Peruvian border.

Cuenca was proving to be a delightful old city and its grand Spanish colonial buildings, one of which we were staying in apparently, had gained UNESCO World Cultural Heritage status since 1999.

Just a few hundred yards from our hotel, and visible by hanging out of the window and looking to your right, was the huge white church of Santo Domingo. This church had a huge statue of Christ dominating its façade and at first I mistook it for the Catedral de la Immaculada, so impressive did it look.

Cuenca is Ecuador's third largest city and sits on the banks of the Rio Tomebamba. It was built upon the site of an Inca city ordered to be built under the rule of Tupac-Yupanqui, one of the more powerful Inca warlords. This city, then known as Tomebamba, was so magnificent that it rivalled the imperial capital of the Inca people at Cusco.

Its decline is shrouded in mystery however, and by the time that the Spaniards arrived in 1547 it lay mostly in ruins. Only a few excavated walls, uncovered near the river, remain of the original city.

We wandered around the city and experienced our first 'menu de hoy' (menu of the day). We enjoyed a set lunch of fruit juice, a thin vegetable soup and bread, boiled rice and beef and banana fritters to finish, all for $1.50. This was excellent value and these set meals are well worth looking out for. The other advantage was that we were eating with local people and were able to talk a little with them. They seemed equally pleased that we were eating with them as opposed to finding one of the many tourist restaurants. Someone once told me that if the food is good enough for the locals then it is good enough for you - sound advice, I'd say.

After more wandering and sightseeing, we stumbled across a Nativity Parade featuring hundreds of school children. With Christmas approaching and being a heavily Catholic country, these parades are apparently quite common. The children were accompanied by proud camera and video toting parents and seemed to be enjoying the occasion, judging by the laughter and sheer joy that they exhibited. It made me think of home and family Christmases, despite the fact that the temperature was approaching 30C.

We finalised our bus schedules for the onward haul to Huaquillas, the Ecuadorian/Peruvian border, and then onwards from Tumbes to Trujillo. We were going to have to catch a bus at 5.40am the next morning and would most likely be travelling until well into the evening before arriving at our destination. A nice dinner and an early night were needed as we pondered what excitement the next twenty four hours would provide.

Cuenca to Trujillo.

We checked out of the Hotel Chordeleg at 5am after an early breakfast that they had left out for us by prior arrangement. The bus to Huaquillas and the Ecuadorian/Peruvian border left at 5.40am from the nearby central bus station.

The journey was spent mainly in slumber and we arrived at Huaquillas at 10.30am. Our backpacks had been strapped securely (we trusted) on the roof of the bus. We waited for them to be lowered (thrown actually) from the roof storage space and were immediately engulfed by hordes of men all offering to carry our bags, give us directions, and get us to exchange currency.

Hands were grabbing everywhere and it very quickly became quite scary. Ann may be a slight lady, but she is quite feisty. Even so, it was worrying to almost lose her in the scrum of bodies around us. Refusing help politely just wasn't working and as we were getting ready to become more forceful, two young lads approached speaking very good English. They were obviously known to most of the mob and seemed to restore some order to proceedings.

They explained that we would need to have Peruvian Soles, as US dollars were not accepted here. I didn't have many dollars at all as I had a problem using my bank card to access money from ATMs and had only travellers' cheques. Anne had more dollars and we were ushered to a chap armed with a calculator and wads of currency.

In hindsight we were so naïve. We really hadn't researched this eventuality or seen the warning signs. Tapping into his calculator he showed us a figure for exchange. Neither of us really knew what rate we could expect not having anticipated being faced with a transaction out in the open. We were both wary but agreed to exchange a small sum each, and in my case, very small.

This chap would have done credit to a professional card sharp as without doubt he palmed some of the notes that he was counting out for us and, as we thought of afterwards, the calculator was probably fixed to display an amount in their favour. Anne was encouraged to change more as, with it being the 22 December and with Christmas approaching the banks would be closed.

The transactions completed, our two boys said they could see us safely through the market place of Huaquillas, and onwards by taxi to catch our bus from Zarumilla for a fee of $20 for them and $20 for the driver. It was a pretty hostile environment and we decided it may be the best of few options. A small cart appeared and we were told to put our backpacks onto them. We did so, keeping our day sacks close to our chests and began moving off through the throng of stalls, vendors and lots of people going about their daily business.

We got to the Ecuadorian border office and insisted on taking our backpacks inside with us as we were stamped out of Ecuador. Once outside again, our boys explained congenially that the Peruvian border office was located four kilometres away and that they had a taxi (unofficial) that would drive us across the neutral zone to it, wait, and then take us on again to Tumbes and not Zarumilla as, according to them, our onward bus had already departed from Zarumilla bus station.

The driver was an older chap and seemed to speak very little if any English. In fact he spoke very little at all. The backpacks had to go in the boot space and Anne sat between our two boys in the rear and I sat upfront with the driver, whom I nicknamed 'Smiler'. The boys kept up a genial conversation with us as far as the Peruvian Immigration Post. We did not want to leave our backpacks in the car with the driver and so, in a moment of genius or bravado, I grabbed the keys from the ignition saying I would look after them until we returned.

Formalities completed we returned to the car and the keys were returned to Smiler. We drove out further into No Man's Land, at which point the car stopped on a bridge. Our boys calmly said that they had to return to Ecuador as they would have problems crossing back into the country if they went further, but that the driver would take us to Tumbes as agreed. In hindsight they were probably known to the police and feared possible arrest, although I feel sure a few dollars would have eased any problem.

They wanted their cash and it was then that they said that surely it was worth more than $20 for their trouble. We argued but eventually gave them $20 each, mainly to get rid of them, and with a smile they left. Nice little earner for them I guess, but at least we still had all our gear and the car and Smiler to take us to Tumbes.

As we drove on into Peru he seemed almost ashamed of his part in the whole transaction and just said "too much" as we swore openly about his mates. As we were driving, we saw a bus coming from the other direction and saw it was the bus for Trujillo. This was strange as that bus had supposedly already departed from Zarumilla, so we made Smiler turn around and take us back in pursuit of the bus. At Zarumilla bus station Smiler, perhaps in an act of contrition, went with Anne to the ticket office and, once she was assured that it was our bus and had purchased two tickets for 50 soles each, we took our backpacks, paid him his $20, and he left.

I don't know about Anne, but I felt drained as we boarded the bus for Trujillo. The border experience was not one that I would wish to repeat. I am just thankful that we had not been physically mugged or lost any of our belongings. We are fairly sensible people and older than many of the backpackers who will negotiate this particular border crossing. However, if you are unprepared and naïve then there are always people who will try to take advantage of you. Another lesson in life and travelling learned.

We were now travelling on the Pan-American Highway that runs North-South, hugging the Peruvian coast. The road has a fairly good surface, and work was being undertaken to improve some parts, but it is no European motorway, let me say. We had left Zarumilla at 12am and anticipated a twelve hour journey before arriving at Trujillo. Nothing for it other than to sit back, sleep, read and look out of the window.

Two lads from Hungary were also travelling on the bus, and they told us that they hadn't had quite the drama that we had experienced at the border, but that they had certainly been pestered. We were a softer target undoubtedly!

They were going to Huaraz and the Cordillera Blanca, arguably Peru's most beautiful area with wonderful lakes, snowy mountain peaks and wonderful hiking opportunities. It was an area that we had identified as a potential 'must visit' at our planning stage, and I would have liked to have seen the pre-Inca sites at Chavin de Huantar, reputedly over 3,000 years old. However, it just didn't fit into our time frame and the boys told us that they planned to spend about three weeks in this area alone. They left us at the town of Pativilca and we continued on our hot and dusty journey south.

It was at times like these that I wished that I had purchased a mini-disc player before leaving the U.K. My friend Semi had recorded some music discs for me that I had with me, but I had reasoned that I could buy the actual player cheaper at a duty free shop. This hadn't happened - in fact I hadn't even been able to locate a mini-disc player, let alone buy one, up to now. The hours passed and we stopped occasionally at some small town or other to collect new passengers, and so that the driver could rest and get a drink and a meal.

We had decided that when we reached Chiclayo, this was roughly three quarters of the journey, and we would try to contact our host in Trujillo, Michael, to advise him of our estimated arrival time. We warned him that it would be late, and he didn't seem bothered. Just knock on the door of his premises and he would get up and let us in.

I was continually struck by the ramshackle housing and seeming poverty of the towns we passed through. Whole families were sitting outside in the warm evening air where it was probably cooler than inside. I doubted if air-conditioning was affordable to these people and judging by my brief experience of South American television, they probably didn't think it worth watching anyway, assuming that they even had one. This was a complete eye opener to me and so different from our comfortable Western lifestyles.

It was past 1am when the bus entered the city of Trujillo. We wearily disembarked, retrieved our dusty backpacks, and found a number of taxis waiting for the arrival of this 'stagecoach' from the North.

We eventually found Michael's accommodation, and after a lot of knocking, roused him from his slumber. He showed us to our respective rooms, advised us that he would be off early in the morning, as he was an archaeological guide and had a tour to lead, and told us he would leave breakfast for us to have at our leisure.

Christmas 2001 in Trujillo.

Michael had left us breakfast as promised. There were fresh rolls, jam and marmalade, a flask of coffee and orange juice. The accommodation was fine but obviously a home for working people as opposed to a guest house, and letting the rooms supplemented their income. Michael's wife was away for the Christmas period visiting relatives so we would not have the pleasure of meeting her.

Still feeling shattered from our previous day's long journey, we lazed around until about 2pm, reading the notes on Trujillo that Michael had left for us. His brother-in-law owned a small restaurant across the road from our accommodation and we decided to visit this for lunch. The 'menu de hoy' was chosen, and was acceptable fare for a very modest outlay. The locals there seemed fascinated by our presence in this part of Trujillo, situated as it is a 20 minute walk from the centre. The young children in particular seemed curious and emboldened by our smiling demeanours, took great delight in patting my tummy and then giggling uncontrollably. This was to become something of a regular occurrence over the coming days and I suppose I didn't see many large local people about and certainly not many Europeans at this time, either.

Despite the very warm weather of nearly 30c, the Plaza De Armas (Main Square) was looking very festive. Christmas decorations and bunting hung everywhere, complete with reindeer and a Father Christmas. Local schools had been encouraged to add their own decorations and these were proudly displayed along with the placards of local businesses, which had provided sponsorship.

The centrepiece of the square is a large statue topped by a man holding a torch depicting liberty. The statue also represents agriculture, commerce, education, art, slavery, action and liberation. What a busy statue! The city of Trujillo was founded in 1534 by a Spaniard, Pizarro, after his home town in Estremadura. It has always had a reputation for being a hotbed of revolt and in 1820 it was the first Peruvian city to declare independence from Spain.

Fronting one side of the Plaza de Armas is the large and beautiful cathedral dating from 1666. This imposing building has the most unusual colour of any cathedral I have ever seen, being an almost mustard yellow with white relief. Also on the Plaza are grand Spanish colonial buildings in the form of the Hotel Libertador and the Universidad de la Libertad.

With over 300 days of sunshine and a pleasant daily temperature, Trujillo is known as the 'city of eternal spring' and is Peru's third largest. We took the opportunity of using an internet café that was packed with children playing games, and had to wait some time for a free terminal.

That evening we had the opportunity over drinks to get to know Michael a little better. He was originally from Birmingham but had been living in Peru for many years. His 'brummie' accent however, was detectable and seemed to grow stronger the more he talked. He invited us to join him the following day to visit the ancient adobe walled city of Chan Chan, where he was to give a guided tour to an English group travelling with Toucan Tours. A free tour to one of Peru's major archaeological sites is not to be sniffed at, so we gratefully accepted.

The remains of the imperial city of the Chimu people, Chan Chan, is the largest adobe city in the world. It covers 21km and consists of nine great compounds. Within these compounds they would have stored the agricultural wealth of the kingdom, which stretched 1000km along the coast from near Guayaquil in Ecuador to the Carabayllo Valley, north of Lima.

Each of the compounds had a burial mound for each of the respective Chimu Kings and their possessions and treasure. Much has been destroyed or stolen due to the ravages of time, weather and 'huaqueros' (grave looters). What has been found and can be seen, are some of the moulded decorations of fish and other animals on the walls and painted pottery of varying colourful designs.

It would seem that the Incas almost certainly copied the style of Chan Chan after the Chimu surrendered to them around 1471 after the city was under siege for 11 years. Similar large compounds can be found in Cusco, to which the last of the Incas retreated.

Michael knew his stuff alright but his delivery was rather monotone in his 'brummie' English and I wasn't the only one who was rather bored by the end of the tour. If that sounds mean-spirited, then it is not meant to be, as Michael was good enough to show us this remarkable site.

In the afternoon, after we had been to the bank and were once again solvent, Michael took us to see two pyramids dating to the Moche civilisation, which pre-dated the Chimu civilisation. These pyramids are known as Huaca del Sol and Huaca de la Luna (temples of the sun and moon). Excavation of these sites had only begun in the early 1990's and, since the Huaca del Sol had been partly destroyed and looted by the Spanish conquistadors in the 17th century, they had concentrated on excavation of the Huaca de la Luna.

It would seem that the Huaca de la Luna served a predominantly ceremonial and religious function, and we were able to see some of the richly decorated murals that have been uncovered. One in particular, known as 'Ayapec', was deemed of some importance, and is visible in a number of places. It is thought to be of an all-knowing deity revered by the Moche.

I was so tired that evening that, after a meal and a couple of glasses of wine, I wasn't even able to see in Christmas Day. Happy Christmas one and all, I miss you.

Christmas Day was a pretty quiet affair. After making a call to home to wish the family all the best, I did my laundry. Michael has a rooftop area where it is possible to hang your clothing to dry in the sun. Michael's dog also lives here and is tethered to a chain that allows him a reasonable amount of freedom.

After the initial barking, he settled down and I hung out my clothing. My stomach had been a little upset for the last day or so and I had a sudden violent stomach cramp. To my horror, I realised that I was not going to be able to make it to the first floor toilet and had no option other than to allow nature to take over. The roof area is completely private but I still felt incredibly vulnerable and embarrassed by what had occurred. I quickly went off to fetch a bowl of water and a broom to make good my actions. It was only a matter of minutes before I returned to the roof but could find no trace of the offending diarrhoea. Surely it couldn't have evaporated in the hot sun could it? It was then I realised that the dog was within roaming distance of my mishap! He seemed fine, but to this day I have said nothing to a soul about this most embarrassing of incidents. My conscience is now partially clear.

For the rest of the afternoon I just dozed and kept out of the sun. Michael's in-laws called around at about 6pm with a special fruit cake and hot chocolate as is the Peruvian Christmas tradition. Afterwards, Anne and I walked into the Plaza de Armas to view the Christmas

Parade and lights. We were surprised to find hundreds of families there and enjoyed a very pleasant couple of hours.

Boxing Day, 26th December and Michael had again kindly offered us an excursion to visit the temple of Huaca El Dragon (Dragon Temple), also known as Huaca Arco Iris (Rainbow Temple) after the shape of the friezes that decorate it. This partly restored site dates from AD1000-1470. It was then on to the temple complex at El Brujo, some 60km north of Trujillo.

This site, as with the others, was only partly excavated to date and already some fantastic friezes had been uncovered, and more were literally being unearthed weekly. Michael told us that the whole area needed UNESCO World Heritage Site status in order to gather a much needed cash injection to assist with archaeological work. It indeed seemed such a shame to have these potentially priceless sites as yet fully undiscovered.

We were able to go to the Linea Buses office in Trujillo and with Michael's assistance sorted out an overnight bus to take us to Lima the following day. The cost of 35 soles was more expensive than travelling by day; however, we would save on one night of accommodation cost, so it evened itself out.

We did little the next day other than visit the bank, as they were open again after Christmas. Everyone else had the same idea and we were there for nearly two hours just to change our travellers' cheques, which resulted in faxes having to be sent to their head office in Lima for authorisation.

Michel kindly drove us to the bus station to catch our bus for Lima that was scheduled to leave at 11pm. The journey was due to take eight hours but the bus was equipped with a toilet, which was as well as my stomach was still feeling poorly. When I eventually managed to get my seat to recline, I was able to get some sleep and the journey passed peacefully enough and we arrived in Lima at 7am, on schedule and just as the sun was rising.

Happy New Year.

We had pre-booked accommodation in Lima at the Hostal Mami Panchita. This hostel is owned by a Dutch/Peruvian couple and they also operate a travel agency from the premises. This was a plus factor, as far as Anne and I was concerned, as we still had some travel arrangements that needed to be made.

Our rooms were excellent - clean, bright and with plentiful hot water. This was the best accommodation that I had stayed in within South America so far. We sought out our host Toon, in his travel office, as he had arranged our return flights to Cusco. We were to depart the following day, spend New Year in Cusco getting used to the altitude and then depart on the Inca Trail for Machu Picchu on 2nd January.

Yes, the lost but now found city of Machu Picchu, the biggest single reason for my entire journey. I had been captivated by stories of, and documentaries on, the fabled lost city of the Incas for many years, and very soon I was to realise my dream.

Financial transactions completed, we went for a walk to look over the Pacific Ocean from the cliffs found along this part of the Lima coastline. It was only one block, however the mist we had been told about was omnipresent and blocked out not only the ocean but the sun. This reduced the temperature by a few degrees and it gave the atmosphere a moist and cool feeling.

I had not been happy with the walking boots that I had purchased and christened on the Orwell 25 Walk back in October, and had decided against bringing them with me. Virtually on the eve of the two-day Inca Trail hike, I now decided that I would indeed need something more robust than my training shoes for what might lay ahead.

We took a taxi to Plaza San Miguel where Toon had advised me that I would find a large shopping mall, and purchased a lighter pair of Hi-Tec walking boots. I put them on immediately and they felt pretty comfortable. They had better be, as I only had a few days to break them in before the big event.

After a siesta back at Mami Panchita and a meal at Pizza Hut (yes, that's right), we sat up on the hostel's roof terrace reading and writing postcards until sunset over the nearby Pacific. We had a 7am departure for the airport next morning so a good night's sleep was the order of the day.

Our flight with LAN Airlines departed on time at 9.10am and we landed in Cusco promptly at 10.45am. The tour operator with whom we had booked our Inca Trail hike met us from the flight, and drove us to our accommodation in Cusco, the Hostal Amaru.

This hostel is situated on a quaint, cobblestoned and very narrow, steep hill. The rooms were of typical Peruvian style with thick, white stone walls, and felt very cool. It was clean and each room had a television and private facilities. Once settled, we made our way down the hill into the Plaza de Armas where Andean Life, our tour operator, had its office.

Rather unsettlingly, they were closed for the rest of the day, but one thing that Cusco doesn't lack is travel agencies, so we had a number to choose from in gathering information on train and bus services to Puno, on the shores of Lake Titicaca, and Arequipa, from where I planned to fly back to Lima. I wanted to visit the floating reed islands on Lake Titicaca and visit the 'White City' of Arequipa after completing the Inca Trail. Anne had a desire to spend a few days in the Amazon Jungle, and was looking at these possibilities prior to flying home to Scotland on 8th January.

Considering that Cusco is 3,400m (11,200ft) above sea level, I was feeling remarkably well so far, with little effect from that altitude. With our travel arrangements completed, we had the opportunity to actually look around the Plaza de Armas properly.

It's more a rectangle than a square, and is dominated on the north-eastern side by the early 17th century Cathedral de Santo Domingo, built on the site of the Palace of Inca Kiswarkancha. Amongst its many fine artefacts, the Black crucifix of El Senor de los Temblores is revered all over Peru as a guardian against earthquakes. It is paraded each year in the Lord of Miracles Procession in October, in commemoration of the 1650 earthquake.

In the sacristy there are many valuable works of art, amongst them, the Pintura Senor de los Temblores, which is acknowledged as being Cusco's oldest surviving art work, and is attributed to the Dutch artist Van Dyke. (I thought he was in Mary Poppins!).

The two altars are both magnificent in their own right. The high altar, originally of cedar wood covered in gold flakes, was subsequently embossed in silver in 1803. The rear altar is carved from alder-tree (lambran) and is a classic example of Andean wood craftsmanship.

The Maria Angola Bell housed in the right tower of the cathedral is named after an Angolan slave who threw gold into the crucible where it was being made, it stands at 2.5m high and weighs 5980kg and it is claimed that it can be heard from more than 20 miles away. As it is cracked, it is only rung on special occasions nowadays.

On the south-eastern side of the Plaza stands the church La Compania de Jesus, built in the late 17th century on the site of the Palace of Serpents. The Jesuits wanted this to be the most beautiful church in Cusco, and its twin towers, facing the Plaza, are indeed most graceful and inside are yet more fine works of art and superb altars.

The other sides of the Plaza have Spanish colonial style balconied buildings, formerly mansions but now a collection of shops, restaurants and even an Irish Pub! It was in one of these restaurants that we dined before retiring back to the Amaru. It was as I was walking back up the hill to the hostel that I began to feel the effect of the altitude. My breathing, with the effort of a steep incline, had become much laboured, and I gulped down plenty of water when I got to my room.

Next morning after a simple breakfast of rock hard roll and jam, we went back to the Plaza de Armas to use an internet café that we had spotted the previous day. I was feeling decidedly dizzy and short of breath which, together with the heat (close to 30c) and humidity, was really draining.

Neither Anne nor I were particularly impressed with the Hostal Amaru or its location, and agreed to search out new accommodation. We found the splendidly named Colonial Palace had rooms available and after inspecting them, booked a twin share on cost grounds, for 31st December, 1st January and 3rd January. By then we would have returned from our two day Inca Trail hike to Machu Picchu.

New Year's Eve in Cusco seemed like any other day to me and after we checked out of the Hostal Amaru and moved into the Colonial Palace, we had a 'menu de hoy' at a restaurant on the Plaza de Armas. Although the meal was relatively meagre, we both struggled to eat it. Anne in particular was really feeling unwell with the altitude and returned to the hotel to rest.

That evening I sat in the room with a bottle of beer but just struggled to drink it and phoned home to wish my mother and sister a Happy New Year. It was lovely to hear their voices and for a while afterwards, I felt rather emotional and eventually fell asleep well before New Year actually arrived in Cusco.

The Inca Trail and Machu Picchu.

Anne, normally a sweet-natured lady, was not in a particularly good mood this morning. She had not slept at all well the previous night due to my snoring, and was up and about early, muttering and cursing me. Snoring is an unfortunate affliction that usually affects others rather than the perpetrator. This was obviously the case in this situation and, whilst I was apologetic, I didn't see what I could do to rectify it. (Who said, a pillow over the face?)

We went for a long walk around Cusco and found it to be relatively quiet this early New Year's Day. Standing above the city is a large white statue of Christ (Christo Blanco) so common in Latin and South American countries. From our viewpoint above the city we were able to look down on the rooftops and see how the Plaza de Armas becomes easily identifiable with the cathedral dominating the vista.

Anne's mood had mellowed (well whose wouldn't in my company?) and we made our way back to the Plaza for lunch, as breakfast had been pathetic at our new hotel. At one of the restaurants we met up once again with a tour group whom we had encountered on our first day in Quito. They were travelling with an adventure company called Dragoman, whose headquarters are in Debenham, Suffolk, England, just ten miles from my home in Ipswich. I had visited them prior to leaving, with the view of joining one of their overland tours of South America, but their route and timings did not quite match my own.

Whilst having our lunch, one of the funnier moments of our trip occurred, and one that Anne and I always remember. Whilst eating a rather delicious looking slice of cake, Anne suddenly recoiled in horror as a long black hair was seen protruding from the aforementioned cake. That was it, no more would she eat, and we managed to laugh ourselves silly despite the waste of cake and money.

While Anne was using the internet, I sat on a bench in the Plaza enjoying the warm sunshine. Two young boys that I had seen around the Plaza on a few occasions selling postcards and offering a shoe-shine service came over to see if I was now willing to buy something from them.

They both spoke good English and told me they had learnt English at school and were keen to know if I knew the England football captain, David Beckham. Not personally, I told them, so they then inquired about Princess Diana. Their knowledge of England and the Royal

Family was quite surprising and they said that they were sad at Princess Diana's death.

I asked them about the two flags that are flown above the Plaza. One was the Peruvian National flag but they were not sure about the other. This flag has the seven colours of the rainbow upon it in horizontal bands and according to my research is meant to represent Inca territory (Tawantisuyo).

Not to be distracted from their main objective of getting some 'soles' out of me, one of my young friends exclaimed, "Hey Mister, shit on shoe". I was wearing open toed sandals, but as I looked down, there was indeed dirt on my foot, cunningly put there while I was staring up at the flags, no doubt. I gave these young entrepreneurs a few soles to clean off the 'shit' and also agreed to buy a few of their very dated post cards.

They were only young lads after all and so I offered them a sweet each. Big mistake as walking back across the square a short time later I had acquired a small entourage of local children all begging for a sweet. I must have looked like the Pied Piper of Hamelin, as my dancing throng followed in my wake.

At 5.30am on the 2nd January 2002, the day that I had planned for and travelled to South America for had begun. We made our way to Cusco railway station to catch the train bound for Aguas Calientes.

The 6.30am train was packed with a mixture of nationalities all heading for, arguably, South America's most famous archaeological site, Machu Picchu. There are a number of ways in which you can visit Machu Picchu; a four-day, 45km hike commencing at km 84 of the rail route; a two-day hike commencing at km104; or the easiest, stay on the train all the way to Aguas Calientes and then take a bus to the ruins of Machu Picchu.

We had opted for the two-day short hike option, which according to Andean Adventures blurb, is a moderate hike and should be undertaken by people who are fairly fit and take regular exercise. Well, I had been playing local league badminton on a regular basis for over fifteen years so I felt reasonably confident.

My small backpack was relatively light, the main weight being my video camera and water bottle, as my spare underwear, socks, t-shirt and necessary toiletries didn't amount to much.

The train journey is very scenic as it rumbles up the valley for about three and a half hours via Urubamba and Ollantaytambo, names I had heard mentioned by Michael Palin whilst undertaking the same journey on his Pole to Pole adventure series for the BBC.

When we reached km104 I was surprised by how few people alighted to join Anne and me. As the train disappeared into the distance twelve of us remained and were met by a lady called Suzanna, representing Andean Adventures, who was to be our guide. The group was of mixed ages and were all British, American or Canadian.

An offer was made for a porter to carry your backpack for an extra fee, but I felt in no need of such assistance. Our oldest members did avail themselves of this service and I wondered if they would manage to keep up. I shouldn't have worried about them but about my own fitness, as became evident after the first half an hour of steady ascent.

The two porters were to carry our lunch and utensils as well as any extra backpacks and were both wiry local men. They gave us a good start but were soon overtaking all of us to set up lunch at a pre-arranged point on the trail before we arrived.

The trail starts gently enough, crossing the Rio Vilcanota before heading uphill to the ruins of Chachabamba. Our guide explained that these ruins were a religious site and also acted as a gatehouse to Machu Picchu itself.

From here on in, the going became more rugged, and we were advised to walk at our own pace. Our guide would wait for any stragglers to ensure that we all arrived safely for our lunch stop, which we couldn't possibly miss, as the trail was well worn and clear. It is suggested that hikers carry a whistle to attract attention should they get into difficulties. I didn't have one, but had settled into a small rearguard party with the two seniors and a youngish Canadian woman. Anne and the other fitter members of the party had moved ahead at their own pace.

It was a further hour and a half walk in hot sunshine until we came to a grass covered hut where our porters had set up lunch. I had foolishly drunk a good proportion of my water already, so was glad to see that, along with bread and fruit, some juice was also available.

Having arrived sometime after the vanguard of walkers, our rest time was less, although our ever-smiling guide once again advised us to proceed at our own pace, and said that as long as we reached the ruins of Winya Wanya before dark, then all would be well. It was only a relatively short walk onwards from there to our overnight hostel.

The going had been fairly tough, but was to get increasingly so as we continued upwards. Crossing a small stream, we continued on and out onto open grassland, the trail hugging the hillside, but climbing ever higher. The views were stunning and I hoped that my video footage and gasped commentary would do justice to the vista.

Through the video camera I was able to follow the trail for some way ahead and pick out the small ant like figures of fellow hikers and then finally, at the extreme of the camera's magnification, Winya Wanya. I wondered how far that was, and how much longer it would take us to reach it.

After another hour and half or so, we arrived at the ruins and terraces known as Choquesuysuy where the Inca Trail leads onto Winya Wanya. The scenery here was stunning and as we looked upwards, we could just see Winya Wanya in what still looked like the far distance.

Suzanna had told us that when we reached this point, we were well on the way to our overnight Trekker's Hostal about thirty minutes further on from Winya Wanya. Maybe if I was a mountain goat it might take about thirty minutes but, I was finding this hard going, and to make matters worse, I had drunk all of my water. Some passing porters saw us sitting by the side of the trail, and stopped to make sure we were ok. They gave us some coca leaves and told us to chew them as they would help with energy and combat the effects of thinner air. It is from these leaves that cocaine is eventually produced. I hadn't expected to be offered drugs half way up the Inca Trail, that's for sure!

Whether it was the coca leaves I don't know, but our small group of four found renewed vigour and we headed onwards to Winya Wanya. I had discovered that the young Canadian woman wore callipers on her leg as a result of polio, hence her slower pace and she was carrying a bigger backpack than mine. I found that I had great admiration for her and the older couple with us, none of whom complained at all.

We reached the bottom terraces of Winya Wanya after we had been hiking for about six hours. These terraces are really an incredible sight and the Inca people who would have built and then farmed these must have been both ingenious and hardy. An irrigation system would have been devised to get water up to the very top terraces to help their crops grow in the sunshine.

We had to climb up these terraces, about a 100 deep steps, that rise steeply. After six hours my energy levels were low and my fitness, or lack of it, was to be sorely tested. Suzanna had waited for us at the summit and shouted encouragement as one by one we took on the climb. I stopped a few times, with the excuse of taking video footage, to gasp in a lungful of air and gather myself for the next section of steps. I had the feeling of being very insignificant as I climbed these terraces and tried to imagine what life must have been like for the average Inca.

At the top as I lay pretty nearly exhausted, the thought occurred to me of what I had achieved and I sat up and just took in the loveliest view. It was worth every tired step. Nearly to your overnight stop, a beer, food and bed, called Suzanna. Those last thirty minutes seemed to pass quite quickly and as we emerged into the Trekker's Hostal and campsite I could see Anne sipping a beer and looking as fresh as a daisy. She had probably been here for hours. Just over seven hours for me and it was coming up to sunset.

The view from the hostel was fantastic as the sun shone onto the white, snow-capped Andes across the valley. That was all that was fantastic about the hostel. It was run down and very basic. The toilets were disgusting and the shower, assuming it did work, was filthy.

The dormitory rooms consisted of three-high bunks, were mixed sex and took about forty persons. It looked as though I would have to take a 'high rise' top bunk but Anne took pity on me so that I could stay on the bottom row. Probably just as well for the other folk that I would have had to clamber up and over!

Our porter made us a reasonable meal of soup, spaghetti bolognaise and peaches to follow. No one stayed up late as we were scheduled to be up at 4am the next morning to ensure we arrived at Intipunku (Gateway to the Sun) for sunrise.

As we retired the mosquitoes were having a field day and I decided to sleep fully clothed on my less than comfortable bunk bed. Despite all the noises of my fellow guests, and the constant whine and irritation of the mozzies, I soon gave way to deep sleep.

I have rarely, if ever, been so glad to get up in the morning. It wasn't the excitement of the forthcoming day, but the desire to try and get to the toilet before many others. No toilet seat and of course no toilet paper, but this was the norm for South America. The shower did work, just, but was freezing cold. At least I felt a little cleaner and used yet more bottled water to clean my teeth.

We left with Suzanna at 5am and if I never see this hostel again it will be too soon. (After numerous complaints, it was closed and demolished in 2005). An easy two hour and slightly uphill walk she told us. Heard that before, I thought, but we actually made it in the dark by 6.30am.

It was nice and cool, and as we waited for the sunrise, I began to have a sinking feeling that the penultimate moment of this hike was going to be ruined by the heavy mist that was rolling around us. At sunrise, the sun shines gloriously through the Intipunku Gateway and reveals Machu Picchu, the ancient and fabled lost city of the Incas, in all of its glory. This is the view shown in all the travel brochures, magazines and television footage….we saw sod all!!

The disappointment for all there was 'deafening' in our silence. We all just sat or stood staring hopefully into the mist for some time. All at once my exhaustion returned and my left heel was by now very sore. It was downhill from here to the city and we headed off, a very quiet and deflated bunch. The trail winds down through the forest and soon enough comes to a fairly narrow stone-stepped path with huge drops into the valley below to your right.

As well as being rather slippery due to the mist and foliage, we also had the added hazard in the form of wild Alpacas, who had no intention of giving way to us. Good video opportunity however, and then the sun burst through the mist and parts of the city were revealed. The swirling mist in the valley and the sun burning through to hit the famous old ruins and the Huayana Picchu (the cone shaped mountain behind it) was unforgettable for me and my spirits soared appreciably. This was what I had come to see...thank you, God, for getting me this far.

It took me a further two hours to slowly complete the downhill journey into the city of Machu Picchu and then followed a further two hour guided tour of the ruins. Whilst this was fascinating, I was tired and sweaty and longing just to sit down and rest. The buildings and their uses are fully explained but when the rain came, as with any ruins, there is no shelter. Now I could add wet and cold to tired and sweaty.

Having said our goodbyes to Suzanna and other members of our group, we boarded the bus that would take us to the train stop at Aguas Calientes. The rain had caused a few problems and had contributed to a massive rock fall that had completely blocked the road further down before Aguas Calientes. We had to disembark and walk carefully, in single file, around the fall, then board another bus to continue the trip down.

I said train stop as opposed to station, as frankly that is what it is. The village of Aguas Calientes straddles the rail track and is a hive of activity for the vendors, cafes and market stall holders who make their living from Machu Picchu. As we sat waiting for the train, keen t-shirt vendors draped their wares over me in an effort to elicit a sale. "Bueno, bueno", the gap-toothed crone uttered encouragingly. It must have been a medium if that and, when I stretched it over my tummy she laughed and disappeared.

I had nodded off in the humid air when I felt another garment being laid across me. This time, I knew by the giggles of the young girl who was with her, that the size wasn't good. Undeterred, the lady stretched the shirt as wide as her arms would allow and smiled at me. I shook my head and shrugged my shoulders and again she disappeared leaving her juvenile assistant at my feet.

A truck loaded with crates and boxes was lurching over the tracks, and should it break down now, it would cause yet more mayhem, I thought. It was a yet another typical scene here to be photographed and remembered.

Just as my vendor returned with four different shirts, the train from Cusco pulled into view. Suddenly, the previously lethargic trackside community sprang to life. New visitors, new opportunities, and so life goes on.

Tourists who had been sauntering through the stalls, or like me, having a fitting service at their café table, appeared trackside, ready to replace the hordes of expectant people disgorging from the train. Like a plague of mosquitoes, the traders were upon them, and the wheel turned full-circle again.

The journey back to Cusco was uneventful, and spent in quiet reflection on a memorable couple of days that somehow seemed much longer. Machu Picchu, the lost Inca City, had been my driving force and the main catalyst for my entire trip. Now it lay behind me and I felt completely drained but euphoric.

The Incas' Revenge.

We had arrived back at the Colonial Palace at 8.45pm only to discover that our pre-paid train and flight tickets had not been delivered as promised. A quick, sharp phone call from Anne soon rectified the problem, and they were delivered within the half hour. Then it was time for a quick sandwich, and then to bed to recuperate prior to the next phase.

My snoring, which I mentioned previously, had now frayed Anne's nerves to the point where a constant barrage of shoes and shouts finally drove me to dress and sleep on a couch in the lobby near the room. (When I think about it, my friend Carlton had treated me in much the same disdain on a previous holiday!).

Anne was off to catch a flight to the Amazon where she was confident that the jungle creatures wouldn't make as much noise as me, whilst my itinerary was to take me to Puno and Lake Titicaca. If things went to plan, we would rendezvous briefly at Hostal Mami Panchita, Lima on 7th January.

My train was due to depart at 8am, so I took a taxi to the rail station, being fully laden once again. My seat was pre-booked and I found this at a table for four persons. As the train filled, to my relief, no one took the seat next to me. My table companions were an American guy and his Columbian girlfriend.

We had nine and a half hours to become acquainted and it was nice to have friendly, English speaking companions. They too were planning a tour out onto the lake to visit the 'floating reed islands' of the Uros Indians and kindly invited me to join them. As Maria spoke Spanish, this would also make things somewhat easier.

The train passed through flat plains, where from time to time you would see small groups of traditionally dressed Peruvian women and children, but very few men, herding goats or alpacas.

The scenery changed as we gained altitude, and we stopped for, presumably, photographs and a driver break, at La Raya. The altitude here is recorded as 4,345m (about 14,000ft) and you can feel the chill in the air as you gaze up at the snow- capped Andes Mountains rising behind you.

Frankly, I didn't care why we had stopped, I was just grateful to be outside and stretch my legs and ease my aching bottom. This train was somewhat unforgiving in that respect.

85

I was hungry, and my meagre sandwich and apple lunch seemed hours away. Apparently, our stay here would be for longer than normal, as another train had broken down nearer to Juliaca and, being a single track, we would had to wait until it was underway and would reach the spur at Juliaca where the line split.

Various ladies were trotting up and down with small baskets that Maria confirmed contained empanadas. These are small pasty-like stuffed bread or pastry. The ones I succumbed to buying had meat, cheese and vegetable fillings and were still warm. I was breaking one of my golden rules on buying food from a street vendor; namely, if you haven't seen it being cooked, then don't buy it.

In this instance I was hungry and let that get the better of my caution. They were delicious and together with a couple of bananas, this would have to see me through to Puno. As it transpired, this was probably a good thing as the train made another unscheduled stop in the middle of nowhere for about an hour and a half. There was nothing either side of the train for as far as I could see and yet a small group of women carrying baskets of empanadas appeared. I could only conclude that they were travelling on the train somewhere.

We passed through Juliaca, quite a busy junction and the train slowly winds its way through the busy market of the city. Vendors actually have their wares in the centre of the track and the train just rumbles over them. Everywhere there are people; women wearing the traditional bowler-style hat of the Andean Peruvians, people huddled under ponchos and children waving and holding out their hands hopefully to the train's passengers.

Once through this maze of humanity, it is not much longer to Puno. Our nine and a half hour journey has stretched to thirteen hours and it was gone 9.30pm by the time I bade Alan and Maria goodnight and arranged to meet them in the morning for the floating islands tour on the lake. My hostel, Q'oni Wasi, was not far from the station, so I checked in and basically crashed out soon after.

My slumber was interrupted time after time, but not by any outside noises. The Incas' revenge had struck. Up and down to the bathroom so many times that I lost count (not that I normally count!). All I'd had to eat in the previous 24 hours was a cheese sandwich, a couple of bananas and....two empanadas.

I had broken my rules on eating 'street' food. Had it come back to bite me on the bottom (not a good analogy!)? I had a few Imodium tablets for just such occasions, and confidently assumed they would control this situation.

In the morning I was still making regular visits, and felt terrible. There was no way that I was going to be able to go out onto the lake in this condition, so I struggled downstairs to find a telephone. I called Alan and Maria's hotel, left a message of apology and wished them well on their continued journey.

By mid-afternoon I was feeling worse, if possible, and had also exhausted my supply of Imodium. I dragged myself up and went in search of a pharmacy for supplies.

Armed with a Spanish phrase book, I tried to explain to the lady assistant my predicament and requirements as I could see nothing on the shelves that looked familiar (well, condoms but I didn't see how they would help!).

We were getting nowhere as this desperate game of charades became ever more comical. Holding my stomach and doubling over, pointing to my bottom and pulling a face had her on the phone to the men in white coats. Sounds like, 'Snips'! Come on dear, first syllable….Shh. Just as I thought that I might be forced into a practical demonstration, an older man, who I guessed was the pharmacist, appeared and took over. He produced six huge tablets, rattled off something in Spanish and pointed at the till.

Was I to swallow these, grind them down or insert them? Either way, I paid him and hurried, as quickly as I could in the circumstances (short steps with buttocks clenched) back to the hostel. The lady owner eyed me suspiciously as I retreated to my room. Who was this 'gringo' who had spent nearly all his time in his room to date?

By the time I ventured downstairs again it was dark outside and I went only as far as a shop to purchase some bottled water. Later, there was a knocking outside my room and I opened the door in my shorts (funny place for a door…old ones are the best!) to find the owner and a young girl carrying a tray.

The tray had a vase of flowers on it and a thermos flask. Nice touch I thought, perhaps they thought I was dying? Taking a large glass, the owner crumpled some of the flowers into it and then poured boiling water from the thermos over them gave it a stir and then motioned for me to drink it.

Call me old fashioned, but I prefer to look at my flowers whilst I drink my tea. This was obviously a Peruvian herbal cure and my host made rubbing motions on her stomach, smiled and nodded. "Gracias Senora", I mumbled. I also asked, well I hoped I had, for some more toilet paper ("el papel higienio, por favor"). As happened whenever I tried to use Spanish, I received a quizzical look, but she smiled, and they left. It obviously worked, as a little later there was a small tap on the door (funny place for a tap) and when I looked out, there was a catering-sized packet of toilet paper!

My cramps subsided at last. Whether it was the combined effect of the 'horse' tablets and the herbal infusion, I didn't care, as at least I was able to get a little undisturbed sleep. In the morning, I took the tray and thermos back to reception. Breakfast had long since finished but my kindly host ushered me through to the kitchen and produced a roll, jam and some fruit juice. How kind she was.

All I can tell you about Puno is what you can read in a guide, as regrettably I saw none of it. I didn't even get to the shores of Lake Titicaca much less actually spend time on it. The rest of my day was spent in and close to the hostel, as I was still not free of the Incas' curse.

I had pre-booked an overnight bus from Puno to Arequipa and decided to contact them to ensure that it had a toilet on board. I was assured that it did, and that at least gave me some comfort for the ten hour journey to come that evening.

A nightmare on a night bus.

boarded my bus for Arequipa and found my allotted seat. It was certainly more comfortable than other buses I had been on so far in South America. I spied the toilet at the rear and noticed a TV monitor at the front. My seat even reclined easily and I felt slightly easier about what was to come, famous last words.

The bus left at 7.30pm and was about half full. The seat next to me was still vacant, so all was well and I settled down to try and sleep. In deference to my delicate condition, I had devised a form of 'nappy' safety device that I wore under my trousers.

After a couple of stops to collect new passengers the bus had rapidly filled. As with all South American buses, it seemed, luggage was not confined to the underneath luggage compartments or the overhead parcel shelves. Boxes, suitcases and even babies were placed in the aisle or wherever space permitted.

Adjacent to my seat, a Peruvian lady in traditional costume complete with bowler hat had placed a tiny baby on a large bundle of blankets in the aisle. Bless its little heart, it was sleeping peacefully, as was its mother, who was snoring quite loudly.

The inevitable happened about 4 hours into the trip, I needed to visit the toilet. I would need to wake the mother and ask her to move the baby to allow me to get up. This I did as delicately as possible, but I had to shake her quite forcibly to rouse her. She was not amused, lifted the baby and muttered her obvious annoyance at this interruption to her dreams.

The lights had been switched off and the bus was in complete darkness as I started towards the back of the bus. I had to negotiate various obstacles and at least one sleeping person along the aisle. It is not easy to climb over obstacles when you are in the state I was, as to stretch one's legs is very dangerous.

When I made the rear of the bus I pulled the toilet door only to have it snapped back shut by someone inside. "Oops"! I offered to no one in particular, and waited patiently.

My stomach was cramping quite badly now and I looked desperately at the door of the toilet. A young girl seated adjacent to the toilet looked at me and said, "Senor, hombre he live there!" What was that I thought? Hombre, he live there? Then it came to me, she meant he was using the toilet as his seat, rather than for its intended purpose.

I knocked and receiving no response took hold of the handle and pulled. A pathetic trial of strength ensued. I had to be careful as too much effort may well result in the exercise being pointless! My greater need won the day and the door flew open, revealing a short, swarthy guy clutching a big bag to his chest.

I gestured for him to vacate, but he just shook his head. I asked him "hablas Ingles" (do you speak English). He shook his head and so, in desperation, I told him that unless he moved I was going to shit on him. I physically lifted him by the arms and dumped him and his bag into the aisle, entered the toilet, closed the door shut, and used my universal door lock to secure it.

As I opened the door he was still there with his bag, and I said to him, "Muchas Gracias hombre" and left him to it. Rather him than me, I thought!

The journey back to my seat on the speeding and lurching bus was completed and the baby, still asleep, had been replaced in the aisle. Someone was sitting in my seat, head bowed beneath a cap. I tapped him gently on the shoulder and then more urgently until he raised the peak of cap and squinted at me before completely ignoring me.

I was tired, and getting angry and in a loud voice told him it was my seat and to please get up. He totally ignored me and once again I had to tug him to his feet and slip into my seat. He didn't argue, and disappeared into the darkness - what a chancer!

So, I'd made at least two enemies on the bus and the lady opposite me wasn't exactly my best friend either. I tried to sleep with one eye open but eventually succumbed to slumber and awoke only when the bus pulled into a rest area. I decided I would stay in my seat for fear of having to fight for it again.

It was 4.30am when the bus rolled into Arequipa's bus terminal, an apt term when you looked around at bodies huddled at varying points, presumably waiting for their bus. I found a taxi and explained that I wanted to find a hostel for just a few hours so I could get a little proper sleep and a shower prior to catching a flight back to Lima later that afternoon.

He took me on a fairly long journey before stopping outside a hostel by the name of Santa Catalina. He got out and rang the bell and banged on the locked doors. A head eventually appeared from an upstairs window and, after what sounded like a heated conversation an old chap opened the door in his dressing gown. (I know...we've done this joke!).

With the taxi paid off I was shown to a large dormitory style room with six beds. All were empty and with that the old chap retired back to bed no doubt. It was clean and cool and I virtually fell asleep as soon as my feet touched the pillow!

I was awoken by the clanging of a church bell. It was very loud and upon opening the window and looking out I could see the church just off to the right. It was 10am and I had managed a few hours of blessed sleep and felt relatively well.

I finished my water and took a couple more of the 'horse' tablets and decided to have a shave and shower.

Clean and in new clothes, I felt better than I had for days, and decided that I needed to explore some of the city of Arequipa.

At the hostel reception I saw the old chap who had let me in earlier, and agreed a fee to keep the room until 2pm that afternoon. The hostel was only a few blocks from the Plaza des Armas, and the TANS Airlines office was a couple of blocks off this. TANS is an acronym for Transportes Aeros Nacionales de Selva, a Lima based airline

My flight was scheduled to depart for Lima at 4.50pm, and I was reconfirmed and told to report to the airport at 2pm. It seemed excessively early for a domestic flight, but this was South America, so better be early than miss it.

Arequipa is known as 'The White City' or 'La Ciudad Blanca' because of its many glistening white buildings that are made from 'sillar', a white volcanic rock. (The only Cilla I know is the Liverpudlian lady famed for her 'Surprise, Surprise' catch phrase). The city is situated in a valley surrounded by three volcanoes; El Misti (5,882m), Chanchani (6,075m) and Pichu-Pichu (5,669m).

It is El Misti that is featured prominently on postcards of Arequipa with its snow–capped cone. It was clearly visible above the city and was as described. The Plaza des Armas is reputedly one of the most beautiful in South America and certainly exuded a feeling of wealth and elegance.

Even the citizens of Arequipa seemed to be more affluent in their dress and manner, or maybe they were better at hiding the less fortunate of the populace.

Founded in 1540, Arequipa is Peru's second city and much of its prosperity was based upon its ability to trade between Bolivia and Lima.

The twin-towered Cathedral covers one entire side of the Plaza, unusual in itself, with the other three sides filled with colonial arcaded buildings, housing shops, cafes and offices. The central Plaza is a pleasant mix of shady trees and seats, and was a popular place for Arequipa's citizens and visitors to promenade or rest.

From a photographic viewpoint, the scaffolding covering the Cathedral's façade spoilt the effect. I took a pot of tea and water at a café under the arcaded side of the Plaza opposite the Cathedral and rested, as I was feeling a little weak and had a slight ache in my lower left leg.

I should have liked to have visited the nearby Colca Canyon and witness the flights of the Andean Condor as they rise up effortlessly on the hot morning thermals, however, this was another 'must see' attraction that I just wouldn't see this time.

While I was sitting resting I read about the Santa Catalina Convent that is described as being the most remarkable sight in Arequipa. Guided tours were given, but in my current state and with the lack of time available to me, this would also have to be missed.

I arrived at the airport at 1.50pm and checked in for my flight at the TANS desk. My ticket was looked at and then I was told to take a seat and wait. My backpack was not checked in so I slumped into a seating area and waited.

The TANS desk seemed to be closed and various passengers milled about looking for anyone in uniform to ask. No flight information was displayed on the arrivals or departures screen and as time went by I started to get a bad feeling about the ongoing situation.

I presented myself and passport to a general desk but the chap there seemed evasive and implied I needed to speak to someone from TANS. It was now 3.30pm and a minibus with TANS Air symbol on the side arrived with what looked like a flight crew aboard.

This looked a bit more promising, but forty five minutes later came the news that all TANS flights had been cancelled and it would appear that TANS had failed financially. A sacrificial TANS employee had now appeared at the desk and, considering the situation, a relatively orderly queue had formed to discuss alternatives. The crowd's mood may have been tempered by the presence of two policemen toting semi-automatic weapons.

When my time came, he asked to take my ticket and passport and said he would call me back to the desk. When I was called back about twenty minutes later it was to tell me that I was provisionally rebooked on a flight to Lima leaving at about 6.45pm. This was at least some positive news and I got a coffee and a cheese roll and waited.

I eventually arrived in Lima at 8pm and took a taxi to Mami Panchita. It felt good to be back there and Anne had emailed the hostel to advise that her Tans flight had also been cancelled. Her flight home with KLM Royal

Dutch Airlines was due to depart tomorrow, 8th January so I hoped she would make it.

Lima, Peru.

My stomach problems improved slightly but I now had a painful left leg, and it had become quite red. Toon and Monica, the owners of Mami Panchita, persuaded me to see a doctor, and arranged for one to visit me that evening.

Anne had called to say she had paid $300 to get an alternative flight to Lima, and was at the airport trying to get on a standby flight to Amsterdam. If she hadn't turned up at the hostel by 10pm, then she had been successful.

The doctor arrived at 9pm and with Monica to help with translation, he advised that I had a blood infection, should rest with my leg elevated as much as possible, and he prescribed me some antibiotics. He would return in 4 days and check on my progress. Today was 8th January and I had booked to fly to Santiago, Chile on15th January. At this stage the doctor had ruled against flying, so I had seven days to recover sufficiently.

Lima, the capital city of Peru, has a population of about eight million. It was founded by the Spanish conquistador Francisco Pizarro in 1535, and until a major earthquake in 1746, which destroyed all but 20 houses and killed 4,000 people, it was the most important city in Spanish South America.

Lima is built on both sides of the Rio Rimac and its main suburbs are Miraflores, which sits on the coast about 15km south of the centre and San Isidro, a few kilometres north of here.

As in a number of Latin and South American cities, Lima has several squatter settlements or 'Pueblos Jovenes' that fringe the city in the hills. These people have migrated from the Sierra (countryside) in search of work over many years.

I was staying in the suburb of San Miguel to the west of the city centre and close to the Pacific coastline. It is mainly a middle-income residential area and thought to be relatively safe, which I was pleased to hear.

A short taxi ride from the hostel was the San Miguel Plaza. Here there were various shops and restaurants and internet cafes. I visited the Plaza on a number of occasions over the following days, partly for something to do and as a change of scenery from Mami Panchita.

As new guests arrived at the hostel so I, as a longer term resident, was able to pass on some tips on the area and also to make some new acquaintances. Because of the Dutch/Peruvian ownership, the main nationality of guests tended to be Dutch, German or British. It was nice for me to have this company and I went for meals and little sightseeing trips with various people.

I hadn't had my hair cut since leaving the UK and by now it had grown very thick. (Imagine Boris Johnson!). Monica arranged for her hairdresser to cut my hair at the hostel and as I sat outside in the garden, a short and loud lady set about me with her scissors and a razor blade. I had been visiting the same hairdresser in Ipswich since I was 16 years old and they knew my hair intimately. With no mirror to check progress, all I could do was sit and watch the mass of blond locks falling onto the ground around me. I decided that I had got a good 15 Soles worth and went in search of a mirror! (Imagine Johnny Rotten!)

Miraflores became one of my favourite destinations and with its hotels, restaurants and park areas, it reminded me more of a Mediterranean beach resort. One such park overlooking the ocean is the Parque del Amor (Park of Love). This, as you can imagine, is a romantic place, and extremely popular for wedding parties to have photographs taken by the statue of a loving couple entwined in, shall we say, an embrace.

The days went by and guests came and went. One English girl called Lisa was staying for 5 days, as she had been studying an intensive Spanish language course, and was going into the Amazon jungle to take part in a voluntary conservation programme. How these could be called voluntary when you have to pay a considerable sum for your board and lodgings (a tent) beats me.

It was nice to have a longer term buddy and we got on well together and visited some old and new haunts. One visit was to the Museo Nacionale de Antropologia, Arqueologia e Historia (Museum of Anthropology and Archaeology).

This huge museum was excellent and cheap and we spent quite a few hours wandering through the exhibits. As one would expect, there were various ceramic pieces from the Chimu and Moche culture as well as Inca works of art and textiles. An excellent model had been made of Machu Picchu and I was able to tell Lisa about my adventures on the Inca Trail. Another whole gallery was given over to the Amazon, with displays of fauna and flora found in the rain forest, which Lisa would soon be visiting.

On another day we visited Lima Zoo. This was a huge disappointment to us and could definitely do with some money being spent on tidying the place up. It was rundown and scruffy but could have been made to look very nice with just a little effort, we felt. Even the poor animals looked listless and unhappy, that is except for the various monkeys cavorting in quite a large open area.

The doctor gave me the news I didn't want to hear and told me I shouldn't fly for a while yet. Toon cancelled my flight to Santiago through his travel office, but I would need to present myself at LAN Chile's office in Miraflores to rebook that flight and the onward flights to Easter Island and Rio de Janerio. This was done with a minimum of fuss and a penalty payment as per the conditions of my One World RTW ticket.

I continued to rest and read and watch films at Mami Panchita until I was given the all clear to fly on 21st

January to Santiago. It was sad leaving Mami Panchita and the friendly Toon and Monica but I needed to move on.

Anything but Chile.

It was good to be on the road again, even if it did mean getting up at 4am. My flight was at 7.50am and check-in was advised for 5.30am. My goodbyes to Toon and Monica had been the previous night and they had really made my stay at Mami Panchita as comfortable as it could be.

The flight time to Santiago was to be three and a half hours and I had managed to secure a row to myself, which allowed me to spread out, especially good for my left leg. This thankfully was showing no ill effects from the infection and my stomach had settled down, so all in all, I was in pretty good fettle.

The flight arrived on time and with the time difference, the local time was 1.10pm as we taxied up to our arrival gate. I had been impressed with LAN Chile and their Boeing 767 aircraft.

I took my time at the airport, and changed some money into Chilean Pesos before finally entering the arrivals hall. This was reasonably busy and was, as usual, full of annoying taxi/minicab drivers touting for business.

I had been researching accommodation and phoned a hostel advertising a single room for $10 per night, but with a shared bathroom. I had actually phoned them from the airport, and they had rooms available and suggested that I take a taxi to them.

One driver who was dressed fairly smartly introduced himself to me and spoke good English. His name was Gustavo and I gave him the address of the hostel. On the way to the taxi, he asked me if I knew this hostel, and then asked me if I realised how far out of the centre it was.

He suggested a hotel much nearer the centre and told me that although it would be more expensive, I would save on costly taxi fares to and from my original choice. He rang this hotel for me and advised that they had a room with private bathroom for 16,000 pesos per night. I would only be three blocks from the Plaza de Armas so I would be able to walk easily for sightseeing, restaurants and the internet.

I agreed to his suggestion and on the journey from the airport he told me that he was also a guide and would be willing to take me on private sightseeing tours in and around Santiago. I mentioned to him that I intended to go south to visit the city of Valparaiso and he said he could drive me there also, and give me a tour on route.

The hotel room was comfortable enough and after freshening up, I went to seek out the Plaza de Armas. The weather was sweltering; 37c was showing on a digital display along the main road leading into the centre so I kept to the shade wherever possible. (Makes me sound like The Phantom of the Opera!).

I found a busy restaurant in the Plaza de Armas and had a couple of lovely cool beers and generally took in the atmosphere. Office workers were taking an early evening meal and beer before heading home, and it was quite a peaceful scene.

I returned to the Los Arcos Hotel via an internet café where I was able to catch up with various people and let them know that I was on the road again. The sun sets much later here in Santiago than in Lima and is only three hours behind GMT.

I slept well, too well, and didn't get up until 11am. I then walked into the Plaza De Armas in search of brunch. It was baking hot again, and a display showed the temperature as being 39c. It was a dry heat and not too humid, but I still sought as much shade as possible.

Whilst letting my brunch settle, I was reading up on Santiago and Chile in general. Chile covers over half of the South American continent stretching 4,300km. It is a relatively narrow country sitting between the Andes Mountains to the east, and the Pacific Ocean to the west.

It has the world's driest desert, the Atacama, in the far north of the country leading from the Peruvian border, whilst Santiago has grown to become South America's fifth largest city with a population of nearly five million.

Going further south, Chile has its own Lake District. Many lakes provide wonderful settings for all manner of water-based sports, fishing and hiking. From here you go further south into Chilean Patagonia and the dramatic and world renowned national park that is the Torres del Paine. This journey involves either a flight or a four-day sea voyage to the main city of this region, Punta Arenas.

Finally, at the extreme south of the Chilean territory, is the island of Tierra del Fuego. This large island is Chilean sovereign territory on its western side and Argentinean territory to the east. The island is surrounded by the Magellan Strait to the north, the Atlantic Ocean to the east, the Beagle Channel to the south and various other channels to the east. As well as being a rich habitat for wildlife and birds, it also produces most of Chile's oil.

I would have loved to see more of these magical sounding places, but my enforced incarceration in Lima had impinged on my timetable somewhat. I decided I would have to make do with Valparaiso, before heading to the remote and enigmatic Easter Island.

Santiago was founded by Pedro de Valdivia in 1541 and sits on the Rio Mapocho. It is a modern city with many skyscrapers in the central business district and has many lovely public gardens filled with well-tended flower borders and places to sit and relax. In the background, away to the east, are the ever impressive snow-capped Andes, providing a superb vista.

I decided to ring my taxi driver, Gustavo, and discuss the possibility of him driving me to Valparaiso the day after tomorrow. He was not in, but I left a message with a lady, who I think understood my message asking Gustavo to call me at the hotel. He called and left me a message saying that he would call to see me the next morning at 10am, and that he could do this journey for $100.

The hotel receptionist seemed to indicate that this was too high a price and overnight, after thinking about it, I agreed with her. When Gustavo arrived I tried to negotiate a new price and he became quite animated and started throwing his arms about in a typical Latin manner. Eventually we agreed on a fee of $70 to include a two-hour tour of the vineyards on the way. He was most reluctant about this additional side trip and then said I should pay him 10,000 peso (£8.50) to cover the cancelled work in coming to see me. Now I was furious, and gave him 5,000 peso and said I would see him the next morning at 9.30am.

I was still fuming over Gustavo's attitude as I walked into the city centre, and it wasn't just the sun that made me feel hot under the collar. I had a distinctly bad feeling about friend Gustavo, and made enquiries about getting to Valparaiso using public transport.

I had read that a typical Chilean dish is 'cazuela de ave', a stew with chicken, potatoes, rice and peppers. I found this on the 'menu de hoy' at a shaded restaurant just off the Plaza de Armas and ordered this together with a carafe of cabernet sauvignon. This, the waiter assured me, came from the central valley vineyards that I hoped to visit tomorrow.

I purchased some rolls, ham and fruit to take with me the next day, and a large bottle of water. Back at the hotel, I watched the second half of the Manchester

United and Liverpool game live with a screaming Chilean commentator. The Scouses won 1-0 and the commentator did his 'goaaaaaaaaal' celebration as is common in South America. Football is the national sport here, but the season had not yet begun.

I was up, packed and checked out ready for Gustavo's arrival but by 10am he had not shown up. The hotel rang his number for me but it was not answered. The bastard had stood me up, so I decided to get another taxi to the bus station and purchased a return ticket to Valparaiso for $23.50, a fraction of the cost that I had agreed for a one-way trip, albeit with a vineyard tour thrown in. I somehow felt that it would have cost me more than the agreed figure.

I had picked up a leaflet on backpacker accommodation in Valparaiso and read this on the hour and 45 minute bus journey. A nice sounding hostel called Casa Aventura set on the hilly streets of central Valparaiso caught my eye and the rates seemed reasonable.

The taxi ride there was certainly uphill, and we came to the hostel on a steep street. They only had a room to share, but for 6,000 peso including breakfast, I accepted, and met my roommate, a ginger-haired German guy by the name of Willy. He was travelling with another German couple, and they were travelling down to the Lake District and Patagonia where they planned to hike and camp.

Situated in the old part of the city, I was able to take a long walk and look over the city from various lookout points, served by funicular railways. Although the weather was bright and sunny, there wasn't the intense heat that I had experienced in Santiago, and the temperature was a more moderate 28c, still plenty warm enough.

The upper city, made up of 'cerros', clings to the hills surrounding the port of Valparaiso, and there are fifteen funicular railways or ascensores dating from the period 1880 to 1914. I was staying in Cerro Alegre/Cerro Concepcion, colonised by the Europeans in the 19th century, and it is now popular with artists and students.

This area is served by Valparaiso's oldest and most famous Ascensore, the Ascensore Concepcion, also known as the Ascensore Turri, and from here I was able to descend to the new city and Plaza Sotomayor, which houses the Naval Headquarters, and where every evening a ceremonial lowering of the Chilean flag is performed by naval ratings.

I hadn't realised that Valparaiso was the main port of the Chilean Navy, hence the naval headquarters. It had also become a major cruise port, especially for trips to Antarctica, a few thousand miles to the south.

I booked onto a harbour cruise, and once out on the ocean, I was able to see the way that the houses of the cerros clung to the hills above the old city. The cruise lasted for thirty minutes and the wind was cooling, but far from cold.

I had spied a restaurant sitting virtually on top of Ascensore Concepcion, and decided that this would be an ideal place for a meal with a view, so returned to the Café Turri that evening before sunset. I was lucky enough to get a table on their terrace and had a blowout meal of steak, washed down with a bottle of cabernet sauvignon. It cost me more than my accommodation, but what the hay, it was a fabulous meal, and a fantastic setting.

My cousin Margaret had sent me some money prior to my departure from the UK, encouraging me to put it towards a nice meal and a bottle of cabernet sauvignon whilst in Chile, so here's to you Margaret, cheers and 'salute'. The lights below and above the restaurant were twinkling and it all added to a magical moment, one of the best so far on my trip.

I had breakfast in the company of the Germans and one of the hostel owners, Christian, discussed with us the places that he had visited, and made suggestions for the Germans about their onward journey south.

After they had departed, an Australian couple, Helen and Geoff pitched up for a late breakfast. They had got in last evening whilst I was out at dinner, and were joining the cruise ship that I could see at the passenger terminal below. Their cruise would take them to Patagonia and Antarctica and I was really envious of their itinerary.

We talked for ages about their travels and mine, and gave me an invitation to go and stay with them when I arrived in Australia. They lived in a suburb of Sydney called Fairlight and gave me their contact details. They were lovely people and very well-travelled and before we realised it, the time had come for them to take a taxi to the port.

I had a light lunch and a beer or two, changed some pesos into US dollars in preparation for Easter Island, and booked a room at a hostel called Scott's Place in Santiago. I had a bed in a shared room for 5,000 peso including breakfast.

They had a minibus to collect guests from the airport and I was soon at the hostel. I had a bottom bunk in a room with 1 guy, 2 girls and a couple in a double bed. Interesting, but all seemed friendly enough, and it was for only one night after all.

The hostel had a large kitchen where you could prepare your own meals and a part- covered common area. It all had a nice feel to it, and I was soon in various conversations with my fellow guests. A stadium was located nearby and, along with an Irish lad and an American girl, we walked the short distance to it and watched part of a game. Entrance appeared to be free, or to put it another way, nobody stopped us walking in and sitting on the concrete terrace.

I met my fellow 'dorm-mates' and settled down to sleep. I slept fitfully and couldn't help but listen to the couple in their double bed who had erected a rough privacy sheet around their bed. Hope my snoring didn't keep anyone awake? Having said that I doubt if they could hear me above the sounds of passion from the 'happy' couple!

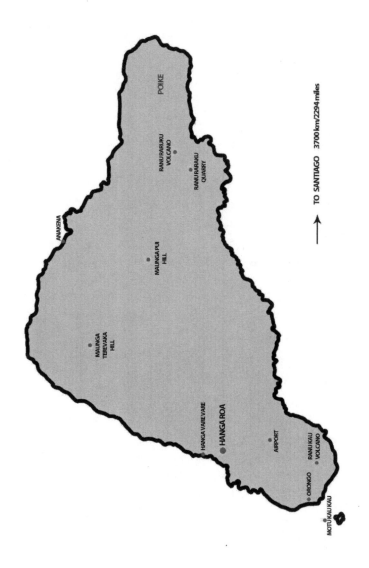

Rapa Nui, Easter Island, or Isla De Pascua.

My LAN Chile flight to Rapa Nui (Easter Island) was scheduled for 10am, and I was able to share a 'colectivo' taxi to the airport with some other backpackers. The flight left on schedule, and I settled back for the five and a half-hour flight. With a time difference of minus five hours GMT, the flight arrived at 1.30pm local Rapa Nui time.

The runway at Rapa Nui's airport is huge for such a small island. This phenomenon was to allow for the possible emergency landing of the US space shuttles. The arrival terminal at the airport is basically an open-sided thatched barn and despite this informality, the Chilean customs performed their task in a professional manner.

A tractor and trailer delivered the luggage and, once you had collected it, you were faced with a number of small kiosks representing tour operators and hoteliers. I hadn't pre-booked any accommodation, so wandered along the various kiosks.

I opted for a guesthouse and, together with a young Norwegian couple, was bundled into the open back of a Ute and driven to the accommodation. Rapa Nui consists of one main settlement, Hanga Roa, where the majority of the locals live and accommodation is to be found.

Our chosen accommodation was somewhat further away from central Hanga Roa than I had thought and upon arrival, the Norwegian couple were given a room within the main house, whilst my room was about 100m away in a sort of outbuilding. My first impression was that the accommodation was very basic. My host told me that she would make up the room whilst I was exploring Hanga Roa with the two Norwegians.

Her husband gave us a lift down to the small harbour of Hanga Roa and told us to get a taxi back to the guest house when we were ready. My Norwegian friends seemed happy with their room in the main house, but I was not feeling particularly impressed with mine. We went our separate ways and I took in the first of the Moai, the huge stone statues for which Rapa Nui is famous. There were in fact two Moai on this platform or Ahu and, if I was reading my map correctly, it was called Ahu Tautira (more on these iconic statutes later).

I found a bar and had a few beers, which were quite expensive, but since everything is imported to Rapa Nui this was to be expected. A small café sold pizza, and after eating one of these and experiencing a fabulous sunset, I caught a taxi back to my boarding house, Chez Cecilia.

By now it was dark and I made my way carefully towards my room. Opening the door and finding the light switch, the room looked much as I had left it. The bed had not been made up; there were no towels, no toilet paper and a solid line of ants marching right over the bed!

It was stifling hot and I went to the window and as I went to slide it open the entire window pane fell out and disappeared outside. I didn't hear the sound of breaking glass and found the pane unbroken lying on the grass outside. Relieved, I replaced it against the window frame and hurried over to the main house.

With many apologies, my host (possibly Cecilia) returned with me, carrying bed linen, towels and the all-important toilet roll. She produced a can and sprayed the room and the bed liberally causing the ants some consternation, but it did clear them. Cecilia laid a sheet over the mattress and asked if I wanted the window opened. I said I did and waited for the glass to fall but, she gently lifted it out and laid it against the wall. (Obviously she was aware of the problem). "My husband fix later, yes?" she said. Before or after every mosquito on the island arrived for a feast, I wondered.

I really needed a shower and went into the small bathroom and turned the shower tap. Other than a shuddering noise nothing happened, not a drop of water fell, great! I had got used to saying 'no hay aqua caliente' (no hot water), but this was a case of 'no hay aqua' (no water, full stop!).

Nothing else for it, I cleaned my teeth using some bottled water, applied some mosquito repellent to my exposed parts and lay down on the bed fully clothed. I eventually fell asleep to the sound of whining mozzies.

The next morning, I went over to the main house for breakfast to find the Norwegian couple looking refreshed and happy. I must have looked a fright, unwashed and still in my crumpled clothing of yesterday.

They had hired a couple of motorbikes and were soon zooming off to explore the island. Meanwhile I told Cecilia about the lack of water and she disappeared and returned with a huge wrench. Back at the room, instead of loosening any nuts and connectors with the wrench, she just belted the shower pipes with it. There was a shudder and a rusty coloured liquid dribbled from the shower head. Call me picky if you will, but this just wasn't on. I was allowed to use the bathroom in the main house, which was quite luxurious. There was plenty of hot water, and suitably refreshed and shaved, I set off to walk into Hanga Roa.

I couldn't stay at Chez Cecilia another night, and whilst having a coffee started a conversation with an American lady who suggested another residence called Vai Ka Pua, situated nearby on Avenue Te Pito Te Henua. (What a mouthful).I made my way there and it looked quite nice with lots of flowers and greenery leading up to the door. A small dark haired woman called Lucy welcomed me and showed me a room with private bathroom for $20 per night including breakfast. She didn't bat an eyelid when I asked to try the shower, which worked splendidly. I explained as best I could that I was billeted at Chez Cecilia and that all was not well. No problem, Lucy knew Cecilia, telephoned her and then told me she would drive me to collect my luggage and return here. Being such a small island it made sense that everyone knew each other and, as I was later to discover, many are related. Cecilia was fine and even gave me a $5 discount on my agreed $15 per night charge for the problems with the room. Lucy explained to me that they hadn't actually had guests staying other than in the main house for some time. (No kidding!).

I was so pleased to be resettled that I lay on the bed and slept for about three hours before heading towards the harbour area in search of dinner. I found a restaurant that overlooked the ocean just west of the harbour called 'Pea'. Despite any misgivings over the name I had a nice meal, once I had found out what dishes were actually available from their extensive menu. My first three choices were unavailable, again a norm, as I was to discover over the coming days.

The next morning I had a really nice breakfast at Vai Ka Pua and met some of my fellow guests. It was good to be feeling comfortable, and Lucy booked me a full day tour of the Island. I joined an English speaking tour made up of a group travelling with Journey Latin America, a tour operator I knew well from my travel days. Our local guide spoke excellent English and it turned out that he had studied at the University of East Anglia, Norwich, only an hour from my home in Ipswich. He had picked up on the rivalry between Norwich and Ipswich whilst living there, and was quick to remind me of the 'Canaries', Norwich's football team.

Our first stop was the Ahu Hanga Te'e o Vahihu on the island's south coast. An Ahu is the platform upon which the Moai (stone head) is placed. It is thought that they were used for ritual ceremonies, initiations and food distribution celebrations, and the earliest date from the 6th century.

The Moai are believed to represent and perpetuate the memory of an ancestor. They are all male heads and most have the characteristic long nose and ear lobes. The earliest Moai were smaller, with wider heads and short ear lobes. This could be accounted for by fashion, especially the ears, which some cultures today use weights to stretch and elongate.

Some of the Moai had coral eyes added and also had a Pukao (large hat or top-knot). This would seem to indicate that person's tribe and importance, e.g. a priest or leader. The Pukao was a latter addition, as not all Moai had them. Certainly all had the white coral eyes, as these huge stones fitted exactly into the eye sockets, and would perhaps have given the appearance of a watching guardian. The Moai at Ahu Hanga Te'e o Vahihu are all on their sides, and the Pukaos are spread about them, again showing that they were added after the Moai were erected. We were told that this Ahu was a representation of the destruction of the culture or religion that the Moai represented.

From here we were taken to the southernmost tip of the island, to the Rano Kau volcano. (Rano means volcano, and Kau, wide or vast). Within the volcano's crater is a lagoon, which apparently has a depth of 280m. As we looked down on it, it appeared to be a horrid green colour. This is caused by extensive vegetation that supposedly can support the weight of a man or animal.

Our guide looked for a volunteer to test this theory and eyed me, his new Ipswich buddy. He explained that people actually used to slide down the smooth slopes on sledges made from banana leaves as a form of competition. (I will tell you more about this type of competition later).

Close by to Rano Kau is an old ceremonial village by the name of Orongo. The 'O' is a place, while 'Rongo' is a message or messenger, therefore, Orongo means 'place of the messenger'. From this lofty site, they would watch for the arrival of frigate birds, signalling the arrival of spring. These birds would nest on the craggy islets off the coast, and collecting the first egg of the breeding season would become a major ceremonial event. The houses of Orongo, of which there are about fifty, are well preserved with ornate carvings on the walls. They face the islets, and have incredibly small entrances - I certainly wouldn't be able to crawl into one!

From here, we were driven along the southern coastal road to view Ahu Tongariki. This has the biggest and most complete Ahu of any on Rapa Nui. It is situated at the foot of the Rano Raraku volcano, from where all the Moai were carved and transported. We were to visit the volcano next.

Ahu Tongariki has fifteen Moai standing on its 200-metre platform and these were fully restored by Chilean archaeologists, with financial support from the Japanese, who wanted to make a documentary featuring them. As I took video footage of them I couldn't help but liken them to friends and relatives, and even to the cartoon

Trumpton firemen in the BBC children's television programme of the 1960s.

We walked up towards the main crater of the Rano Raraku volcano and strewn about on their sides or partly standing, were hundreds of Moai. They seemed to have been abandoned where they fell, perhaps in the transportation stage of getting them to an Ahu somewhere on the island.

It was fascinating to see some Moai in the process of being sculpted from the rock of the volcano and then just left unfinished. To imagine the manpower needed to work on such an undertaking is staggering, as is the method of transporting these huge and enormously heavy heads over the island.

This leads to the theory of deforestation that occurred on the island and helped to nearly end civilisation on Rapa Nui. Logs would be used as rollers to transport the Moai from Rano Raraku to the different Ahu around the island. Trees were cut down and huge armies of slaves and workers would pull these huge statues. It is a matter of conjecture as to whether they were transported in an upright position, or lying down. Either way, the workload would have been immense.

For fear of boring you with details of the Moai, let me just say that whilst the average height of each one was about four metres, there was one in the quarry of some twenty two metres and, as we were to see for ourselves, one of ten metres sited on the northern coast. The weight would therefore be colossal, maybe as much as 50,000kg

Over the centuries, the need for wooden rollers consumed their every thought, and eventually, there were no trees left. Could they not have realised that their actions would mean no bird life, that the ground would be barren and useless, and that ultimately, they would have no materials to make boats to fish and travel? Did the need to follow a religion or cult virtually destroy the people of Rapa Nui?

This was quite fascinating, and I found myself bound up in the mythology of Rapa Nui and its iconic Moai. Our guide was excellent (despite his preference for Norwich over Ipswich). He tried to give us a balanced overview and made reference to his own ancestral teachings. It was becoming clearer to me that the Rapa Nui heritage and culture were still very much alive, and he mentioned a festival called Tapati, held annually on Rapa Nui, that celebrated that heritage.

Our tour continued to Anakena, a beautiful, wide, sandy beach with turquoise water. We ate our packed lunch here, and were able to enjoy a swim. The water was surprisingly cool, despite the very warm sunshine, but it was wonderfully clear and sandy underfoot, gently shelving to a greater depth.

The Ahu Nau Nau is found here behind the beach and has seven Moai, of which four are large, two medium, one of which has no head, and the seventh is missing half of its body. The four large Moai are complete with Pukao and are in good condition, having remained buried in an accumulation of sand until 1980, when they were uncovered and restored by an archaeological team.

We were shown several petroglyphs (carvings) depicting fish and the Tangata Moko (Lizard Man). Again, interpretation of these symbols is unclear, however they are to found all round the island and on the walls of the houses at Orongo.

There is another Ahu close by on the beach, Ahu Ature Huki, with one Moai standing on it. This Moai was restored to an upright position with the help of the Norwegian explorer and anthropologist Thor Heyerdahl, who visited the island in 1947.

Heyerdahl's expedition undertook the building of a reed and balsawood raft, similar to the raw materials available centuries before. He then sailed it from South America to Rapa Nui, thereby reasoning that the island could have been populated in this way originally. DNA tests would however seem to indicate that the original inhabitants came from the scattered islands of Pacific Polynesia.

That evening I visited a café with an internet and spent an hour catching up with the world. The young lady who served me at the café was very endearing and most interested in me and my journey. She was certainly a most lovely girl and I promised to return to use the internet and because her English was so good. (If you believe that, you'll believe anything!).

Back at Vai Ka Pua, I was invited to join Veronica and Thomas, a young Norwegian/Swedish couple, for a meal. They had hired a jeep and we drove into Hanga Roa to a restaurant called Aloha that Lucy had recommended. It was a good meal and a lovely evening to finish off a fantastic day.

Going Native.

It was my fourth day on Rapa Nui, and I had a flight booked back to Santiago three days later. I had booked this on the basis that Rapa Nui was so small and that the average stay on the island was no more than a week. I was beginning to consider the possibility of extending that stay for a few days as I was starting to feel quite comfortable here.

That morning I had a half-day tour booked to complete the island's main sites. We visited Puna Pau, a small volcanic crater of red scoria rock. This is where the Pukao were quarried. From here we visited Ahu Akivi, the only Ahu situated in the middle of the island. It has seven Moai that uniquely face the ocean as opposed to the rest, which face inland to look over and protect the islanders. They are lined up with the sun rising behind them and may have been used as some form of astronomical guideline. Looking at them is a smaller Moai, Ahu Vaiteka.

Finally, we were taken to Ana te Pahu. This is a network of lava tubes leading to a large cavern, where islanders would have hidden from raids by slave traders. They are also called the banana caves as bananas and other vegetation grow abundantly in the entrances to the tubes.

Back in Hanga Roa, I needed to go to the bank. The one bank on the island, Banca del Estado, was heaving with people and I needed to queue to be seen by the foreign exchange cashier. As I was sitting patiently reading up on the island, I was greeted warmly by a young lady, who kissed me on the cheek and hugged me.

I was completely taken aback by this act of friendliness, and for quite a few moments, had no idea who this person was. It then dawned on me that this was Maria, the young woman from the internet café that I had visited the previous evening. I was introduced to her mother, who was doing her banking business. (What else in a bank, the laundry?).

Maria sat with me, and said that she had been to Europe, as she had a German boyfriend, whom she had met when he had visited the island. This explained her good English, as this was the language that she used to communicate with him.

We talked about my thoughts of extending my stay on the island. Maria's mother, Elena, had a friend who worked at the local LAN Chile office, so she called her and arranged for me to go and see her later. Maria was lovely and her mother was also very friendly, such was the way of the people of Rapa Nui.

The LAN Chile office was very busy and, after a long wait, I saw Elena's friend and checked out the options available to me. If I decided to stay longer on Rapa Nui, I would be able to see the festival of Tapati starting on 9th February. It would mean missing out on the Rio Carnival in Brazil, but the accommodation situation in Rio was proving to be a nightmare, either full or horrendously expensive.

It was suggested that I could stay on here, see Tapati and then fly to Tahiti and from there to Auckland. Rosana at LAN Chile would make enquiries to determine the cost and how it would work with my One World ticket rules.

I checked with Lucy about staying for longer at Vai Ka Pua and she said it was no problem. We agreed a new rate of $15 per night and all was set. Elena called Rosana for me and she confirmed that a flight was available to Tahiti on 15th February, and for me to go to the office the following day to finalise details and payment. Elena said she would go with me to help with the transaction. Was I doing the right thing? It felt right, but only time would tell.

Later that day, some new guests arrived at Vai Ka Pua; Steve from New Zealand and Fran his Columbian girlfriend, Heather from the USA and Roald from Norway. Roald was quite a character and had stayed the previous year on Rapa Nui. He was booked for fifty two days and was an ex-teacher. He had the appearance of a 1960s hippie, complete with a guitar that he was soon strumming. We ended up having an impromptu sing-a-long.

Over a few beers the previous evening, I had agreed to join Steve, Fran and Heather in hiring a jeep and exploring the island. We spent all day visiting some of the sights. I had been to some, but not all. We also spent a couple of hours swimming and relaxing on Anakena beach. It was a fun day, and despite my tiredness when we got back, I still walked to Ki-Tai to see Maria and Elena and use the internet. There were no positive messages concerning accommodation in Rio, so my mind was made up to stay on, and besides, my friendship with Maria was going well and I was invited to join her family for a beer.

Meanwhile, Rosana at LAN Chile had faxed a copy of my ticket to the One World Help Desk who said that they would reply the following afternoon with my options. When I returned to LAN Chile the next afternoon, the reply was that I couldn't re-route via Tahiti to Auckland. I left the routing as it was and confirmed the new dates as 15th February to Santiago and 16th February to Rio de Janeiro.

Heather had asked me to accompany her to a folk dance evening at the Copacabana Hotel that evening. I met her at 7.15pm and she looked fantastic. I had previously only seen her in her casual wear and with her hair tied up under a cap, but tonight her hair was down and she was wearing a Chinese-style dress with a sexy split, revealing her tanned legs and thighs. A pair of high-heeled shoes only served to accentuate those legs!

I was completely underdressed in my zip-off cream trousers and a Hawaiian style shirt. I had bought it at the local market and it was rather figure hugging! Never mind, she took my arm and we had a great night laughing and dancing and watching some gorgeous Rapa Nui girls performing the graceful Tamure dance, which apparently originated in Tahiti.

We were all asked to join in the Sau-Sau, which originated in Samoa, and involves couples coming together and apart with quick hip movements in a graceful manner. My hip movements were anything but graceful, being more mindful of 'the bump', made popular in England in the 1970s by a group called 'Kenny'.

Over the evening, Heather told me that she was travelling on her own to get over a failed romance, and wasn't ready for a new relationship yet. Some lucky guy would snap her up for sure when she was ready, but it wouldn't be me, unfortunately. She was leaving the island the next day and we shared a bottle of champagne (well fizzy wine) whilst sitting gazing up at the stars from the harbour of Hanga Roa.

The following day, after a lie-in, I was walking down by the fisherman's cove, dodging the heavy rain showers, when Elena and Maria pulled up beside me and invited me to a party that evening. It was to celebrate Elena's young son Joel's birthday. As well as Joel and Maria, they have a daughter called Margarina, who is twelve years of age. She seemed to take to me immediately and I was seated with her on one side, and Maria sitting very close to me on the other.

We had a sumptuous BBQ and later, Roberto, Elena's husband, produced a bottle of Pisco. (A grape brandy produced in Peru and Chile). This is lovely, but has a real kick, and after the rest of the family had gone to bed, Roberto and I sat drinking until 5.30am.

I had been invited to go to Anakena beach the next day with the family. They take their mobile catering van with them and provide hot dogs and pizzas for the locals, who flock there on a Sunday. I had a lovely afternoon swimming and playing with the children and Elena told me that Maria had told her that she really liked me.

Well, I certainly liked her also and her parents seemed to like me too. Elena told me in confidence that she didn't like Maria's German boyfriend very much, and that he was arriving the following week for a holiday. Alarm bells started ringing, but at that moment I felt good, and ignored them!

The history of Rapa Nui is uncertain, depending on who you talk to. As with all history that is passed from one generation to another, there tend to be more myths and fables than hard facts. This is certainly true of Rapa Nui, but I was interested in reading or hearing about them.

The forthcoming Tapati festival celebrates and traces the island's origins and traditions, and allows every islander to become involved. This annual, weeklong festival is seen as so important to the Rapa Nui people that even islanders who have left and are now working and living away, return and participate. The festival has also in recent year's merited live coverage by Chilean Television.

As Tapati grew closer, I asked my new friends on the island just what it would entail. Basically, the whole island is split between two teams (representing competing clans). Each clan is led by a 'symbolic' queen, (a beautiful young female islander), and they compete to be crowned the queen of the whole island for the next year.

Every islander has the opportunity to use their individual skills to score points for their queen. Competitions would take place using only traditional methods and materials found on the island, thereby recreating and celebrating the island's history and culture.

There would be singing competitions, dancing contests, sculpting, clothes making, fishing, canoe races, horse racing, a form of triathlon, and most intriguingly, a race down the side of a volcano on a home-made sled!

It was becoming evident that practice was taking place amongst the competitors. At Hanga Roa cove, teams were practising their rowing skills in huge traditional canoes. Others were diving in and out of the water with spears to catch fish - no rods or nets in this competition, evidently.

I had managed to be invited to watch the dance practices by some young ladies to whom I had been talking one evening at a local bar. They could certainly dance and their routines varied from rhythmic sashaying to feverish whirling and much gyrating of hips.

They showed little modesty as they changed from outfit to outfit, and I was dragged (screaming) to join the less energetic routines, especially where a male was missing practice. I had a feeling that I was going to enjoy Tapati, and my decision to abandon the much more commercial Rio Carnival was beginning to look a good one.

I was spending many of my days and evenings in the company of Roald, my Norwegian buddy, and together we would entertain (if that's the right word) the locals and tourists with impromptu renditions of well-known songs, Roald on his guitar and me singing along!

The locals seemed to be amused and joined in, as did other tourists. A couple of the bar owners actually gave us free drinks as people flocked (well, not exactly) to hear us. Proves that the Rapa Nui are tone deaf, I reckon!

Other guests came and went at Vai Ka Pau and it was nice as a long term resident to meet and talk with them about their respective journeys. Roald and I joined many of them on tours around the island that made the cost less for all concerned.

Manfred and Andreas from Frankfurt arrived and they, like Roald, had holidayed on Rapa Nui before. We immediately got on brilliantly and we arranged with Lucy to hire her Jeep for the day. I was the only one with a valid driving licence, and was to be the designated driver.

I had never driven a 4WD vehicle before and when I was on the flat and didn't need to use the extra gears, all was well. We drove to the highest point on Rapa Nui, Maunga Terevaka. This hill has a summit height of 511m, and from here you have views over the entire island from coast to coast to coast. (Rapa Nui has the shape of an old ship Captain's hat).

As we started to ascend, so the gravel track petered out altogether, and we were driving through knee high wild grass which meant that I needed to engage the 4WD gears. Only one problem, how? Lucy hadn't shown me how to do this, and in all honesty, I doubt whether she would have known how to either, as I'm sure that she had probably never needed to use them.

I eventually managed to engage them, which made life a lot easier for the engine. By now we were tilting quite alarmingly on this grassy hillside, so much so that my passengers all got out, as they feared that the Jeep was about to topple over. It was a great vote of confidence in my driving, and now I had only my weight to counteract the angle! I eventually made it to the summit and joined the others to be windswept whilst we took our photos and video footage.

It was whilst out of the Jeep that we first noticed the large boulders that were liberally strewn over the terrain. How the hell had we missed them with the Jeep is anyone's guess, but now that I was aware of them, I made the others walk down in front of me as a form of early warning system, since they would have made a nasty mess of Lucy's Jeep had we collided with one.

We then drove to Maunga Poike where the 'banana sled' races were to take place a few days later for Tapati. Are these people nuts? Some contestants were practicing on the bottom section of the hill on what amounted to nothing more than a couple of banana leaves woven together. Already some contestants had suffered broken limbs and would be ruled out of the competition. Wearing only traditional loincloths and no safety gear or helmets, they hurtle down the hill, hoping to avoid the clusters of volcanic rocks present. These 'sleds' have no brakes! I repeat, they're nuts!

We called at Anakena Beach for a swim before going to Rano Raraku where the triathlon would take place down in the crater of the volcano where there is a fresh water lake. The contestants would have to do a circuit of the lake carrying two giant hands of bananas, a circuit without the bananas and finally cross the lake using reed floats. These reeds grow around the lake and once again they would be using the raw materials, as did their ancestors.

As we travelled back via various Ahu, the skies darkened, and we were subjected to a violent downpour. It rained so hard that we had to pull over and wait out the storm, as I couldn't see to drive. As the rain abated, we were left with a magnificent double rainbow. Any gold at the end do you think?

Tapati to the end.

The official opening ceremony of the Tapati Festival 2002 was to take place at 10am on Saturday, 9th February. Together with Roald, Torquil and Marianna, another young Norwegian couple who had arrived recently, I waited outside the Court House. Ceremonial dancers with their skin painted and complete with spears and what looked like paddles but were actually some form of ancient weapon, assembled ready for the dignitaries.

A fearsome dance, not unlike the Maori 'Haka', used as a welcome or challenge, was performed. A traditional offering of food baked in banana leaves was proffered to the Rapa Nui elders and the Mayor of Rapa Nui, a Chilean gentleman. The two young women candidates to become the new Queen were introduced, and the outgoing Queen wished them well. As part of the small audience, we were filmed by the Chilean television crew, and told that it would be shown on national television there, as well as on a special Rapa Nui Tapati channel. Fame at last!

The opening events of Tapati took place on the sports field opposite the Cove, and the   participants were the children. There was much vocal encouragement from parents and not a little overzealous competitive edge displayed by the rival teams.

That evening, events focused on the Hanga Kari Kari stage that had been erected specially for Tapati. A large crowd filled the open-air theatre, and we sat back to enjoy a long evening of dance and songs, telling the story of Rapa Nui's history. I recognised many of the dancers now looking absolutely gorgeous in their traditional costumes. A host and hostess from Chilean Television introduced the various dances in Spanish, whilst a local introduced them in the native Rapa Nui tongue. (I wished I could have understood either).

BBQs and bars surrounded the arena, and did a good trade as the evening progressed. We had a great time and enjoyed mixing with the locals and performers, and eventually got to bed at 4.45am!

The following day I watched the craft competitions. Necklaces and jewellery were made using stones and shells, and wood and stone carvings using only sharpened stone and flint tools.

At 4pm there was to be a BBQ on the playing field, to which all were invited. When we arrived, a giant grill had been erected upon which all of the fish that had been speared during the fishing competition were to be cooked. There were all sorts of exotic looking fish and these were served to you on banana leaves together with yams and other root vegetables.

That evening the events continued at the Hanga Kari Kari with a singing contest. There were individuals and choirs competing for each team, and a panel of judges gave marks to each act. I found the music to be rather boring after a while and so Roald and I made our way to the 'Banana Bar', where it wasn't long before some of the locals were encouraging Roald to play his guitar. Apparently, each team sang a song until the other team gave up, and there was no sign of capitulation so, while the teams sang their hearts out on stage, a Beatles sing-along was in full swing in the bar.

Maria arrived with her German boyfriend, Robert and sat with us. It was a rather strained atmosphere for a while and when Robert was buying a round of drinks, Maria told me that Robert wanted her to go and live in Germany. Her parents were not happy, as they needed her to help run the café.

Then she dropped a real bombshell, by telling me that she had a two-year-old son, and that he lived with the father's grandparents. Robert apparently wasn't aware of this fact, and she asked me if I thought that she should tell him. I told her that I thought she should, and that I hoped that things would work out for them both.

I discovered that Rapa Nui had a high percentage of young single mothers. It was explained to me that by the end of the 19th century, the population had dwindled to fewer than 200 people from a peak of around 10,000. This was due to clan warfare, disease and being taken into slavery to South America.

It would appear that many of the younger Islanders were related, which made normal relationships tricky, and perhaps explains that high number of single mothers. Anyway, this was a journey of discovery for me, and I liked the people and the island, and was not here to pass judgement on them.

Heavy rain caused the next day's Tapati events to be cancelled, and allowed me to catch up on some sleep. The temperature hardly changed, and standing out in the open was actually quite pleasant and refreshing.

The sports field had not fared too well from the deluge, and it was quite comical watching the football event. To see these islanders covered in mud and trying to kick a football around reminded me of matches at the Baseball Ground, the home of Derby County in England, notorious for its muddy, almost unplayable pitch. These guys didn't even have football boots, but played barefoot.

Before I knew it, my departure day was upon me. My flight to Santiago had been rebooked for 15th February, but with the rain delaying the Tapati programme, I was going to miss the end. Roald reckoned that I wouldn't go, and it was a good job that I didn't have a bet with him.

Having said my goodbyes to all my new friends, I was standing in the LAN Chile check-in queue, where a television was showing a recording of some of the Tapati events. To hell with it, I cancelled my flight, and got a taxi back to Vai Ka Pau. Lucy was surprised to see me back, but had no problem with giving me my room back, and at a new reduced rate. That night, some new words were sung to the Eagles classic 'Hotel California'. It became my and Roald's signature tune, and we soon had the locals singing these words.

I went to see Rosana at LAN Chile the next day and rebooked for the 19th February to Santiago and the 20th to Auckland, via Buenos Aries. I had to pay $75 to have my ticket re-issued, but I was happy, and now I could see the remainder of Tapati.

The horse racing event was to be held over on the north coast at Ahu Vai, and Roald and I were given a lift there by the father of Danielle, one of the waitresses at the Pea Restaurant. It's handy to have contacts.

The races were over a distance of about half a mile, and the track was a dirt road that rose uphill to the finishing line. The horsemen rode bareback and in bare feet, and it is a testament to their skill that no one fell off or was injured as they thundered past us.

Our lift had left before the completion of the last race, and we started to walk back towards Hanga Roa, but managed to hitch a lift on the open back of a truck with some rather excited children and a dog. Their parents owned a small restaurant, and we were invited in for a lunch of kebabs and salad, which we got at a discounted rate. The young girls served us, and it was a fun couple of hours.

Later we made our way to the harbour area where we watched the end of the canoe race. They had rowed these craft all the way around the island in quite heavy seas, and two entire crews had to be rescued after capsizing their canoes. Reminiscent of the annual University Boat Race, the victorious crew threw themselves into the water at the finish. Then the vanquished crews did so also, and an impromptu game of 'drown your opponents' ensued!

The big event at Hanga Kari Kari was a fashion show, where the respective Queens paraded in clothing handmade by their teams. Some of this was quite unusual, and some very skimpy! The dialogue that went with each creation was obviously telling us how the garments were made and with what. Audience cheering and whistling was used to judge each outfit.

The big finale was the banana sled racing, followed by the triathlon event at Rano Raraku. It seemed that the whole population had de-camped to this crater to watch, and cheer on their team.

The sled racers were brave, but completely bonkers, as they hurtled down the entire slope without any seeming regard for their own safety. It made great filming for me, and doubtless great television too, as very few made it to the bottom without mishap.

The triathlon was a tense affair and people were screaming themselves hoarse in an attempt to will their men to victory. A European tri-athlete had been given permission to compete, but he found the somewhat unusual events more difficult than those he was accustomed to. Despite his obvious physical fitness, he was no match for the local champions, in this, their home event.

So Tapati had ended. I did not know which of the Queens would be crowned at that evening's closing ceremony, but it had been great fun, and an insight into the past culture of Rapa Nui.

The closing ceremony was cancelled due to more heavy rain, and I didn't venture far from Vai Ka Pau. I had no chance to visit Maria and her family before I left the island, but I did give Roald some money to give to Margarina and Joel from me. Margarina had done some drawings of dragons for me to illustrate a story that I had written about the island, and had sent to my niece, Nicole, for her birthday.

Roald accompanied me to the airport, mainly to make sure that I left, and we had a final sing along of the now infamous "Hotel Rapa Nui". I had been twenty five days on Rapa Nui and was really sad to be leaving. I doubted if I would ever return, but it had been a memorable visit, that is for sure.

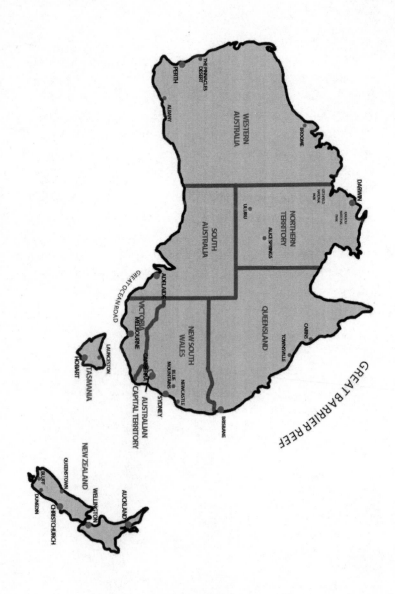

Kia Ora-New Zealand.

QF 116 touched down thirty minutes early at Auckland International Airport at 4.40am on Friday, 22nd February. Somewhere on the incredibly long flight that commenced on 20th February from Santiago, Chile via Buenos Aires, Argentina, I lost the 21st February in its entirety.

This is caused by the phenomenon known as crossing the International Date Line. I had spent many years as a travel trainer explaining to my students how days are either gained or lost depending on which direction you cross it.

It is an imaginary line that sits on the 180 degree of longitude in the middle of the Pacific Ocean. As you look at the International Date Line, anything to its left is in the Eastern Hemisphere, and always one day ahead of the date immediately to the right in the Western Hemisphere.

Are you with me so far? Ok, therefore, if you cross from the Western Hemisphere, South America, to the Eastern Hemisphere, New Zealand, the date advances by one day. The line has been moved slightly over the years, at the request of various Pacific Island countries, to avoid their territory having two different dates. However much you understand the principle, nothing prepares you for it actually happening. Let's face it, at my age I can ill afford to lose any days in my life.

I had, for me, slept quite a lot throughout the flight, having managed to get a row of four seats to myself (must check my personal hygiene!), allowing me to stretch out along them. My gratitude goes to the Qantas flight crew, who didn't wake me at the due meal times, after I left a polite note for them before falling into a deep sleep.

I was now feeling surprisingly alert as I passed through immigration control and collected my backpack. There was just one further requirement for arriving passengers, and that was to walk through a cattle grid style disinfectant bath, to ensure that we had no infectious diseases with us.

With some 50 million sheep living on some 24,000 farms, not to mention 2.8 million cattle, I suppose you can understand their concern. Still, at least my walking boots were now nicely cleaned.

Whilst in Santiago, I had pre-booked accommodation at the Auckland Central City Backpackers' hostel. I took the cheap shuttle minibus that drops off at this as well as other establishments in the city. Your luggage travels in an enclosed trailer behind the bus.

On arrival, the reception staff could find no record of my booking, but I insisted that they should have it, as I had made the reservation via e-mail. (I found out later that I had actually made the reservation at the Queen Street City Backpackers'...oops!).

Tactfully, I was told that I should be ok for a bed in a shared dormitory, but the existing guests had until 10.30am to check out. In the meantime I was welcome to use their left luggage room and make use of the shower and toilet facilities. This was most welcome, and I felt much refreshed after all that travelling.

The hostel seemed well appointed; with a travel/tours desk, cellar bar, laundry, internet access, TV room and large common room/lounge. Apparently, each floor had a communal kitchen equipped with fridges, cookers, microwave, crockery and utensils. You are asked to clean and return items when you have finished with them for your fellow backpackers to use. Items in the fridges should be labelled, and a form of honesty policy is followed.

At this early hour, some of the young guests were only just returning after a night on the town. A slight disturbance just outside was dealt with by the police, as two young British girls were finding it difficult to persuade some local guys that their company was not required any further than the hostel's front door.

I was sitting in the reception area, so was given a ringside seat to these events, and chatted to the two girls, who were undoubtedly slightly the worse for wear, but had nevertheless been shaken by the amorous attentions of their 'new friends'.

I guess it's a problem worldwide, with a combination of alcohol and young people out for a good time. The girls were both attractive and dressed in what seems to be the norm outfits nowadays; mini skirt and plunging crop-tops. As a friend of mine once remarked, "I have more cloth in my handkerchief than in that lass's skirt".

I know that it's not an excuse for every low-life to hit on them, but it can be very provocative. They were nice girls, and over the next few days we had a number of chats, when I bumped into them at different times. They were both trainee nurses and were taking a few months between their studies to see Australia. I must have seemed a bit like a father figure to them, but it was nice to be approached and introduced to their friends by these attractive girls whilst out and about.

I was eventually given a bed in a five-bedded dormitory room, sharing with a French lad, a German and two Irish lads. All of them were friendly, but as you can imagine, I was the only one who spoke English as my natural tongue. The two Irish boys were more difficult to understand than the other two, especially when they were tanked up, which seemed to be most of the time.

My first task was to undertake my laundry duties, and the facilities were excellent. This onerous chore completed, I went out for a walk. The hostel was indeed ideally situated just off Queen Street, Auckland's main shopping street. After being on Rapa Nui for the best part of a month, all of these shops, fast food outlets, modern buildings and people took a little getting used to.

I had run out of digital video film towards the end of my stay on Rapa Nui, and had been unable to obtain a new supply. Here, there were four or five camera shops within a five-minute walk of the hostel, that all stocked what I needed.

Something else I was in need of was a haircut, and I found a barber's shop complete with the red and white striped pole outside. I am indebted to my sister Sandra for the origins of the barber's pole. Barbers were usually also traditionally surgeons, and the red and white pole represents the blood and bandages of their profession! (Now, I know I have been scalped a few times but to be fair, no one has ever drawn blood...yet!).

Perhaps with the state of the National Health Service in the UK, doctors will once again revert to haircutting to make ends meet. I suppose this would be preferable to vice versa. To all my good friends at Gino's Hair Salon in Ipswich, please keep to what you know, thank you!

Anyway, my Kiwi barber turned out to be Iranian, and for $12, he gave me an excellent cut and a most relaxing head massage. It seemed that all the flying and time differences suddenly caught up with me, and I was close to nodding off right there in the chair.

Another plus after life on Rapa Nui, was the number of low cost internet locations available. There was almost a sale going on, with rival sites vying to outbid each other and gain your custom. Most also offered private telephone booths, and sold really cheap phone cards.

The café that I used was huge, and had at least fifty computers, all equipped with headphones, microphones and cameras. In this way you could not only talk to your loved ones, but see and speak to them if they had reciprocal equipment. It was a Chinese run establishment and much patronised by the many immigrant Chinese here in Auckland.

It was becoming clear what a cosmopolitan population Auckland has. It is believed that the Maori people originated in eastern Polynesia, possibly from the Marquesas Islands. As expert sailors, the Polynesians often made long sea voyages, sometimes discovering new lands by accident.

It is believed that the Polynesian explorer Kupe was the first to discover New Zealand in about AD950. He explored the coast and sailed inland up the Whanganui River before returning to 'Hawaki' (a general term used to describe Polynesian homeland), with information on how to reach this new land. Legend has it that his wife named the new land 'Aoteoroa' or 'Land of the Long White Cloud', a nickname that New Zealand uses to this day.

The first European to visit New Zealand was the Dutch explorer, Abel Tasman, in 1642. He sailed up the west coast, but his only landing resulted in three of his crew being killed by Maori warriors. He named this land 'Niuew Zeeland' after the Netherlands province of Zeeland.

This disastrous first contact deterred the Dutch from returning, and it was Captain Cook who was the next European visitor in 1769, in his ship 'Endeavour'. After sailing completely around both the North and South

Islands, he claimed the entire land for the British Crown. (What a magnanimous gesture on behalf of his Country!).

The early settlers encountered harsh conditions, and during the 19th century, following deterioration in relationships with the Maori, the British decided that they needed to establish law and order and to protect the settlers. It was the threat of French colonisation on the South Island that prompted the dispatch of Captain William Hobson to New Zealand, to persuade the Maori chiefs to relinquish their sovereignty to Britain. (Another magnanimous gesture!).

The Treaty of Waitangi was drawn up in 1840 and agreed and signed by forty five Maori chiefs. The treaty was carried throughout New Zealand, eventually being signed by over 500 chiefs, and Hobson was to become the first governor of New Zealand and to set up his capital at Kororareka (now called Russell) in the Bay of Islands on North Island. The following year, the capital was moved to Auckland. In 1865, the seat of government was moved from Auckland to Wellington, on the southern tip of North Island, where it remains to this day. By the 1920s, it controlled most of its affairs, but did not become a fully independent country until 1947.

The City of Sails.

I had been doing my usual research on the places that I was visiting and read that Auckland's population of just over a million represents about a third of the country's total population.

Named after Lord Auckland, the Viceroy of India, by Governor Hobson on 18th September 1840, the city sprawls across a narrow volcanic isthmus facing two huge natural harbours. These harbours are Waitemata to the east and Manukau to the west.

I had designated my first full day as a sightseeing and orientation day and decided that the best place to start was 'the beginning, a very good place to start' (according to Julie Andrews in the 'Sound of Music')! Well, the nearby Skytower, actually. Part of the Sky City casino, hotel and shopping complex, it is reputedly the Southern Hemisphere's highest building at 328m.

It has two enclosed observation decks and a revolving bar and restaurant offering 360 –degree panoramic views of the city. The Maori gods were smiling on me today, as the sun burst through the cloud to leave me with fantastically clear views across the city and harbour.

From my vantage point, I realised why Auckland is referred to as the 'City of Sails'. There were yachts everywhere, and it is reckoned to have over 90,000 seaborne craft. The vista that was laid out before me was impressive, and with the aid of the maps around the observation decks, I was able to orientate myself around the major sites.

At this particular time, the England cricket team was in Auckland to play a one-day International with the 'Black Caps', New Zealand's national cricket team. A party of English supporters arrived with a guide, and I was able to listen in on the commentary to receive some free information.

Far from being the boisterous followers infamously dubbed the 'Barmy Army', these folk were all cricket club members sporting their club ties from different counties around the UK. They told me that Ian Botham and Allan Lamb, two legendary English players of a few years ago, were officially accompanying them on the tour.

Perhaps the most exciting thing you can do at the Skytower is to jump off it! Yes, in the land of the 'bungee' you can participate in what is known as a 'controlled bungee' whereby you are supported by two lines, which take the strain and help to lower you somewhat more gently than a freefall leap would.

Even so, it looks a terrifying ordeal to me and the old maxim of 'if we were meant to fly then we would have wings' always comes to mind. I was able to get some great video footage of descents from both above and below. A large bulls-eye is painted on a platform at the base of the Skytower, onto which participants are lowered, they hope!

Before leaving the Skytower I was able to send an e.card to friends from the tallest building in the Southern Hemisphere. Quite neat, I thought.

I made my way to the Auckland Visitor Centre for some more ideas on things to see in the city, and the best way of achieving this. It is a grand old building in itself, having been the original Town Hall, and dates from 1911.

I was able to pick up quite a lot of information, and a kindly assistant helped me plan a route using the Auckland Explorer bus. To make the most of this, I decided to wait until the next day, and in the meantime, I walked down to the waterfront. Here I found the National Maritime Museum and spent some time looking around the exhibits for free.

As the weather was looking rather threatening, I made my way in and out of shops before heading back to the hostel. I used the travel desk to make enquiries about hostels in Christchurch on the South Island, where I was going to meet my friend, Anne once again in a few days' time.

For the record, England beat the Kiwis in the one-day cricket. I watched the end of the match whilst having dinner at an Indian restaurant with the owner and his children. They were obviously supporting their adopted country and were somewhat disappointed when the last New Zealand wicket fell, still short of England's total.

Gupta (I swear to you that was the owner's name) and I had a good chat about cricket and then about the UK, where he has many relatives living in the London and Birmingham areas. He would love to visit them, but is put off by the long flight, and instead hopes that they will visit him one day.

I was up early the next morning, after the two Irish lads crashed into the dormitory at about 5am, following a particularly good night! I took breakfast with my new 'ami Francais', Sebastian, at a café a couple of doors down from the hostel. They did a 'backpackers special' consisting of; fruit juice, eggs how you like them, (cooked preferably), bacon, sausage, fried bread, beans, toast and tea or coffee for $4.50.

After this I was raring to go, and did (phew!), before leaving to catch the Explorer bus from the nearest stop on Queen Street outside the Tourist Office. The route takes you out of the Central Business District (CBD), along the waterfront eastwards to Mission Bay. This is one of the popular beaches around the city.

Situated on the curve of Okahu Bay and with superb views of Waitemata Harbour and the high-rise buildings of the CBD, is Kelly Tarlton's Antarctic Encounter and Underwater World. This is an excellent place to lose a few hours, and you start off by riding a heated snow-cat through a simulated snowstorm to an Antarctic landscape, complete with a breeding colony of King Penguins.

These funny fellows, who are so ungainly on land, are majestic when swimming and diving in the water. There was real excitement at this time as they had just had a successful birth of a penguin chick and we were amongst the first visitors to see it.

From the penguin aquarium, you are taken on a moving walkway within a glass tunnel, where you have absolutely marvellous views of all manner of reef fish, huge stingrays floating above your head and several species of shark. Everything was so clear and the accompanying music was almost hypnotic.

Once through this part of the Aquarium, you enter an area with numerous small theatres showing films on varying aquatic topics and Antarctic exploration. Small tanks with tiny sea horses and other micro fish could be viewed, and I managed to take some excellent close-up video footage.

I rejoined the Explorer bus, and we travelled through some lovely suburbs and up to Mount Eden, Auckland's highest volcanic cone, standing at 196m. Offering panoramic views of the city and harbour, this is a popular place for Aucklanders at weekends. Many bring their picnics to the grassy terraces that are protected from the wind by the walls of the volcano.

I decided that the city and harbour backdrop would make an excellent photo opportunity for me with my 'Cross of St.George', English flag. I just needed to find someone to take the photo, and just as I found a chap willing to assist me, a coach load of Japanese tourists arrived. They all had the same idea, but had no notion of the term 'queuing'.

Mount Eden is just one of 48 volcanic cones that surround the city. The summit crater is sacred to the Maori and known as Te Ipu a Mataaho (the Bowl of Mataaho), after the god of volcanoes.

From Mount Eden, the only way is down, and I re-boarded the bus before disembarking again in the suburb of Parnell. This is reputedly a trendy area with many cafes, restaurants and smart bars. It was such a beautiful afternoon that I wandered for some way down the hill towards the harbour, stopping here and there for a refreshment or three!

I got back to the hostel at about 6.30pm and met a fellow Brit called Dave. Whilst chatting I discovered that although he hailed from Middlesbrough, he had been living in Ipswich for the previous five years, whilst working at the British Telecom Research Centre at Martlesham Heath.

It's hard to believe that I had travelled to the other side of the world only to bump into someone from my home town. We decided to go out for a drink, and having found a bar selling Kilkenny Irish Ale and Guinness, we enjoyed a few pints as we chatted about our respective journeys.

Whilst in this pub I came across 'pokies' for the first time, the local name for one-armed bandits or fruit machines. A huge area at the rear of the pub was devoted to them, and eager punters were dutifully feeding each machine. There are no licensed betting shops in New

Zealand, so pubs and clubs offer this facility on an official basis called the tote.

It is possible to win big money on the ' pokies', but like all forms of betting, you are likely to lose far more than you are ever likely to win. Either way, the machines earn the establishment, and the government via tax revenue, huge sums. It is sad to think that many gamblers will put their entire weekly wages into the 'pokies' at just one session.

I was due to meet up with Anne in three days' time on 27th February, as she was joining me again for a few weeks after a visit to the world-famous Kota Knabala National Park in Borneo, where she was going to the Orang-Utan Rehabilitation Centre.

I had decided to bring my flight to Christchurch forward by one day, as I felt that I would have seen most of Auckland's sights by then, so visited the Qantas Airlines office in Queen Street. There was a monster queue, and I had no option but to sit and wait my turn. (Not that I'm a monster you understand!).

The flight change was completed in a matter of minutes but my wait had been an hour and three quarters. I hadn't had to pay anything, as my RTW ticket was changeable without penalty, as long as the routing wasn't changed.

This task completed I was able to pre-book a hostel in Christchurch that the travel desk at the hostel had recommended to me. They only had twin share rooms available at $52 per night, which meant that I might need to share with another guy, if there was anyone wishing to do the same. If there was, then the room cost would be halved, so I decided to take this option. Finally, I ordered the shuttle bus to the airport and I was advised that a 10.15am pick-up would be sufficient time for me to check-in by 11am.

These little details taken care of, it was time for more sightseeing. Dave accompanied me as we walked to the Auckland Art Gallery. I know I've said that I am not a great art lover, but this one had a whole floor that did interest me. This part of the gallery was devoted to comic books from around the world. The names of many were familiar to me; 'Eagle', 'Beano', 'Dandy', 'Beezer', 'Hotspur', and many of the American comic book heroes.

A small theatre was showing old black and white cartoons of Mickey Mouse, which reminded me of the film shows that used to be shown at St. Thomas's Church in Ipswich by choirmaster Chris Smith, when I was a choir boy and that so enthralled us all.

From the Art Gallery we continued north and walked across a large parkland area known as the Auckland Domain. These undulating grounds cover eighty hectares of cycle and jogging paths, sports fields, landscaped gardens and wooded areas. At the crest of this lies the impressive Auckland Museum.

There was only a small charge for entry, but it is one of the most interesting museums that I have ever visited. I was especially interested in the displays of Maori arts and culture. There was even a huge, magnificently carved meeting house or 'Hotuni', built in 1878.

Another superb exhibit was the Great War Canoe, 'Te Toki a Tapiri' (Tapiri's battle-axe), built in 1836 and capable of carrying a hundred warriors. It was no wonder that the early explorers like Abel Tasman and Captain Cook were often unable to land when faced with a few of these great war canoes filled with fierce, strangely painted Maori warriors.

After a long walk back to the hostel, we were both ready for a beer or three and after an early meal we returned to the QF Bar where we had been the previous evening and enjoyed a few pints, as Dave told me more details of his journey thus far.

His trip started in North America before he headed to Australia and then here, to New Zealand. It was good to hear about his experiences in Australia as I was soon to be headed there myself. He had worked in far North Queensland on a Sheep Station, (not a place where sheep wait for a train, but a huge ranch covering thousands of kilometres!)

The sheep all have to be accounted for and periodically rounded up for sale and shearing. (Here is the old joke: Two Kiwis are walking towards each other and one has a sheep over his shoulder. "Guday mate, are you shearing?" one asks. The other replies, "No mate, get your own!")

Anyway, I digress as usual. Over such large areas, the only feasible way of doing this is by using quad-bikes, motorbikes and even helicopters. This sounded like a great adventure, not unlike the movies, but Dave was quick to tell me that it was incredibly hard work. Workers live in large, basic bunkhouses and have their meals included in their wages. Day-to-day life is very tough, and work is manual and undertaken in some pretty inhospitable conditions. These stations are miles from any major towns, but at least you can save your money as, apart from gambling, a major side occupation, there is precious little else to spend your wages on.

Dave started off by going out on work parties erecting fencing, but his computer skills allowed him to be re-housed in the main ranch house, where he was put to work helping with the paperwork and administration. Still, it was a fascinating experience for him. I will not be officially allowed to work under the terms of my tourist visa for Australia, due to my age, however, there are undoubtedly ways and means should I wish to.

I had really enjoyed Dave's company and we exchanged contact details and promised to keep in touch and hopefully meet up again at some stage in the future back home.

Christchurch to Queenstown.

My Qantas flight from Auckland to Christchurch was scheduled for an 11.30am departure. The shuttle bus had collected me at 10.15am, and I had been assured that this was plenty of time to comply with my check-in time of 11am.

What the shuttle company and I had not taken into consideration was the small matter of a State visit by HRH Queen Elizabeth II. As the senior British subject moving around Auckland, I had to accept the traffic congestion and road closures, and very nearly didn't make the flight.

It was 11.10am when I presented myself at the Qantas desk, and although allowed to board, I had to run to the aircraft. In my haste I had forgotten to place my knife, fork and spoon set in the backpack and these were confiscated, as I had them in my carry-on baggage.

Christchurch is located on the East coast and has a population of 331,000. It is reputed to be the most English of New Zealand's cities, complete with punts gliding down the Avon River. Founded in 1852, the settlement was designed to be a model of class-structured England in the South Pacific, unlike most of the scruffy colonial outposts common at that time. Land was given to the gentry, and churches rather than pubs were built. (What a pleasant but slightly boring place to have lived in me thinks!)

Christchurch lies in the region of Canterbury that is dominated by the dead-flat farming lands backed by the Southern Alps and known as the Canterbury Plains. As I have previously mentioned, some 50 million sheep are to be found in New Zealand. The Canterbury Plains contain a good proportion of these, and helped to make early settlers in Christchurch very wealthy.

My hostel was situated about a 20 minute walk from Cathedral Square, which is the heart of Christchurch and not surprisingly, dominated by Christchurch Cathedral. This Anglican cathedral was consecrated in 1881, and for $4, you can climb the 133 steps to the viewing balconies. (Guess who didn't spend $4?)

Whilst in the nearby visitor centre, I had found a leaflet on the Christchurch Gondola. No, this is not a ride down the Avon River, but a cable car ride high above the city, giving 360 degree views. I decided that this was for me (no step climbing) and caught a local bus to the Heathcote Valley Gondola terminal and for $12, I was whisked up and up on a ride that took only about five minutes to complete.

On a clear day you are able to see all the way to the Southern Alps, and although the weather was bright and sunny there was a slight haze and I doubted if it was possible today. For those of a more adventurous nature, as an alternative to catching the gondola back down, you can hire a mountain bike or paraglide down. Call me chicken-hearted if you will, but the gondola sounded fine to me, especially after seeing a party hurtling off down the track on two wheels at a tremendous speed.

I could see right down onto the city and could clearly make out the grid-style layout of the streets. New Brighton Pier was identifiable, as was Christchurch's harbour of Lyttleton, hidden from the city by large hills.

Back in Cathedral Square, I met my friend Anne strolling along, having just arrived from Borneo. We adjourned for coffee and caught up on matters at home and in Borneo, which Anne enthused, had been fantastic.

Anne had booked a trek along one of New Zealand's iconic walks, the Routeburn Track. This thirty two kilometre 'tramp' as they like to call it takes about four days and runs from near Glenorchy to a place known as 'The Divide' near to Te Anau. The track passes through some spectacular mountain scenery, but after the Inca Trail, I just wasn't up for more track walking.

Instead I intended to use the time exploring the South Island to its southern tip in the rental car that we had decided to hire to take us from Christchurch. Now I knew Anne's dates and movements, I could start to plan my route more exactly.

The following day we decided to visit the International Antarctic Centre. Built to house the administration and warehousing of the New Zealand, United States and

Italian Antarctic programmes, this huge complex has been developed into a major tourist and educational centre.

It was an excellent venue for a couple of hours, and gives an insight into this vast continent. We were able to see the equipment and vehicles that Antarctic researchers use, as well as watch video presentations on the sights and sounds of this huge continent. I was particularly interested to read how Australia and New Zealand were once part of a 'super continent' named 'Gondwana', which also included Antarctica.

In the afternoon, we caught a free shuttle bus to Lyttleton Harbour where we had booked onto a Wildlife Harbour Cruise. Lyttleton is situated twelve kilometres from the city centre of Christchurch and is an attractive small town. The first settlers landed here in 1850 and trekked over Port Hills to found Christchurch. Nowadays, there is an impressive road tunnel that takes you between the two.

We were hoping to have a glimpse of one of the world's smallest dolphin species, the Hector's Dolphin. Found only off the coast of New Zealand these dolphins can fit into a bath tub. (Different to a rubber duck I suppose!)

As we headed out of the shelter of the harbour and the wind picked up, the temperature dropped, and I was glad of the windcheater that I had decided to bring along despite the earlier warm sunshine. We had been going for about twenty five minutes when the Captain advised us that they had spotted a pod of Hector's Dolphins, and we would slow to see if they wanted to play. As if on cue, these tiny dolphins came alongside and just like their larger cousins, jumped and careered around the boat. The only problem was that when we stopped, the boat rocked in the swell and made videoing and photography tricky.

Back on dry land in Christchurch, we sat by the Avon River in the warm sun before finding a Thai restaurant for our dinner. We had planned our route to Queenstown, and would collect our car from Avis Rentals the following morning. There was still time for some last minute sightseeing around this lovely city, and we walked along Oxford Terrace to Victoria Square, where there is a statue of Captain James Cook. We should have liked to visit the Canterbury Museum and the next door Botanic Gardens, but not this time. Maybe I will get back to Christchurch before heading back to the North Island and my flight to Australia.

I met Anne at the Avis Rental Station and they gave us a free upgrade to a Toyota Corolla hatchback. We were impressed with this vehicle, and after collecting our belongings from our respective accommodations, we headed for Highway 1 out of the city.

It felt good to be back behind the wheel of a vehicle, despite the unfamiliar roads. At least we had no problems with driving, as New Zealand drives on the left, as in the U.K. We followed this road as far as Geraldine, passing through the vast Canterbury Plains dotted with sheep and cattle. At Geraldine we turned onto Highway 79, marked as the scenic route to Lake Tekapo. We had been blessed with glorious weather for our road trip and the Southern Alps were visible in the distance.

As you approach Lake Tekapo, the first thing that strikes you is the incredible colour of the water, a beautiful turquoise, which is due to the lake being fed by snow melt from the distant Southern Alps. It is one of three lakes in the Mackenzie Basin, as this area is referred to, and covers an area of 83sq km (32 sq mi). As we drove around the lake, we came to a statue of a collie dog. This statue was commissioned in 1968 to represent the working collie dogs so beloved in this area.

We also came upon a small church called The Church of the Good Shepherd. It was the first church to be built in the Mackenzie Basin in 1935, and is dedicated to the men who work these vast open lands. It has the most beautiful views of the lake and the mountains through its Altar window. As we left this serene vista behind, I was once again reminded of how fortunate I was to have witnessed it with my own eyes.

We were now following Highway 8 that would take us through the Lindis Pass to Lake Pukaki. This route was twisty and getting ever higher, and offered initially rolling hills covered in tussock grass and little else. The mountains, many snow-capped, were becoming closer in the background and it was quite a sight to behold.

Lake Pukaki came into view and once again, being a glacial lake, it had an incredibly milky-blue colour. With an area of 169 sq km (65sq mi) it is larger than Lake Tekapo and is 70m (229ft) at its deepest point.

We got our first view of Mount Cook, New Zealand's highest mountain at 3,754m (12,316ft), and of course had to stop for photographs of it soaring majestically above the lake. This was a 'wow' moment for sure. Following the shore of the lake we continued onwards towards Queenstown along Highway 8. This route takes you to the quaint-sounding town of Twizel and then to Omarama. Now we had crossed into the Province of Otago, and we had about another two hours before we reached Queenstown.

Upon arrival in Queenstown, we navigated first to Anne's hostel and then to mine. Anne had reserved her accommodation from the U.K., whilst I had been reserving mine as I went. My hostel was called Southern Laughter (well I hoped it would be) but regrettably it was not exactly as I had hoped. It was well situated near to the centre and gondola lift, but the accommodation reserved for me was a bunk in a five bunk room. The added twist was that it was a mixed gender room but, as I was discover I was the odd man out (literally!).

My fellow backpackers comprised of two American girls, a French girl and a German girl. Add to this that the spare bunk was on the top and my spirits dropped. Physically it was not easy for me to clamber up onto this bunk and the French girl below me was quite possibly going to be in mortal danger!

When I walked in, the two American girls made it plainly obvious that I was not welcome in their domain, as they were both scantily clad and perhaps not expecting a male roommate. The German girl was friendly, and we spoke for a while about our respective trips before I left to meet Anne for a walk and dinner.

Queenstown is the self-proclaimed adventure capital of the world. As we walked into the centre, it soon became apparent why. On the corner of the main streets of 'Shotover' and 'Camp', we found the huge visitor centre. Here it is possible to get information on and book every conceivable adventure that Queenstown and the area has to offer.

From gentle rowing on the lake to the 'ultimate bungee' experience, adrenaline junkies are well catered for. A.J.Hackett is the name of the company who have made 'bungee' a household name. They have the 'Nevis Bungee' at 134m (440ft) above the Nevis River. This is the highest bungee in New Zealand, and is all over in 8.5 seconds!

Would you jump with just a large rubber band attached to your ankles? If yes, then this is the place for you. If we were meant to fly, then we would have been given wings, so call me faint hearted if you will, but I think I'll find some other form of thrill, thank you.

That evening, after our dinner, we returned to our respective hostels, and I received a somewhat frosty reception from the American girls. You would think that they would be pleased to be sharing a room with a hunk like me! I put my belongings into a locker and decided to sleep in the car that night.

I found a large car park on the outskirts of the town and parked up between two trucks, reclined the seat and settled down to sleep. All was well for a few hours until I was awoken by the sound of a vehicle being driven at high speed around the car park.

Peeking out from my hiding place I could see a car being driven in circles at great speed sending up clouds of dust and gravel. That was all I needed, joy-riders. Had they stolen the car or were just locals out for some fun? Either way I thought that they might attract the police and I didn't want to be discovered sleeping in this truck park.

I carefully drove out of the park and made my way back towards town. As I was about half a mile from the truck park a car whizzed past with blue lights flashing...the police investigating? I found a quiet road close to one of the larger hotels, parked up, and managed to get a few hours' sleep before dawn. Whilst driving around, I had seen another hostel with a vacancy sign illuminated, and decided that this would be where I would move to for my second night, if the accommodation was ok.

I returned to Southern Laughter at about 7.30am and the girls were all sleeping soundly. I used the facilities to shave and shower and checked out and into my new accommodation, the Alpine Lodge, where I booked a male share room for four people at the same rate as Southern Laughter. As I had checked in early, I had the choice of bunks, and grabbed a bottom one.

I picked Anne up and we drove to Glenorchy, a forty-minute drive from Queenstown. This small town sits at the head of Lake Wakatipu, at the opposite end of the lake from Queenstown. With the mountains as a backdrop, Glenorchy is a picturesque setting, but today the weather had closed in, and the low cloud and cool wind made the lake's waters somewhat rough. As the rain fell, we retreated back to Queenstown, and took lunch at

Anne's hostel, which had lovely views from its large balcony - obviously the benefit of being able to spend some extra time finding a place to stay.

The rain had set in for the day and so we spent the time resting, reading and for myself, planning how to spend the next few days while Anne was hiking the Routeburn Track.

South Island Road Trip.

Anne was off hiking, and I was off to see as much of the rest of South Island as I could in the next four days. I skirted Lake Wakatipu and followed the signs for Highway 6 past Frankton and carried on until I came to the small town of Lumsden.

Lumsden is roughly halfway between Queenstown and Invercargill, my destination for that night, and it sits at a main crossroads for the Province of Southland that I had now entered. The old railway station, once an important hub, is now the Visitor Information centre and it was here that I enjoyed a break and some refreshment. Southland is a small Province, surrounded by the larger Province of Otago and occupies the central south area of South Island.

I drove the remaining ninety kilometres at a steady pace and found my pre-booked hostel without any trouble. The Tuatara Lodge is part of the Youth Hostellers Association (YHA), and this one had recently been refurbished. The facilities were excellent and it was also centrally situated in the city on the main street.

Invercargill is the southernmost city in New Zealand, and one of the most southerly in the world. Its main industry is farming, and it has a reputation for being somewhat old-fashioned, and even backward. Living in a rural area myself, Ipswich people have become accustomed to jibes of being 'Sleepy Suffolk Yokels'.

There was still a lot of daylight left and so I decided to make the short journey to Bluff, New Zealand's southernmost town on the mainland. Stewart Island, which lies off the coast of South Island, and is reached by ferry from Bluff, is technically the most southern point, and the town of Oban lays claim to the title of southernmost town.

The weather was dull, and it was raining sporadically as I parked up at the foot of Stirling Point. Here there is a large signpost indicating distances and directions to major cities worldwide, including the Equator and the South Pole. London was shown as being 18,858 km (11,556 miles) away - quite a thought!

As I made my way up to the lookout point over the Southern Pacific Ocean, the force of the wind was incredible, and the rain was actually stinging my face. I had to shout whilst videoing, in the hope that my voice might be heard above the howling wind. It was sobering to think that some 3,000 miles to the south lay the South Pole and I could only imagine what the seas between here and there would be like, especially in the winter months.

Bluff is the main port for the New Zealand ships that replenish the Antarctic survey teams. Bluff's main claim to fame lies in its oysters, found in the Foveaux Strait. The Bluff oyster is renowned for its succulence and flavour. I have tried oysters, as the Blackwater River oyster beds in Essex are near to home, but personally, I can do without them. If it has a large pearl inside, then fair enough, but knowing my luck I'd swallow it and choke! I had read that there was a bungalow in Bluff that had been completely covered in Paua shells (sea snails), and had become a tourist attraction. I was freezing cold, wet, and frankly this did not cause me any great excitement, despite having travelled nearly 12,000 miles from home.

I drove back to Invercargill and after a quick food shopping expedition at Woolworths I made myself a dinner of noodles, tuna and salad followed by a banana and some hot chocolate - the basic backpacker fare.

Interestingly, the Tuatara Lodge is named after the reptile similar to a lizard, but a throwback to creatures that lived 200 million years ago. The Tuatara is endemic to New Zealand and has been a protected species since as long ago as 1895. It has a prominent spiny back from which it derives its name. In the Maori language it means 'peaks on the back'.

Invercargill didn't excite me, and after a brief walk the following morning, I drove away towards Dunedin. I had decided that I would follow the Southern Scenic Route along the coast and through a wilderness area known as the Catlins. This route is not much longer than the main Highway, but can take considerably longer, as some roads are unsealed and require much slower speeds.

The Catlins start at a point called Waipapa Point, a really wild promontory over the Ocean. Signs here warn travellers that there are twenty two kilometres of unsealed roads ahead, and it is recommended that 4WD vehicles be used. My little Toyota Corolla had four wheels, so I reasoned it would be alright to continue!

The weather was pretty poor, with gusting winds and heavy rain showers, interspersed with sunshine. There were very few other vehicles about - hardly surprising, I suppose, but this did allow me to stop frequently for photo opportunities. One such stop was at Curio Bay and then again at Porpoise Bay. I guess that these creatures might frequent the bay, but if they were today good luck to them, as the seas were really wild.

According to my guidebook, the Catlins are a haven for visitors interested in the fauna and flora of New Zealand, with some 22,250 hectacres of forest. There is also a plethora of bird life around the coast, including the endangered yellow-eyed penguin.

I was looking for the turn-off to McLean Falls and when I came to the sign it indicated five kilometres. I turned off an unsealed road onto a very dodgy dirt road, and coaxed the Toyota gingerly along this track until it came to a dead end. Another sign informed me that there was now a thirty-minute walk to reach the Falls. I'd come this far, so it seemed a shame not to go any further, and after all, I needed some exercise! The walk, as it transpired, was quite pleasant, winding up through a dense forest. The large ferns, so synonymous with New Zealand, are really very attractive, and with the raindrops clinging to them, made for good photographs, especially as the sun broke through the dark clouds. I don't know about plentiful birdlife, but to me it sounded very quiet apart from the distant roar of the waterfall.

I suppose that these are some of the oldest rainforests in the world and there I was, a lad from Ipswich, walking amongst them. Humbling, somehow, and it did make me feel very lucky to be there. I was jogged out of my reverie by a sudden and heavy downpour that very quickly left me drenched. Nothing for it but to trudge on, and hope that the falls did not disappoint. They didn't disappoint, and whilst not Victoria or Niagara, they were pretty impressive and, I felt, well worth the effort. Impressive or not, I was glad to get back to the car, remove my wet fleece and find some dry clothing from my backpack.

The unsealed road continued, and there was evidence of some slight flooding in parts, that I carefully avoided. Papatowai, Owaku and Balclutha were passed, and despite the signs for nature walks and trails at various points, I decided that the Catlins had seen enough of me in this weather, as I had of them.

By the time I reached Dunedin, the weather had cleared and I was greeted by bright sunshine. I had booked into the Downtown Backpackers, which turned out to be a rather large and old style property. My shared room had a really high ceiling and eight beds in bunk style. My only room-mate was a young English girl who had taken a lower bunk at the window end of the room, so I took a lower bunk at the door end to help preserve our respective privacy.

I went out for a walk whilst the weather was dry to explore this most Celtic of cities. Founded by Scottish settlers, Dunedin means Edinburgh in the Celtic language. There is even a large statue of Robert Burns, the famous Scottish poet, in the main square and apparently the city has a whisky distillery and holds haggis ceremonies.

It has a very Victorian feel about it, and the Railway Station is a classic example of Victorian architecture, but there are plenty of modern buildings as well. Dunedin is the second largest city of the South Island, and houses New Zealand's first university.

With a large student population, the city has a thriving pub and café culture. I decided to visit one such pub, and enjoyed a very nice steak and kidney pie with mashed potatoes and vegetables. Afterwards I went to the cinema and watched a film about diamond smuggling in South Africa, but I must admit to falling asleep well before the end, following my brush with the wild nature of the Catlins earlier in the day.

The next day I picked up Highway 8 at Milton and headed back towards Queenstown. The weather had started dull and cold, but as I made my way across Central Otago Province through first Lawrence and then Roxburgh, the skies turned blue and the temperature rose appreciably. The mountain scenery was stunning in these conditions, and I was soon coming towards the town of Alexander. Originally, it was gold that lured people to Central Otago, but today, Alexandra is an oasis of orchards amidst the surrounding mountains. The Alexandra Historical Museum has a good collection of mining memorabilia, and for the more adventurous, there is the opportunity to follow a rugged road called the Dunstan Trail into the old Dunstan goldfields. A 4WD vehicle is very definitely needed to undertake this route.

My little Toyota was cruising happily towards Cromwell and, as is evidenced by the outsized fruit sculpture, (a bit like Carmen Miranda's hat), it is the centre of fruit country. This is the main route for Wanaka, and it was here that I had reserved accommodation for the night.

As I drove into the outskirts of Wanaka I was immediately given the impression that this was a much quieter resort than Queenstown, but beautiful nonetheless. The chalet style houses along the road were reminiscent of Alpine homes, and as I wound down towards the centre, the lake came into view. What a beautiful sight in the sunshine. The waters were a shimmering blue and a small beach ran opposite a number of shops and cafes. Large-wheeled water bicycles and pedalos sat ready for hire and I could now see a few people paddling along the shore.

I checked into my hostel, the Bullock Creek Lodge, and had a two-bedded room to share. It was situated on the ground floor, and faced out onto a large grassy paddock. My roommate was a Dutch lad called Rolly, who was very chatty, and we agreed to meet up later and go for something to eat in the town.

Wanaka is, like Queenstown, a popular winter sports venue, but without the razzmatazz of its larger neighbour. It was also becoming popular as an ideal place for people to retire to, and this could account for the well-ordered properties that I noticed on my arrival. The tourist brochures claim that Wanaka has one of the sunniest climates in New Zealand, and today it was certainly living up to that claim. I had actually taken off my fleece and it was lovely to feel the sun on my face and arms as I wandered down to the lakeside. A large digital display showed the temperature as being 25c as I sat down for a pot of tea and a scone. (How quintessentially English of me!)

Covering an area of 192 sq.km (74 sq.mi), Lake Wanaka is New Zealand's fourth largest lake. Wanaka sits at the south end of the lake and is in a U-shaped basin formed by glacial erosion during the last ice-age (just like a couple of days ago in the Catlins, perhaps!).

My evening meal turned out to be tuna, noodles and salad, accompanied by a bottle of red wine that I shared with Rolly. We then went and found a couple of bars, where we spent the money that we had saved on our meal on a few jugs of beer.

I thought that it would have been very pleasant to spend a few days here, just relaxing and exploring a few of the walking trails around Wanaka, but I had arranged to meet Anne back in Queenstown after her hiking experience along the Routeburn Track, so tomorrow I would be heading up the Cardrona Valley and over the highest sealed road in New Zealand, promising yet more spectacular scenery.

Queenstown to Wellington.

I awoke to a glorious day in Wanaka. After breakfast, I walked the short distance down to the lakeside and just took in the majestic scenery. The mountains made a fabulous backdrop to the lake, which reflected the strong sunshine, causing me to squint, even with sunglasses on. It was only 8am, but already the temperature reading on the digital display was showing 22c, with a promise of higher temperatures to come as the sun reached its zenith.

I said my goodbyes to Rolly and checked out of the Bullock Creek Lodge. Before heading to Queenstown, I decided to pay a visit to one of Wanaka's stranger attractions, Puzzling World, just off the main road out of Wanaka towards Cromwell, and set in seven acres of grounds.

The brightly painted, outrageously tilted houses are an attraction in themselves. Entering one of the tilted rooms, set at fifteen degrees, is a weird experience. All of the displays are normal, but the illusion created is so strong that you are convinced that the room cannot be sloping. Your brain automatically straightens the room and leaves the displays hanging at some impossible angle, a quite remarkable illusion.

Another room is called the Hall of Following Faces where a plethora of famous faces appear to follow your every move and after a while, this can become quite disconcerting. Imagine the feeling of being watched in minute detail, and you can begin to understand the illusion created here.

Other rooms show various visual puzzles and there is plenty of opportunity for hands-on logic puzzles. As someone who struggled to make one side of a Rubik cube all the same colour, most of these left me stumped.

The biggest attraction at Puzzling World is the Great Maze. Built using wooden panels, and with four large towers at each corner, you are advised to allow between thirty minutes and one hour to find your way through to the exit. Even from the vantage point of one of the towers, I was struggling to see a clear route, and sadly admit to using one of the emergency doors, as I was mindful of my time dwindling away and wanted to continue my journey to Queenstown.

It was in some ways a relief to have my vision fixed once again on what lay around me. One of these sights was Mount Aspiring, which at 3,033 mt or 9,950 ft, is the second highest peak in New Zealand after Mount Cook.

As I continued towards Cardrona, there were signs for various ski fields, once again reminding me of the winter sports opportunities here. I had read about a rather odd attraction in the Cardrona area, the Cardrona Bra Fence. Apparently, in 1999 four bras had been attached to a length of fence alongside the road and by February of the following year this number had risen to sixty. No one ever gave a logical reason for these actions, but when they were removed anonymously, it was reported in the local newspaper. It then became a newsworthy item across New Zealand, and more and more bras were left hanging on this stretch of fence, becoming a quirky tourist attraction.

I could find no trace of bras hanging from any fences, and can only assume that they had been removed for fear of offending anyone or sullying the area's reputation. If you found a glove or handkerchief it was common to hang this item on a wall or fence so that its owner might recover it later, but a bra...!

I was now following the Crown Range road that leads to the summit of the highest sealed road in New Zealand at 1,121 mt (3,667 ft). You can only imagine the views at this height, so I had to stop and do some videoing and just take it all in. Arrowtown and Queenstown were visible in the distance as I gazed down into the Wakatipu valley. The landscape was an unremarkable brown, being mainly tussock grass and scrub, but this only served to emphasis the beauty of the scene.

What surprised me was to see a group of cyclists. Must they ever be fit to cycle up this road? They stopped at my lookout spot to take some much needed liquid refreshment, and I found out that they were from England, and had been cycling all over New Zealand. They told me that it was tough riding, especially with the windy and wet weather, but the views and scenery were simply spectacular.

I wished them well and continued on my way, thankful for the four wheels I had. The road was now winding steeply ever downwards towards the valley floor, and made me even more amazed by the stamina of those cyclists. I bypassed Arrowtown and headed for Lake Hayes, reputedly the most photographed lake in New Zealand. It must be something well worth seeing, I reasoned, if it is more photogenic than the lakes that I had already marvelled at.

It was without doubt a beautiful setting, with the omnipresent mountains providing a thrilling backdrop. It has more trees and foliage around its shores and therefore more colour, and perhaps this is why it is rated so highly. An exclusive estate on the shores caters for weddings, and I can only imagine the superb backdrop for one's wedding photographs. It was only a relatively short drive now into Queenstown and because of this, Lake Hayes is a popular weekend and holiday destination for local people to come to picnic and swim.

Back in Queenstown once more, I made my way back to Southern Laughter despite my previous experience of not actually having slept there! This time I had managed to get a bed in a four-bedded dormitory with three other males. (Who would have thought I would have preferred this to sharing with females?).

I had time to complete my laundry duties before Anne arrived. She was bubbling about the Routeburn Track and had arranged to have dinner with one of the guys on the trip. In the meantime, we had some exploring of the town to do, and in sparkling weather, unlike a few days previously.

We took the Skyline Gondola ride situated close to my hostel, and rode to the summit of the hill overlooking the town. It wasn't cheap at $15 return but wow! the views were marvellous, and made it more than worthwhile in my opinion. Lake Wakatipu is framed by the aptly named Remarkables and the Eyre Mountains, and from my eyrie it was fascinating to watch the craft coming and going down on the lake.

There is no bungee jumping from this point but adrenaline chasers can try out the Luge track. This is a three-wheel cart that zooms you along an 800m track. There is one track called the scenic, and one more blood pressure rising for the 'advanced' nutcase! It is based on the Olympic sport where the competitor lies on his back on what looks like a tray, and shoots down an ice track, feet first!

While Anne was being wined and dined, I busied myself booking accommodation at Franz Josef, Greymouth and Nelson as we were heading up the west coast of South Island in readiness for catching the car ferry to the North Island from Picton.

I had my dinner and a few beers at a small restaurant near to the lake shores, and afterwards walked down by the lake to watch the paddle steamer arrive back with a party of tourists. A group of kilted pipers was performing, and reminded me of my dear friends Tom, Maisie, Ian and

George back in Ipswich, who hail from Kirkcaldy, Fife, in Scotland.

The next morning, I had expected to be making a visit to Milford Sound, one of New Zealand's most famous tourist attractions. However, Anne had gone there with some of her fellow hikers after the Routeburn Track, so if I wanted to go, it would be on my own. I was disappointed to miss out, and annoyed that Anne hadn't stuck to our original plan, but the drive to Franz Josef was about four and half hours, and there was plenty to see on the way that would necessitate stopping, so I would have to forgo this particular bit of scenery.

Retracing my route of the previous day, we climbed back up past Lake Hayes and Arrowtown to the lofty views over the Cardrona Valley and onto Wanaka. As a form of retribution for missing out on Milford Sound, I had considered trying to rush this section to deny Anne the stupendous views and beauty of the area, but I didn't, and enjoyed them all over again.

From Wanaka the road continues towards the west coast and Haast. The Haast Pass road was opened in 1965, before which the only southern link to the west coast was an old cattle track. This is all part of the Mt. Aspiring National Park, and as we headed down towards the coast, the scenery changed from the snow-covered peaks to forests and waterfalls.

Haast itself was rather disappointing, and I thought it rather scruffy, but there are not many other stopping places for petrol between there and Franz Josef. From

Haast, Highway 6 follows the coast mostly, with thick-forested areas inland.

Franz Joseph is reached in about an hour and three quarters, and as you drive into the small township, the mountains loom over you. Our hostel was the YHA, and it was as well that we had booked ahead, as the place was crowded. This was a very modern building with excellent amenities, and key cards to all the rooms, somewhat like a more expensive hotel.

There was a different feel about this area, a more alpine feel. The weather had closed in as well, and this gave it a different feeling also. The glacier is situated five kilometres from the town and there are various ways of viewing it. We opted for a helicopter ride that would allow us to land on the glacier and walk on it. We would also be able to fly over the nearby Fox Glacier. The flight was scheduled for thirty minute duration and was subject to weather conditions on the day.

That evening, we expressed a hope that the following day's weather would be good, but the staff at the YHA said that a completely clear day was unlikely, as rain was forecast.

Anne had told me that one of her girlfriends was arriving in Wellington, and would be travelling with her through to Sydney and her return to the U.K. I had my own ideas and plans for the rest of my time in New Zealand, but Anne was unsure of her friend's plans until she met up with her.

I decided that perhaps this was the time to strike out on my own once more, and leave the girls to enjoy their respective holidays together. I used the travel desk at the YHA, and arranged accommodation from Wellington. I booked a bus journey from Wellington to Rotorua and then onwards to Auckland. From Auckland I booked another bus to the Bay of Islands in the far north of the North Island. They recommended a hostel in Rotorua called Cactus Jack's, that I booked, and I rebooked into the Queen Street Backpackers in Auckland. Finally, I booked into a lodge in Paihia, in the Bay of Islands.

I would leave Anne with the car, and her friend could take over my share until they got to Auckland, where we had arranged to return it to Avis before leaving for Sydney. I now had a firm plan and felt quite pleased at my decisiveness. To celebrate, I went out for a few beers with one of new roommates, a lad from Denver, Colorado. This turned into quite a few and I eventually made it back to the YHA at 1am.

The weather wasn't perfect the following morning, and I was feeling the effects of my indulgences of the previous evening. Anne and I walked to the tour office on the main street and checked in for our 8.15am flight. We had heard helicopters flying as we left the YHA, which we thought was a positive sign. The flight was going ahead as planned, but it would be the pilot's decision as to whether we would actually land on the glacier. It was made clear to us that safety was their first priority, and that no refunds would be made if it was deemed unsafe to land on the glacier.

That was fair enough, at least we had been forewarned and you can't afford to play with people's lives. The helicopter sat four people and after deciding the loading pattern, I was seated behind the pilot, with two Japanese girls on my left. Anne had a prime seat up front, next to the pilot. Safety procedures were explained and once we had fastened our seat belts and donned our earmuffs with built-in radio, we were ready for take-off.

This was not my first time in a helicopter, having enjoyed the experience a few years previously when visiting the Grand Canyon, in Arizona. The noise is unbelievable, hence the ear protectors and built-in radio microphone. Without this you would be unable to hear the commentary and instructions of the pilot.

As we rose into the air and pulled away from the town it became obvious that the low clouds were possibly going to be a problem. Our pilot informed us that with luck, we would be landing on the glacier - not the Franz Josef, but the larger Fox Glacier. Conditions and wind direction were more favourable here for a landing, and a previous flight had landed there successfully a little while earlier.

The sun had actually begun to penetrate the clouds and the visibility was fairly good now. Our pilot /guide explained how the Franz Josef glacier was named. In 1865, the German explorer Julius von Haast named this glacier after the then Emperor of Austria, Franz Josef I. (I presume that the Haast Pass that we travelled across a few days ago was named after that same German explorer).

The glacier is approximately twelve kilometres (seven and a half miles) in length and reaches almost to the coast, quite unusual for a glacier. I had read that The

Maori name for the glacier is Ka Roimata o Hinehukatere (The tears of Hinehukatere). Legend has it that Hinehukatere loved to climb in these mountains and persuaded her lover, Wawe to climb with her. They were caught in an avalanche and Wawe was swept to his death. Hinehukatere was devastated and wept so much that her tears flowed down the mountain, froze and formed the glacier. Maybe not the accepted scientific answer for why and how glaciers are formed, but I like this version.

We went first to the Fox Glacier or, Te Moeka o Tuawe, to give it its Maori name. Imagine my disappointment to learn that it was not named after a fox and a polar bear of the famous clear mint brand, but rather boringly, after Sir William Fox the Prime Minister of New Zealand in 1872.

Good news, we were going to land on the glacier and have the opportunity to take some unique photographs. The glacier is approximately thirteen kilometres (eight miles) in length and falls 2,600 m (8,500 ft) down to the rainforest, which is just 300 m (980 ft) above sea level.

It was extremely windy out on the glacier, but not as cold as I had imagined. There were already two other helicopters on the snow, and we were told that when we were called back to re-board, we should do so without delay, as other helicopters would be arriving. (Busy, busy place and plenty of tourist dollars being made, doubtless).

We were not technically on the glacier itself, as this is the pure ice flow or moraine that moves down through the valley and which can be seen from the air as a blue colour against the grey/white of the surrounding snow and ice. This is caused by trapped water that freezes to a pure ice block and reflects the light, giving a blue appearance. (I prefer the tear drops theory put forward by the Maori!)

I had the opportunity to have a photograph with my Cross of St. George flag and of course to reciprocate for our Japanese ladies, who posed with the 'V for whatever' sign that they so favour.

As we took off, so other helicopters were landing, and the tourist trade continued unabated. It is also possible to 'heli-hike', where you are taken by helicopter to a certain point, and then hike up part of the glacier with a qualified guide. Anne would have liked to do this, but the cost and time were prohibitive. I was fascinated to see the Tasman Sea so close to these glaciers, something that you wouldn't see in the European Alps or in the Rocky Mountains of North America. It was over very quickly, but it had been worth the $190 fee for a once in a lifetime experience.

We left Franz Josef after a leisurely breakfast, checking out of the YHA at about 1pm. The drive to our next stopover at Greymouth was about 180 km (110 miles). Following Highway 6 along the west coast, we were now travelling through 'Lord of the Rings' territory. The film adaptation of the book of the same name by J.R.R. Tolkien was completed entirely in New Zealand, and this part of the coast was used for much of it. I hadn't seen the film yet, but it had been phenomenally successful at the box office, and I looked forward to watching it at some time in the future.

The first major town that we passed through was Whataroa, and then onto Rosa, the area famous for its gold fields. In 1909, New Zealand's largest nugget was found here, and named 'Honourable Roddy' after the west coast politician, Roderick McKenzie.

The next town was Hokitika, once a major township on the west coast, and then we drove on to Kumara Junction. Here there is a strange single-lane bridge to negotiate - strange in so much as it also acts as the rail bridge over the Taramakia River. Trains have right of way, unsurprisingly.

On arrival at Greymouth, so called as it sits at the mouth of the Grey River, they say that first impressions count and I was singularly unimpressed. It looked grey and dowdy, and our hostel, Revingtons didn't look much better from the outside either. Upon checking in, the interior was not better, although the dormitory was clean enough. Never mind, it was for only one night. A walk down by the harbour was no better and there was precious little in the way of attractive architecture to be seen.

We called into a café and, horror of horrors, they didn't have any cakes, and the coffee was distinctly average. A further walk followed and we found a small cinema, where we decided on impulse to watch a film called 'Rat Race'. It was billed as a comedy and was staring John Cleese and Rowan Atkinson. Neither of us had ever heard of it, but in the event, it was absolutely hilarious and upped our spirits no end. Afterwards we found a Mexican-themed restaurant and enjoyed a

Tex/Mex meal that was both spicy and filling, and not too expensive.

We had decide to leave for Nelson fairly early the next morning, and were on the road north by 7.45am. Frankly, we had not enjoyed our visit to Greymouth, as it did little for either Anne or me.

We drove along Highway 6 as far as Rapahoe where we once again skirted the coast. We stopped at a small café for breakfast and then continued on towards Punakaiki. Here the cliffs and crags have been weathered over millions of years to create some fabulous blowholes, known as the Pancake Rocks.

The scenery was wildly beautiful, with the ocean crashing in on one side and mountains and forests rearing up on the other side of the road. Before long we had passed through Charleston and Westport, clocking up 150km since leaving Greymouth.

We were now in the Province of Nelson-Marlborough and the road headed inland slightly as there are no sealed roads up this stretch of the west coast. We reached the coast again when we arrived into Nelson, a city of just over 50,000 inhabitants. Notable for having one of the best climates in New Zealand, one of its nicknames is 'Sunny Nelson'. It was living up to that nickname today, as it had turned warm and sunny for our arrival.

Our pre-booked hostel was situated on the outskirts of the city some six kilometres from the city centre. Being such a lovely afternoon we decided to walk to explore the city, and after a good forty five minutes we had reached the main shopping area, called Trafalgar Street.

It might not surprise you that Nelson was named after Horatio Nelson and many of the public areas and streets bear the names of people and ships associated with the Battle of Trafalgar. It is the oldest settled city on the South Island and the second oldest in New Zealand. The city boasts a number of historic buildings, amongst the best are the restored workers' cottages dating from 1863 to 1867, found on South Street close to the cathedral.

Nelson had a nice feel to it, and had we, or, more accurately, had I the energy, we could have gone to the Botanic Gardens. Here, amongst the splendid floral displays, is an excellent lookout, and a plaque proclaiming the spot to be New Zealand's geographical central point.

The walk back was definitely beyond my stamina or desire, and so we opted for a taxi back to the hostel. That evening, having noticed that the film 'Ali' was being screened at the cinema in the city centre, we decided to go and watch it. Starring Will Smith (of 'Fresh Prince of Bel-Air' fame) the film tells the story of the world-famous American heavyweight boxer, Mohammed Ali. It was well made and well-acted by Smith and an enlightening look at this great sportsman's often controversial, but never dull, life.

That evening, on my return to the hostel, I struck up a conversation with a young Kiwi lad who was working in the area but was actually from near Auckland. We shared a couple of tins of beer before I retired to the dormitory, leaving him watching the television.

The dormitory was the largest that I had used yet, with about twelve single beds within it. My bed was fairly close to the door and I was soon asleep, only to be rudely awakened by having water thrown over my face. I was just aware of a figure jumping back into a bed and, after a few seconds to take in what had happened, I went over to this character, only to discover that it was the young lad from the TV lounge feigning sleep.

I was furious, grabbed him and dragged him outside in to the corridor, preparing to take my anger out on his face. As I drew back my fist I saw real fear in his eyes and hesitated before growling at him and asking him why he had done that? It was my snoring apparently, and he was trying to stop me, as he couldn't sleep through it. I asked him why he hadn't shaken me awake, instead of nearly causing me to have a heart attack. I told him that if he wanted me to have a single room, then he was welcome to pay the supplement, and I would oblige. If not he would just have to put up with it, just as anyone has to put up with other people's nocturnal habits in a shared room! He apologised and I refrained from hitting him, but decided to sleep out on the couch in the lounge, as I just couldn't settle in the dormitory again. Probably to his and everybody else's relief, if the truth were known.

Our inter-island ferry was due to depart Picton at 1.30pm and as Anne had decided to leave the car at the Avis Port Office, we left Nelson early enough to allow for this.

The journey that we should have liked to make was along the Queen Charlotte Drive between Havelock and Picton. This very scenic but winding road covers the last forty kilometres and gives fantastic views over the Marlborough Sound. Unfortunately, we decided that we did not have enough time to do justice to this route, and took the more straightforward highway route.

Picton's little port was quite attractive and the weather had held fine from the previous day. We hoped that it would continue for the four hour crossing to Wellington on the North Island.

Anne had arranged to hire another car from the port to use with her friend for the remainder of their journey in New Zealand, and we drove this to the YHA in the city centre where we were staying, in my case, for just that night.

Rotorua or Rottenrua!

I was up early and grabbed some breakfast before reporting for my bus to Rotorua, which was due to depart at 8am. My scheduled arrival in Rotorua was 3.10pm and involved a change of buses at Taupo.

The bus was less than a quarter full, so I was able to secure two seats for myself and stretch out a little. As we followed Highway 1 north, the driver pointed out interesting facts and views as we came to them, as well as advising us that we would be taking a break at a small town called Bulls.

As we got closer to our rest stop, he told us a little about Bulls. The local tourist office has come up with quite a catchy theme to describe the town he told us. 'Welcome to Bulls, an unforget-a-Bull-town. Our town is live-a-Bull, and the town's folk are hospit-a-Bull and befriend-a-Bull. We have several good eat-a-Bull places, so enjoy the food'.

Bulls was not in fact named after a four-legged animal of the 'ring through the nose' variety, but after one James Bull. Originally from Chelsea, London he was a carpenter, and was commissioned to build a chair for the Parliamentary Speaker in Wellington.

He found the excellent forests of Totura trees along the Rangtikei River and established a timber mill. He then set up a general store, built a courthouse and hotel and became a prominent citizen of the growing township. Visitors would often say that they were going to Bull's and so in 1872 the name of Bulls was accepted as the official name of the township...and that's no Bull!

When we stopped for our break, I was amused to see a sign for the toilets saying 'Reliev-a-Bull' (it certainly was after a few hours on the bus, I can assure you!). In the bakery, I found a leaflet with still more 'Bull' references. The police station was referred to as 'Consta-Bull', the church was 'Forgive-a-Bull' and the medical centre was 'Cure-a-Bull'.

As we drove on after our stop, I was full of admiration for those responsible for these humorous references that would encourage me, for one, to spend some time in the town of Bull. My mind was now in naughty mode, and I remembered a very funny story called 'Have you ever wondered what is meant when someone tells you that you don't know Jack Schitt'. I'll leave you, dear reader, to determine whether you wish to pursue this story via the internet. All I'll say is that it is a little risqué, but very funny.

The drive to Rotorua covers a distance of 450 km (280 miles) and would take about six and a half hours. I settled back after my Bulls extravaganza, and just watched the scenery, wondering how the rest of my overall trip would pan out.

At Taupo it was necessary to change buses for the leg onwards to Rotorua. I was now in the very heart of the North Island and Taupo sits on the north-eastern corner of the Lake of the same name. This lake is the largest of New Zealand's lakes and was formed some 25,000 years ago by what was reckoned to have been one of the biggest volcanic eruptions ever. It left a huge basin that is now filled with the waters of Lake Taupo. This whole area of the Central Plateau is still volcanically active and there are many thermal areas such as those I was looking forward to seeing in Rotorua.

Lake Taupo is a magnet for fishermen, and is widely acknowledged as the trout fishing capital of the world. It is also the source of New Zealand's longest river, the Waikato, which flows through the heart of North Island to the west coast just south of Auckland.

On this leg of the journey, our driver put on a video about Rotorua and its many attractions. It was a well-made documentary, and made me even keener to get there and experience the thermal pools, geysers and of course the 'pong' caused by the sulphur present at the volcanic sites.

We arrived pretty much on time at 3.10pm and I walked to my hostel, Cactus Jack's, from the transit centre. Above the front of the hostel was a large, grinning, unshaven character supposedly depicting Cactus Jack, complete with a sequoia cactus. It looked rather shabby from the outside, and indeed the whole place was rather underwhelming and in need of a refurbishment.

My room, a single, was small and functional, but clean. I had a quick freshen up in the shared bathroom and then asked the receptionist to book me on a Maori Cultural evening that I had picked up a leaflet on.

In the meantime I had a walk to get the stiffness out of my legs after the bus trip. It was only a short way down the main shopping street to reach the shores of Lake Rotorua, where various water craft were plying their way backwards and forwards. A paddle steamer runs breakfast, luncheon and dinner cruises, and self-drive speedboats and kayaks can also be hired.

I could definitely pick up the scent of rotten eggs on the breeze, so Rotorua was living up to its nickname of 'Rottenrua'! My Maori evening included transport to and from Cactus Jack's and this would be at 7pm. I wandered back, looking at the shops, and had a coffee and a sticky bun to fortify myself prior to the meal that was inclusive in the Maori evening.

It was a twenty-minute drive to Rakeiao Marae (sacred meeting place) situated on the shores of Lake Rotoiti, home to the Ngati Rongomai people. As we disembarked from our transport, we were met and treated to the 'Wero' (challenge) before being welcomed to the Marae with the 'Powhiri' (formal welcome), which includes the 'Hongi' (pressing of noses), and told that we were now part of the family for the rest of the evening.

Once inside the Marae, members of the family performing traditional dances and songs entertained us. These included the twirling of 'poi', weighted balls swung in various rhythmical and geometric patterns to the accompaniment of singing. It looks easy until you are given the chance to try it for yourself!

This was followed by stick games, where the performers show great dexterity in moving two sticks, one held in each hand, to the rhythm of music. The finale of this performance involves the sticks being passed back and forth between the performers at great speed, without once dropping them. Again hapless volunteers found out how difficult this skill actually was much to everyone's amusement.

Orators described some of the myths and fables of the Maori culture, and finally a spine-chilling performance of the fierce 'Haka' (war dance) with much sticking out of tongues! I was chosen to join in afterwards, dressed in an ill-fitting beaded skirt. My tongue work needs some work, for sure!

Now as totally one family, we were invited to share the 'hangi' (meal cooked in a traditional earth oven). It was explained that this method of cooking is still used today, but often the food is cooked on gas mark four and instead of wrapping the food in banana leaves, bacofoil is used! The bacofoil was a New Zealand brand, our host added with a grin.

However the food was produced, we enjoyed a wonderful feast of chicken, fish, rice, vegetables, salads and homemade bread. I had thoroughly enjoyed the evening, and left with some excellent video footage and a much better insight into Maori culture.

I had booked a bus to take me to Auckland that left Rotorua at 1.20 pm, so I was up early to see as much of the rest of Rotorua's attractions as possible. First stop was the New Zealand Maori Arts & Crafts Institute. Here I would be able to view Maori carvings and weaving, as well as to walk through the thermal reserve and see some of New Zealand's endemic wildlife species

The first thing to see was the 'Te Aronui a Rua' meeting house. This beautifully carved building was commissioned in 1967, and took trainee and graduate carvers until 1981 to complete. It is deemed to be the pinnacle of a carver's career to work on the 'whare whakairo' (carved house). I guess they would be fully qualified carvers when they had finished this one! What do you do after this? Putting up a set of shelves at home must seem rather mundane!

Next was the thermal reserve. The stench of sulphur was very strong now and from a vantage point I could see that the whole area was covered in a drifting pall of steam. This reserve is called 'Te Whakarewarewa' pronounced 'fa-ka-re wa-re wa'. I was advised that it is best referred to simply as 'Whaka' (fa-ka, careful now!).

I found the cooking pool called 'Ngararatuatara', which derives its name from the texture of the surrounding edges of the pool that resembles the skin of a Tuatara, New Zealand's largest and oldest native lizard. The crystal clear waters of the cooking pool are constantly at between 85 and 90c and nowadays are used to demonstrate how Maori food was cooked.

As I walked through the reserve, the whole ground seemed to be alive and moving, accompanied by the 'bloop, bloop' and gurgle of the mud pools. I know that mud from geothermal pools is used as a skin and beauty treatment but personally I'll stick to Nivea cream for my dry skin, thank you!

I approached one of the Whaka's most spectacular geysers, 'Pohutu' (Big Splash). This geyser explodes between ten and twenty five times per day, spurting steaming water up to twenty five meters into the air. The eruption can last for up to five minutes, and is an incredible spectacle. Close by is the geyser known as 'The Prince of Wales Feathers', so named because when erupting, it resembles the symbol on the Prince of Wales Coat-of-Arms. It was officially named after a visit by the then Prince of Wales in the early 1900's. Its eruption is also an indicator that the Pohutu geyser will erupt shortly afterwards.

The whole reserve is what I would imagine hell to be like, and is one of the most amazing sights that I have ever witnessed. I wonder how many times I have said that on this trip so far and indeed, how many more times I will utter it.

From the Whaka reserve, I caught a taxi to the base of the Rotorua gondola and was soon ascending the hillside for a bird's eye view of the city. I was lucky that the weather was good, with excellent visibility. At the summit is a go-kart track, mainly it would appear, for juniors. The adrenaline-charged Kiwis start them young, so it seems.

I took another taxi back to Cactus Jack's to collect my backpack, and then it was off to the transit centre to catch my bus to Auckland. This journey went via Hamilton, and arrived at 5.40pm.

I had re-booked the Queen Street Backpackers' hostel, and this time had paid a little more to secure a twin room. After showering, I went in search of food, as I had not eaten since 7am, and was famished. A Wendy burger and chips wasn't really very nutritious, but was cheap, filling and easy...oh, and tasted pretty good as well.

The Bay of Islands.

My time in New Zealand was fast coming to an end. Four days from now, on 16th March, I would be flying to Sydney, Australia and meeting up with my old mate, Jonesy

It seemed therefore somehow appropriate to be visiting the north-eastern coast of the North Island, an area known as the Bay of Islands. This was the area where the first permanent European settlement was founded at Russell, formerly Kororareka, and the fledgling country's first capital.

I had booked a bus journey with Northliner Express, leaving Auckland at 8.45am and was due to arrive in Paihia at 12.50pm. We travelled north over the Auckland Harbour Bridge, an eight-lane road completed in 1959, and onwards to the top of the Brynderwyn Ranges.

From here there is a fine view of Bream Bay, as we were at an altitude of 293 metres. Our driver told us that the islands that we could see in the Bay were known as the Hen and Chicken islands. I couldn't see any obvious reason for that, certainly not based on shape. After this the rain settled in and I managed to catch some sleep, as the bus was comfortable and spacious, allowing me to stretch out.

Our arrival in Paihia was a little earlier than scheduled, but the rain was if anything heavier. Even with the rain and low cloud, it was immediately apparent how nice the small town of Paihia was, set against the bay, with islands dotted close to the shore.

I orientated myself and set off on foot, ignoring the taxis waiting at the bus stop for Lodge Eleven, which I calculated wasn't a long walk. It wasn't, but carrying my full backpack, it was still a sweat-inducing stroll, and I was quite wet by the time I arrived at the lodge. I couldn't be bothered to find my 'Batman' cape, as it was somewhere inside the backpack.

I had requested a single room at the lodge after my episode in Nelson, but they told me that the only bed available was in a two-bedded room. I said I didn't mind, but that I did have a snoring problem and was trying to be considerate for others.

The owner had an idea and told me that he had his own caravan on site that wasn't being used and, if I was agreeable, I could use this and be in single accommodation. He showed it to me, and I was quite happy with the prospect. It even had its own small portable television, as well as a kettle and toaster that I was welcome to use. The lodge bathrooms would need to be used, but they were only a short walk from the caravan.

It continued to rain, so I read a little more about the area and possible tours, and then watched some of the New Zealand versus England cricket test match taking place in Napier. It wasn't raining there, but England was not performing particularly well, it had to be said.

I read that the Bay of Islands contained some 150 small islands and was a haven for tourists and sport fishermen alike. The bay and islands were also well populated by both the common and bottle-nosed dolphins, and whale watching was a popular tour during the migration season to and from the winter feeding grounds in the cold waters of Antarctica.

The weather did brighten for a while, and I took the opportunity to walk to a small supermarket and stock up on some basic supplies. Whilst out, I also walked along to the pier where I visited the booking offices for a number of day cruises around the bay and picked up a few leaflets.

I slept well in my little caravan and awoke to the sun streaming in through the curtains. I walked down to the pier and booked myself onto a Bay Cruise, leaving at 10am. The catamaran called first at Russell to collect a few more passengers before heading out into the more open waters of the bay.

We passed Waitangi, where the Maori of New Zealand and the British Crown signed the Treaty of Waitangi, as I mentioned in an earlier chapter of this book. The Treaty House stands here as a memorial to the event and cultural evenings are held depicting those difficult and historic events in New Zealand's history.

Our Captain told us in his commentary to keep a look out for schools of dolphins that frequent these waters. I was sitting on deck, but didn't see any, and besides, I was sure that the watchers in the cockpit would tell us if they saw any.

We headed out through the myriad of islands towards the one called Motukokako. This is where we would see the famous 'Hole in the Rock', an eighteen metre (sixty feet) arch that has been created over millions of years by the action of sea and wind. The water was an incredibly deep blue colour, and as we approached closer and idled in the tide, you could see hundreds of large fish just below the surface. If we had a net we could literally have hauled them out of the water.

Sometimes it is possible for vessels to pass through the hole or 'thread the needle' as our Captain said, but the tide and waves have to be just right. Today was not one of those days, so we had to make do with photographs and video footage.

Heading back towards Russell, we spotted a school of dolphins. They had young calves with them, so we would not be allowed to enter the water and swim with them. They did stay alongside us for about twenty minutes, and provided us with lots of photo opportunities and excitement. These were bottle-nosed dolphins, and were just naturally playful as they swam alongside our catamaran.

There was a special netting suspended over the bow (front, how nautical!) where you could lie, as long as you didn't mind getting wet, and watch the dolphins below you. I joined the queue but by the time it got to me, the dolphins had got bored and gone off to feed. Probably just as well, as more agile people than me were struggling to get off the netting, themselves looking like caught fish.

We landed at a small, sandy beach, where we had our packed lunch and the opportunity to swim and snorkel in the clear warm waters. Good job I had taken my swimmers with me, as I hadn't realised that we would have this opportunity. I didn't have a towel, but the warm sunshine and breeze quickly dried me off.

It was now a glorious afternoon, and the sun was really burning, even though the wind was deceptively cool - great tanning conditions, or in my case vermillion turning. We moored back in Paihia at 4pm after an excellent day, and now I had to do some washing before finding some dinner.

I finished my laundry duties the next morning by using the dryers in the lodge laundry, before leaving my little caravan and catching the bus back to Auckland. The weather had turned cloudy again, so I had been really lucky with my cruise the day before.

On arrival back in Auckland, I stayed for one last night at the now familiar Queen Street Backpackers, and this time I had a single room. I enjoyed a few beers and a meal out, before returning to pack and prepare for my flight to Australia the next day.

Things were now moving quickly, and I had seen so much since leaving home on 9th December 2011. Tomorrow a new country, a big country and, I was sure, more 'wow' moments. I couldn't wait.

G'day Australia!

The flight from Auckland was comfortable and uneventful, and I was excited at the prospect of setting foot on Australian soil for the first time. Having negotiated the baggage carousels and walked nonchalantly through the 'nothing to declare' line, I was through into the arrivals hall of Sydney's Kingsford Smith International Airport. It was early evening, the sun was shining pleasantly, and the temperature was 27c. My friend Neil had arranged to meet me and take me back to his home at Adamstown, New South Wales, so I started to look for him around the terminal. Just as I was thinking of finding a telephone to contact him on his mobile, I saw this smiling figure heading towards me. He had encountered a few problems in finding the right place to park, and was hence a little behind schedule.

It was great to see Neil again, having first met him in England through another friend, Ian. Neil had been over to referee at a youth soccer tournament some years ago and, having an avid interest in the 'beautiful' game, I went along to watch with Ian, who was also officiating at the tournament. After this, Neil returned to England for Ian's wedding, and we renewed our friendship. An open invitation was given to visit Australia (how foolish!) and on Neil's last flying visit to England, we discussed my dreams of a world tour, to include Australia. Well, that dream had become a reality, and here I was.

Neil drove us back to Adamstown, a journey of about 3 hours, and gave me my first views of Sydney. We stopped for a meal, and my first Australian culinary experience was at a Chinese restaurant. It seemed somehow fitting, and judging by the numbers of diners, they are as popular here as in England. I love Chinese food and we had a pleasant meal and a couple of beers, whilst trying to catch up on the news, and with my journey to this point.

We arrived at the "Adamstown Hilton" as Neil refers to his bungalow, and I was shown to my room. Yes, my room, with a double bed, a wardrobe and drawers. What a lovely feeling this was, and I immediately felt at home. It was going to be strange to be able to unpack my backpack completely, and it would be fun to see what clothing was at the bottom that had not seen the light of day since leaving England. I think that this is the norm with backpackers, as you don't want to take out too much, since you have nowhere to store it, and often little time to repack it. Anyway, that was for later, as now was time to stretch out and sleep.

So here I was, alive and kicking in 'the land down under', a land of sun, sand, vegemite, stubbys, tinnies,

BBQs, paddle-pops, and, oh yes, Australians. (Paddle-pops are chocolate ice-lollies and very nice too!).

January 1788, and the first of England's undesirables were exported to Australia, and to Botany Bay in particular. However, Botany Bay was not deemed suitable for our low-life, so a new venue was decided upon called Port Jackson, known better to you and I as Sydney.

This in turn gave birth to the Australian term of endearment reserved for all English subjects - pom or pommy. The word pom is likely to have been a shortening of 'prisoner of mother England', as the convicts were known.

The weather had been really good since I arrived, if anything above average for the time of year, with temperatures around the 27c mark. On one day it reached a sweltering 39c, which was rather unpleasant. The Easter weekend was much like a British Bank Holiday, with torrential rain and cooler winds.

We spent the weekend before Easter in Sydney, staying at a superb apartment overlooking the Sydney Harbour Bridge. Wow, what a view, and best of all, the apartment was free, as the owners were business associates of Neil's.

We took advantage of a Sydney Tourist Ticket that allows for unlimited bus/ferry/train usage for only $13, and did we make use of it! We travelled to famous landmarks such as Bondi Beach, with its surf and beautiful people (should have seen me strutting my stuff there!), the equally nice but lesser known Manly Beach and harbour, and of course the Sydney Opera House.

On a beautiful sunny day, there is no better way to travel than by ferry across Sydney Harbour and the journey to Manly takes 30 minutes. The return journey in the dark was equally impressive, with the City lit up like a giant Christmas scene, and the Opera House looking particularly impressive.

In the evening we just sat on the balcony sipping white wine and watching the traffic on the bay slip past. (The apartment is situated at East Balmain, within 200 metres of the Darling Wharf and local bus stop).

We also went to the top of the Sydney Sky Tower, from where you have excellent views across the whole city and where you can also receive a 35-minute video tour, which takes you through different parts of Australia finishing with a Disney-style 3-D ride around this huge continent.

Finally, we walked through the 'Rocks' area of Sydney, famous for being the first European settlement. It's a bit like walking through Covent Garden in London, with lots of specialist shops, arts and dining, plus a market selling all sorts of tourist goods.

Here is a bit of trivia concerning the Sydney Harbour Bridge. The bridge contains 6,000,000 rivets; construction was started in 1926 and it was officially opened in 1932. It takes 30,000 litres of (stunning grey) paint to cover the bridge's 485,000 square metres of steelwork, (the equivalent of 60 soccer pitches). Paul (Crocodile Dundee) Hogan worked as a bridge painter before he became a film star, so perhaps he should have featured in the film 'A Bridge Too Far'.

Let's Go Off-Road.

Easter had come and gone, and somehow without the same degree of commercial activity here in Australia. At the same time, there did not seem to be the same degree of religious input, certainly not on the TV. The only thing that seemed to be the same about Easter here in the Southern Hemisphere was the weather. It was wretched and somehow reassuring.

On Easter Monday, Neil took me to the 'Sugarloaf' viewing point that gives excellent views over Newcastle and the Hexham Wetlands towards the coast. We were lucky with the weather and the visibility was good, even if it was a little windy.

On the way home we called in to visit some friends of Neil's who were renting a lovely unit overlooking the harbour of Newcastle and Nobbys Head. Michael, Sonya and their children lived in Queensland, but were originally from Newcastle and were taking a few days here to see Sonya's mother. I didn't know it then, but I was to see and enjoy more of these lovely folks' company in the not too distant future.

Back home, Mum's condition after her stroke had deteriorated, and she was going into hospital for tests. It was feared that she might well be kept in for further observation. I could only pray for her full recovery and await further news.

The first week of April arrived, and with Easter over, the weather improved greatly. I enjoyed some lovely warm days with temperatures topping 28c. Over the Easter weekend it had been Neil's intention to take me to visit another friend of his called Peter, who lived a little way up the coast in the resort of Nelson Bay. The foul weather had scuppered these plans, especially as Peter wanted to take us out for a trip on his boat.

Neil gave himself the Friday off but still had to go into the office for a couple of hours first thing. He was back by 9.45 am and we left shortly afterwards for the 50-minute or so journey to Nelson Bay. Peter is a stocky, shaven-headed chap, whom I would have put in his 50s. Neil had told me little about Peter, other than that he was quite a character, a former Naval man, and who had an eye for the ladies.

Peter showed us around his bungalow, which had been tastefully decorated and was large, without being extensive. A lot of building work had been undertaken and more was waiting to be completed, as and when Peter felt like it, so he told us. I had described him as stocky and I could now see that it was all muscle, not a kilo of fat. Peter worked out and was careful what he ate.

He had taught himself physiotherapy and practised from home to a select clientele. I asked him if this was where he met his many girlfriends. He just smiled, wrinkled his nose and left the question unanswered. I couldn't help but notice the twinkle in his eyes.

He showed us his boat, and it was a beauty. He was a little concerned about the weather and made a couple of telephone calls to check the sea conditions. To me the weather seemed perfect - blue sky, really warm sunshine and an inviting blue ocean. So much for what I know, as Peter told us that the sea conditions had become quite choppy and that he felt it too risky to go out and get caught in an autumn squall. Ah yes, autumn. You forget so quickly about the reversal of the seasons in the Southern Hemisphere.

Peter seemed equally as disappointed as I was, and promised us a trip at a later date, but for now we would jump in his "Ute" (four-wheeled drive vehicle) and have some fun anyway. The three of us squeezed into the front of the Ute, (the rear being open for carrying a load) and with a squeal of rubber on tarmac, we were off.

Peter took us first to Stockton Bight, a 32km stretch of beach that runs all the way to Newcastle. He advised us that it is possible to drive all the way along the beach, but not today, as he had another treat in store for us. The dunes that back off from Stockton Bight are the largest anywhere in the Southern Hemisphere and seemed to stretch away forever. Looking up at the huge expanse of undulating sand and with the sun pounding down from a deep blue sky, it was quite easy to imagine oneself in North Africa crossing the Sahara Desert.

Peter drove us along the harder packed sand off the beach before turning inland between two smallish dunes that were topped with coarse, tufted grass. The sand here was much softer, as Peter expertly slewed the Ute upwards, always maintaining an evenly revving engine. We came to a flat area that, it turned out, was a sort of road, running at the foot of the main dunes and the coast.

"Easy, eh?" said Peter. "Fancy a go?" It was quickly decided that Neil should show his prowess and after a little gentle persuasion he agreed, or at least had let himself be led. If we thought that it would be along the same route from the beach to our current position we were mistaken. Leaving the Ute on the side of the track, we alighted and followed our guide up into the dunes.

"Watch out for differences in the sand's surface," Peter told us earnestly, as he pointed out how the sand on closer inspection was much finer and less well-packed than in other areas. An indication was the way the breeze, what little of it there was here, rippled the finer, softer sand. We continued walking; with Peter showing us a pathway of seemingly reasonably firm sand that led to the top of the crescent, whilst pointing out some very dangerous areas where a vehicle could easily come to grief. I was prodding the sand, not unlike a sapper searching for hidden land mines, in an effort to look knowledgeable. Neil meanwhile just kept asking Peter, "You don't seriously expect me to drive up here, do you?" "You'll be alright, son," soothed Peter, as I just wiped the sweat from my brow.

When we reached the top of the dune that we had been climbing, and looked back towards the ocean and the track, our Ute looked really small, and I quickly realised that we had climbed quite a distance. My trainers were full of sand, and as I emptied them out, I could feel how hot the sand actually was on my bare feet. I was going to remain bare-footed until Peter advised against it. "Scorpions love this terrain," he mentioned almost nonchalantly. That convinced me to replace my footwear immediately.

If I had thought that this was to be solely Neil's experience, then I was sadly mistaken, as Peter insisted that I should act as Neil's co-driver and navigator. Now, my experience of 4-wheel driving was exclusively earlier in the year, whilst on Rapa Nui (Easter Island), when I negotiated my way very nearly to the top of the volcano 'Terevaka'.

The terrain there was rocky, and whilst driving across and through some long grass, I managed to miraculously miss any number of large boulders hidden there. The key here again was to keep the revs up, but not to go too hard and lose control. The scariest part for me was traversing the track, where the Jeep was at a precarious angle, and so confident were they in my ability to keep it from toppling over, my three passengers got out and walked! This just made things worse, as I had no ballast to counter-balance the natural lean and my weight!

Anyway, I took my place next to Neil, and took out my video camera, determined not to miss any action. Peter gave last minute instructions as Neil turned the Ute's engine over. Peter set off ahead of us, and now it was down to Neil. We were on the flat, and he started off confidently and began to pick up speed. Despite taking the corner rather wide, we were still moving forward and upward. I could see Peter in the distance shouting encouragement, I hoped, but wouldn't have bet on it! We came to an area where I remembered the sand to our right was finer and encouraged Neil to go to the left, which he did with an over-exaggerated turn of the wheel, whilst at the same time losing the revs. He tried to rectify the situation by going down a gear, but it was too late - we lost our momentum and ground to a halt in the sand.

"Not f***'ing bad for a beginner," shouted Peter, and pushed Neil over to show us how to extricate the Ute from its sandy grave. "Now drive back and have another go, mate," enthused Peter. Neil dared not argue, and we slewed our way back to our relatively flat starting point. Picking up Peter's cudgel, I tried to encourage my Aussie buddy to greater efforts "Go boy, go! Keep your foot down and remember, don't drive in a straight line, try and keep the vehicle moving slightly from side to side". Where the hell I had got that from I don't know, but as if inspired, Neil shot forward and took the first turn well enough.

Now sounding like an extra for Steve 'Crocodile Hunter' Irwin, I was whooping and encouraging Neil to greater heights (quite literally)! We passed the point at which disaster befell us on the previous run, and Peter was equally animated. We came to a point where it became quite steep and where we also needed to go slightly sideways to avoid a miniature mountain. "Keep the foot down," yelled Peter, "Whoooo!" I yelled, "Shit" muttered Neil, as the speed dropped, and he lost his nerve. We suddenly lost our momentum and went nose first into some seriously deep sand. "No, no, no!" yelled Peter followed by a string of the antipodean oaths that so colour the Australian version of English

This time we appeared to be in quite deep, with the sand close to the front axles. Peter tried to rock and coax the Ute out, but only succeeded in forcing more sand under our nose. "Don't worry mate," Peter said to Neil, who was apologizing profusely. "Soon have her out of here," he said as he produced a neat little folding shovel from the rear of the Ute's cab. "Keep this for such emergencies," Peter told us. More likely for creating an emergency 'dunny' (outside toilet), I thought to myself.

As quickly as sand was shovelled from the Ute's wheels, twice as much replaced it. The sun was really scorching down on us now, and there was no shade. Off came our shirts, not a pretty sight in my case, but who was there to see us? Not even a circling vulture, well not yet anyway! We all had a go at removing sand, especially poor Neil who, feeling responsible, was working like a madman. "It's no good, we're stuck good and proper and haven't got a Buckley's!" (Buckley's is Aussie slang for 'no chance at all'). "We'll need a tow out of this one," Peter went on. It was decided that Neil and Peter would head back towards the track, whilst I stayed with the Ute and sunbathed... I mean kept watch. I had my binoculars with me and trained them on the track far below. I had previously noticed a few large bus-like vehicles (buses actually!) driving along, and Peter had explained that this was a popular venue for tours to visit, as it gave them a chance to see the dunes and do some sand-surfing, as well as driving 'off road'.

219

I lay back against the Ute and soon drifted into a light slumber, before being woken by the beeping of a horn and the barking of a dog. Coming up the slope at an appreciable speed was a Ute, with Neil and Peter hanging on in the rear. A dog was running excitedly alongside. They had managed to flag down a guy out for a walk with his dog, well, he drove and the dog basically didn't! A towrope was quickly attached to the special towing attachment at the front of the Ute and the other guy started to rev his engine. Peter's Ute moved as the rope went taut, but the other Ute just didn't have the necessary traction or power to release ours from the grip of the sand.

"I'll go and get my other vehicle," the guy told us. "It's a Range Rover," and winking at me said, "British are best". Would he return, we wondered? I reckoned he would, but after thirty five minutes there was still no sign of him. Suddenly I saw dust rising off the track and bringing my binoculars to bear on the area I could make out a vehicle with something running alongside. Was it our boy? When it turned off and started to make its way towards us we were all sure. Attaching the towrope once again and with Peter at the wheel, the Range Rover gave a throaty roar and as the rope twanged, the Ute literally shot forward, and was free.

After thanking the guy for his trouble, Peter said he would drop him some tinnies off at a later date, and we examined the rather large crater that had held our vehicle so tightly. I had captured our escape on video, and Peter drove us safely back to the track and home to Nelson Bay.

Whilst we showered, Peter displayed his culinary skills and created an excellent curry washed down with some beers and a good bottle of wine. I could have listened to Peter's stories all night, but after agreeing to return for a boat trip (best warn the coast guard in advance), we left after a most enjoyable day, yet another in this great land.

Forth To Queensland.

Prior to leaving the U.K, I had pre-booked a series of flights within Australia called 'Boomerang Flights'. These had originally been on Anset Airlines, but I had heard a whisper that they may have been in financial difficulties, so I protected myself with Qantas Airlines as well. All I had to do once in Australia was to confirm the dates for the flight sectors already booked and pre-paid.

My first flight was from Sydney to Townsville, Queensland. I had decided to travel on Monday, 8th April and had confirmed a flight departing at 8.25 am. This meant an ungodly start time from Newcastle by train to Sydney. Neil, like the true friend he is, insisted on getting up and taking me to Broadmeadow Rail Station for the 3am train. The train was thirty minutes late departing, but somehow we made up the time and arrived in Sydney more or less on time.

It had felt strange leaving Adamstown, Neil and the friends that I had made so quickly. However, I would only be away until the 29th April on this occasion, so it did feel a little as if I was going on holiday. This feeling was reinforced by the fact that Queensland is Australia's holiday state, famous for its incomparable Great Barrier Reef, the fabulous Whitsunday Islands, its wildlife and its human wildlife in such infamous resorts as Surfers Paradise and Cairns. Yes, I was going to have a great holiday within my great odyssey, I could feel it in my bones.

The flight was also delayed by thirty minutes, but once again we arrived at Townsville on schedule at 11.05 am. Whilst resting at Neil's, I had also been busy researching this part of my trip and had pre-booked a room through the YHA at a hostel called Adventurers. From the airport, I was able to catch a shuttle service that called at various backpacker hostels and hotels in and around the centre of Townsville.

In my guidebook, the Adventurers Resort was described as having good facilities but because of its size, it tended to feel impersonal. I arrived and checked in at the reception, where the staff couldn't have been more helpful and welcoming. My room was on the first floor of this large complex and was what I would call functional, rather than comfortable. It had a single bed, small fridge, electric fan and air-conditioning. A toilet block was situated further along the floor. Additionally, there was a small rooftop, outdoor swimming pool that again was situated at the end of my block, a laundry and a well-equipped large dining area and kitchen. It reminded me a little of a Butlins holiday centre over twenty years ago and, in turn reminded me of a couple of holidays taken with my two mates, George and Alan, in the mid-seventies, at Skegness and Minehead respectively. Still, for $25 per night, a special deal on offer when I booked, as I was reserving more than two nights, it seemed fine to me.

I needed some supplies, and decided to walk into the city to explore and to find a supermarket. The Adventurers was situated beside Ross Creek, along which the ferries ran to Magnetic Island, which I intended to visit during my stay. The city centre lay to the north of the creek, reached by crossing the Dean Street Bridge.

Townsville is Queensland's fourth largest city, and its main port. Servicing the agricultural and mining regions of the north, it has a permanent population of a little less than 110,000 and was founded in 1864, having taken its name from a sea captain and financier called Robert Towns.

A few people had told me that as I travelled further north within Australia, especially to Queensland and the Northern Territories that I would encounter more Aboriginal people and my eyes would be opened to their lifestyle. As I walked up Palmer Street towards the Dean Street Bridge, I noticed a rather large sign that read 'Please do not provide alcohol to the Aborigines'. I was frankly surprised and I suppose somewhat shocked to be reading such a sign. It was more like a sign you would expect to read in a zoo next to an animal enclosure. (Not that you would feed alcohol to monkeys or elephants, would you?).

I had read that certain peoples around the world have intolerance to alcohol, possibly caused by missing genes that have never developed, because they had never been exposed to this particular drug. I always remember watching the old 'western' movies, where the North American Indians were always depicted as having a total intolerance to whisky. It would appear that the Australian Aboriginal people fall into this category and these signs, however demeaning, are supposedly placed for their own protection.

I had started to read a book about the Aboriginal people, and it would appear that their lives and heritage went steadily downhill after the arrival and settlement of the British at Botany Bay in 1788. The new settlers considered this new territory to be 'terra nullius', a land belonging to no one. It is believed that they felt justified in this reasoning by the lack of permanent settlements, lack of commerce and lack of land ownership that the Aboriginal people exhibited. The Aboriginal view was that people belonged to the land, were formed by it, and were part of it like everything else.

I have no intention of turning this book into a social and political commentary on Australian Aboriginal rights however, I do feel it is relevant to mention these things as I observe them whilst moving around this continent, for they are as much a part of the experience as the Sydney Harbour Bridge, tinnies and BBQs.

Anyway, back to my exploratory walk round Townsville. It was definitely much warmer here in Queensland than the temperatures that I had become used to in New South Wales and the humidity was also much higher. Palmer Street was pretty uninteresting, with a few tourist businesses dotted along its lower length. As I got nearer to the Dean Street Bridge, there were a few restaurants, bars and a couple of pubs. One Italian restaurant in particular looked quite stylish, and I made a note of this as a potential dining option for that evening.

Once across the bridge it was only a short distance until I reached a pedestrianised area. This was the Flinders Street Mall and the retail heart of the city. It was a pleasant and wide avenue, complete with statues and fountains. It was really deserted however, and the numerous bistros and cafés were empty. I wandered in and out of a few of the boutiques and tourist shops, before stopping for a large ice cream, that I purchased from a kiosk in the middle of the Avenue, and sat in the shade to enjoy it. I found a supermarket further back from the Mall, and purchased water and a few other items before heading back to Adventurers. When I reached the bridge, I could hear a lot of shouting and screaming coming from the underneath, where the shade offered protection from the burning sun. As I crossed the bridge, the people responsible for this disturbance of an otherwise peaceful setting came into view. A group of about 7-10 Aborigines were gathered around, some drinking from bottles and others from cans. One rather wretched-looking woman was cursing one of the men and he responded in like language. The others in the group merely looked on as if this was an everyday occurrence. Maybe it was? Alcohol was obviously the cause of the actual behaviour, but as for the root of the problem, who can say?

Back at Adventurers I stopped to speak with the Reception staff who were only too willing to assist me with things to do whilst in Townsville. They suggested that I make a visit to a popular wildlife sanctuary nearby, and made the necessary arrangements. I was to be collected from the Reception the following morning. With this booked, I decided a swim was in order, and made my way to the rooftop pool. It was deserted, and I had a very pleasant forty five minutes to myself. I shaved and showered, and had a nap in my nice cool room before heading out to the Italian restaurant that I had noticed earlier.

Now it was full with local people, and a lively atmosphere encouraged me to wait for a table. I got talking to a couple on an adjacent table who were fascinated that I was English, and wondered what I thought of Townsville. I told them that I had only arrived that day, but that I had made a quick reconnoitre of the city centre. "See our bloody Abo's, did you?" they asked. I told them that I had, and it soon became clear that these particular Aussies felt that the Aborigines should be rounded up and kept in compounds or reservations, and blamed them for all sorts of local problems. I didn't argue with them, just listened and wondered. I was soon to discover in what low esteem many white Australians regarded these people.

After a breakfast of cereal and fruit, I was ready for my trip to the Billabong Sanctuary. The minibus picked up a couple of other folk, and these turned out to be an American couple from Florida, with whom I had shared the shuttle bus from the airport the previous day. My new companions were called Randy and Honey, and apparently they were on their second honeymoon (now there was a thought? Honey 'mooning', enough to make you...now what was the chap's name?).

Enough of this nonsense, the Billabong Sanctuary was about seventeen kilometres south of Townsville along the Bruce Highway. Let's face it what else would Australians call their highways? At the entrance, we were given a programme of events and met by a greeter/warden. He explained that the sanctuary was not a zoo, but indeed a wildlife sanctuary, where orphaned or injured animals and reptiles were cared for. They had developed a breeding programme for some of the more endangered species and ran an educational programme for children and adults alike. The animals were pretty much left to wander free in the sanctuary that was actually larger than it first appeared.

I had been in Australia for over a month now and had still to sight a koala bear, so I made my way to the marsupial enclosure, where the wardens told us about the life of these cuddly bears. We had the opportunity to hold them and take pictures, so of course I joined the queue (why anyone would want to take pictures of me, I'm not sure!). These 'cute' little fellas have incredibly sharp and strong claws, that they use so successfully to strip the bark from Eucalyptus trees, and the one that I was holding was using these claws to grip my shoulder and arm. Did you know that the word 'koala' is an Aboriginal word meaning 'no water'? It refers to the koala's ability to get all the moisture that it needs from gum leaves. Koalas are a protected species, but large numbers of females are infertile due to Chlamydia, a sexually transmitted disease.

Another of Australia's better-known marsupials is the wombat. Wombats are slow and solid, which is perhaps where the term for someone who exhibits these particular traits comes from. (Well, at least it did in my school!). Wombats again look cute and cuddly but they have extremely sharp teeth and short stumpy legs that they use for digging and burrowing, whilst foraging for their staple diet of grass roots and tree bark. Farmers in particular see wombats as a destructive pest, and will destroy them where possible. The Billabong Sanctuary has taken a lot of these fellas in after they were hit by vehicles as they lumbered slowly across roads.

We went on to the Crocodile Lake where they had a number of 'salties' (salt water crocodiles) and 'freshies' (fresh water crocodiles). The salties are larger, and usually more aggressive, and as the name suggests can be found in salt water, but also thrive in fresh water, especially following floods during the 'wet season' in northern Australia. I was able to pet (if that is the right word) a young fresh water crocodile that had its jaws bound to avoid any little accidents. It was surprisingly smooth to the touch, and felt quite cold. The cooler the crocodile, the less active and aggressive it will be. Crocodiles will lie in the sun warming up, so to speak (I used to have a car like that which would never start on extremely cold mornings). This little fella must have been pretty warmed up as he was wriggling and struggling to be free and I made the almost fatal error of letting it onto the ground where it made straight for the lake. I was saved by the quick reactions of the warden who grabbed its tail, and thwarted its bid for freedom.

I wandered around for a while, awaiting the next event, the presentation on Australia's snakes. The sanctuary has various gates that visitors can go through, but which must always be closed afterwards. Having passed one such gate, I found myself in a fairly densely wooded area. While walking along the track, a large, ugly bird confronted me (my luck just never changes!) It was almost as tall as me, with black coarse-looking feathers and a vivid red neck and head. If it had wings, they were kept close to the body. It had huge feet, with three large toes, and its beak looked as though it could do a lot of damage. I had no idea what it was, and at first thought it was an Emu. It didn't have the height or manic look of an Ostrich, but it did have a wild, calculating stare. It made no attempt to back away, it actually moved towards me. I turned my video camera on to try and capture this strange bird. I became quite concerned, and began looking for an escape route. I started talking quite loudly to this overgrown Chicken, in the hope that it would back away. Just as suddenly as it had appeared, it suddenly lurched to its left and into some thick undergrowth. Relieved, I moved on cautiously, and was later to discover that this was the rare, flightless bird called a Cassowary. They are normally shy of people, but when surprised or threatened, can deliver a fatal attack.

On the subject of potentially dangerous Australian species, the snake exhibition was next on the event list. The warden started off by telling us that most snakes are shy and avoid humans, and to reinforce his point, he produced a sample of pretty, and seemingly harmless, snakes. Then he produced a chart detailing the world's ten most deadly snakes. Oh goody! seven out of the ten are to be found in Australia, with the most deadly, the Taipan, being amongst them. He showed them all to us, Tiger snakes, Death Adder, Brown snakes, Red Bellied Black snakes and Copperheads. I had to admit they were beautiful to look at and all seemed pretty lethargic, luckily. It was a fascinating talk, and despite some goading for a 'big brave pom' to have a Taipan dropped around his neck. I politely declined, adding that I had already eaten lunch, thank you!

Australia's most famous animals, the Kangaroos, were padding around nearby. A few were carrying 'joeys' in their pouches, and I was amazed at how large some of these little fellas were and how they dived back into that protective bag head-first, with hind feet and tail hanging out.. It was easy to tell the Wallabies from the Kangaroos due to their diminutive size.

One of the most amazing, noisy and smelly areas was on the far side of the lake, where up amongst the trees, were hundreds of large fruit bats. It must be quite a sight to see these 'flying rats' depart and arrive back at their roost.

The tour was about over and we were collected from the sanctuary gates at 2.30 pm. It had been an excellent two hours, but I was relieved to be away from the oppressive heat and atmosphere of this slice of rainforest, and the flies and biting insects that inhabit its recesses. I said my farewells to Randy and Honey, who were heading back to spend some time around their luxury hotel swimming pool. I asked our driver to drop me near the city centre, so that I could explore the Strand, a long beachfront area to the northwest of the Flinders Street mall.

I had read there was a large artificial swimming pool called the Coral Memorial Rock Pool at the far end of the Strand. It sits right on the edge of the ocean, and is filled with salt water. The advantage was that you could swim in the ocean here, without the fear of being affected by 'stingers' (a particularly virulent jellyfish capable of inflicting a fatal sting). There were signs all along the beach warning the public to swim only in stinger-free enclosures.

I walked along the promenade, past the strangely named 'Tobruk' Olympic swimming pool and through some splendid gardens, complete with Banyan trees. When I reached the rock pool, the weather had become very oppressive and I was sweating freely. The sun had gone behind some low clouds, but the humidity was very high. Entrance to the rock pool was free, and I was surprised to find very few patrons. Male and female changing rooms, also in the open (that is to say without a roof!), were available, and I quickly changed into my 'swimmers' (swimming shorts). I had to carry all of my valuables with me, but with only a few folk about, I took a chance on leaving my bag and towel near to the edge of the pool whilst I wallowed.

The water was delightfully warm, but you could feel the sand and grit on the pool floor. This was not surprising, given that the ocean water was spilling over into the pool. As this was the case, it could also allow stingers into this pool, so it was with great care that I swam around. With lots of tables, chairs and lounging areas, this really was a great facility for the local folk. It was mid-afternoon, so I guessed that the kids would still be at school, and the adults still at work. It suited me, as I towelled off the excess water, and lay down to finish drying naturally. That didn't take long. 'Aah', lovely!

That evening, back at Adventurers, a BBQ costing $5 had been organised. The staff provided all the food and did the cooking, and guests were invited to bring their own drinks. To get things going a bit, a competition asked for the respective nationalities to sing a song that best represented their country. There were five Brits, a Norwegian couple, some Japanese girls, a couple of Canadians and the rest were Aussies. When it came to our turn, we first sang 'The Archers' theme tune and then 'Swing low, sweet chariot'. It was close between the Aussies and us, so it would be decided on our respective renditions of our National Anthems, with the others now all acting as judges. We belted out 'God Save The Queen' that somehow felt more poignant, given that the Queen Mother's funeral was taking place at more or less the same time. Yes, we did win the competition, seeing off the motley crew from Australia. Our prize was to take a few free jugs of beer at the pub next door, and that's where we all retired to for a rather boozy night. It had certainly got everyone mixing together and I was thoroughly enjoying myself. The night continued at the swimming pool at Adventurers. It was difficult for guests to complain about any excess noise in the early hours, as the manager and a few of his staff were the cause of most of it!

I was feeling rather rough the following morning and did not rise until 9.30am. I did some washing, and then purchased a bus ticket that would take me to Cairns, but also allow me to stop off at Mission Beach. I made reservations at a hostel in Mission Beach for two nights, and then for seven nights at a hotel/hostel in Cairns. The Cairns hotel also helped me to book onto a scuba diving course that would involve two days classroom work, followed by three days out on the Great Barrier Reef to obtain the PADI (Professional Association of Diving Instructors) certificate. It wasn't cheap but it was another ambition that I was about to realise.

Following a relatively early night I felt refreshed and ready for a day trip to nearby Magnetic Island. It was another baking hot day, as I sat on the open deck of the ferry. The journey time was only about twenty minutes, but it was long enough to really feel the force of the sun. My fellow passengers appeared to be a mixture of young, fun-loving tourists and people who, I guessed, made their living by working on the island. We were met on arrival at the pier at Picnic Bay by a variety of car hire, motorbike and bicycle representatives. The little open-topped mini-mokes proved to be the most popular form of transport, but I opted to buy a day pass on a little open bus that trundles around the whole island. The island covers fifty two square kilometres and is one of the larger reef islands, surrounded as it is by the Great Barrier Reef Marine Park. It was given its name by Captain Cook, who thought his ship's compass had gone funny when he sailed by in 1770.

I went first to Horseshoe Bay, passing by some other lovely little bays along the way. There was an excellent beach here, with quite a large number of people on it. Unfortunately, there was only a small stinger enclosure, and that was full of young children. I lay on the beach for a while, but the overwhelming desire to throw myself into the ocean grew too great, and I had to get up and walk along the shoreline through the surf. The wind really got up, but the temperature got even hotter, and I had to seek shade in a café.

After lunch and another walk along the beach, I caught the bus back to Picnic Bay. I did some shopping, purchased my first new t-shirts since leaving the UK, and found an Internet café. It was by no means cheap, but then nothing was on Magnetic Island. One of my travel trainees had told me how idyllic she had found the island. I would agree wholeheartedly, but somehow it was not a place that I would personally choose to stay on for longer than a day.

As we passed Adventurers on our way back along Ross Creek to the Townsville Pier, I wished I could just get off there and save the walk back down Palmer Street. To save a few dollars, I made my own dinner of a green salad, noodles (basic backpacker's fare) and a pork chop. Not exactly gourmet dining, but when washed down with a couple of tinnies, it didn't seem so bad.

I called home and spoke with my sister, Sandra, who told me that Mum was not doing so well, and the chances of her making a full recovery from her stroke were not looking good. Poor Sandra is spending nearly all day at the hospital, although Mum doesn't seem to be particularly appreciative. With these sombre thoughts, I retired to bed, as I was leaving the next day for Mission Beach.

Mission Very Possible.

It was time to leave Townsville, and move further north within Queensland. I took the shuttle bus to the Townsville Transit Centre and checked in for the 11am coach departure for Cairns. This journey goes via the resort of Mission Beach, and it was here that I was going to stay for a couple of nights.

The journey was good, and was broken at the small town of Cardwell, the only coastal town on the Bruce Highway that runs between Brisbane and Cairns. Dating from 1864, it is one of north Queensland's earliest towns, but consists of only one street.

After a coffee and a hot beef sandwich, we continued onward to Mission Beach. I had booked a room at a backpackers' hostel here and a number of minibuses were waiting to collect their guests from the coach stop.

A young bearded guy, who turned out to be the hostel manager, was holding up a sign with 'Mission Beach Backpackers' Lodge' upon it. Myself, and four young

English girls, made our way over to him as the rain began to fall quite heavily. These ladies had kept up a continuous and loud diatribe since we had left Townsville about all the lads that they had slept with since arriving in Australia. Young people today, eh! I obviously wasn't the type of 'young man' that they were interested in, judging by the looks of disdain as I squeezed in beside them!

The hostel was actually situated at Wongaling Beach, one of five beaches or small townships that cover the fourteen kilometre coastal strip known as Mission Beach. My room was situated at the rear of the two-storey building, and consisted of bunk beds and a metal wardrobe. A large floor fan, that wobbled and shook as it swayed from left to right, provided air-conditioning. It was quite effective, even if it did squeak irritatingly as it moved.

I had agreed to share the room, should a suitable person (a male regrettably) wish to take advantage of the same arrangement. This reduced the room cost by 50%, and should no one else turn up, then the room was let as a single at no extra cost. I had experienced room shares in multi-bedded dormitories, and it was not uncommon to have mixed sex sharing, as I had discovered in Queenstown, New Zealand.

Anyway, I placed some belongings on the bottom bunk as a form of reservation, and decided to go out for a stroll to reconnoitre the local area. It was now absolutely pouring in a way that it can only in the tropics and the large pools of water all along the road bore testimony to more recent downpours.

I was wearing my waterproof over-cape and must have looked quite a sight! It was incredibly humid and worse still inside the cape, but at least it was keeping the rain off. Well, off my upper body, but the water ran straight off and onto my legs and socks. I was wearing trousers that zipped off at the knee, so at least it was only my legs that I would need to dry.

As mentioned earlier, Mission Beach is the collective name for four small settlements; South Mission Beach, Bingil Bay, Garners Beach and, here, at Wongaling Beach. I discovered that Mission Beach was named after an Aborigine mission, founded in 1914 and subsequently destroyed in 1918 by a cyclone.

Its main attraction, other than the beaches, is its proximity to the Great Barrier Reef and in particular to Dunk Island. Famed for its bountiful bird life, Dunk Island is only four and a half kilometres off the coast of Wongaling Beach and the Dunk Island Express Water Taxi provides daily services. (I had visions of a London cab shooting down the beach and disappearing beneath the waves, only to reappear on the beach at Dunk Island. "Thanks guv, that'll be a fiver").

Just a short walk from the hostel, there was a small shopping centre, complete with general store, bakery, café and a tourist information bureau. Guess what? That's right, they were all closed, so I headed into the Mission Beach Resort complex that had a lounge bar and restaurant open to the public.

It proved to be a popular watering hole with the locals, and had a number of large television screens showing various sports and music videos. Half a dozen pool tables were all in use, and all in all, it was a lively place. I settled at the bar with a jug of beer, and ordered a steak meal. More people arrived as, being a Friday, the weekend was just beginning. The four girls with whom I had shared the coach journey arrived in their full glory. I had to admit that they were an eye-catching group, and they were soon being chatted up by the local lads. It's the same scene that I have witnessed whilst travelling in the Mediterranean - young, attractive British girls being pursued, or pursuing, the local boys. It doesn't seem fair, where are all the local girls looking for romance?

My steak was excellent and, after finishing my beer and making some small talk with the bar staff, I returned to the hostel. As no further gear had been left in the room, it would appear that I would not be sharing that night. Maybe it was the travelling or the humid atmosphere, or even the beer, but I was feeling incredibly sleepy and fell into a deep sleep.

The next morning it was not raining, and didn't look too bad as I made my way to a small car hire company that I had noticed close by to the hostel. I inquired about a day's rental and the friendly lady owner offered me a deal on their normal rates (they were obviously desperate). She was also interested in my future plans, and explained that they had a car to deliver back to Cairns. If I was interested, and provided I met their deadline, they could arrange for me to have the car for a nominal charge, and deliver it for them. This is an interesting concept of transportation for a backpacker, and one that I was definitely interested in, although not on this occasion. She further explained that a minimum age requirement and a form of guarantee were required for the safe delivery of the vehicle, but most importantly for her was a 'gut feeling' about the person. She told me that she felt that I was a good risk, and that was nice to know. When you consider how large Australia is, even within states, it must present problems with one-way rentals, and this was one cost-effective solution to that problem.

Anyway, with my little Renault Clio secured for a 24-hour period, and with the kind loan of a large cool-box for drinks etc., I set off to make the most of it, after purchasing some provisions from the general store. After visiting the Mission Bay beaches and Bingil Bay, all of which were pretty deserted, I headed north on the Bruce Highway. One of the leaflets that I had picked up earlier was about a rather interesting place called Paronella Park, situated at the small township of Mena Creek. A quick look at my map showed a route across country to Mena Creek, rather than the less-than-inspiring Bruce Highway, and after about ten kilometres, I turned off onto it.

The whole area was devoted to sugar cane production, and the fields bore evidence of this crop. The prosperity of this part of north Queensland was based on sugar cane, and towns like Silkwood, Mourilyan and Mena Creek were historically linked to the industry. I came to the town of Innisfail, the largest town in the area, and stopped for a wander. It sits on the junction of the North and South Johnstone rivers and has a large Italian ex-pat population. In the 1930's, large numbers of Italian immigrants arrived here to work in the cane fields, and settled in the town. Apparently, there was even a local mafia called the 'Black Hand' in Innisfail. Gives a new meaning to the term 'one lump or two', I guess.

Narrow gauge rail-tracks ran alongside the cane fields, and reminded me of those that I had seen in Hawaii some years ago. There, they had an old steam train known as the 'Sugar Cane Express'. It didn't look as if the tracks here were used any more, as they were quite overgrown. Not much further on, I arrived at Mena Creek, and found signs to Paronella Park. In its prime, it must have been quite a sight to see. It was built in the style of an Old Spanish Castle, and had been the pride and joy of Jose Paronella and his wife Margarita.

I joined a tour of the Park, and over the next couple of hours, the story of Jose Paronella was delightfully told as we wandered the grounds. He first arrived in 1913 to work in the cane fields. In 1929, after many years of hard work, he had saved enough to purchase a thirteen acre patch of virgin scrub along Mena Creek for the grand sum of £120. He returned to his native Spain, married Margarita, and returned to set about building his dream home beside the creek. The Park was officially opened to the public in 1935, complete with a theatre showing films every Saturday night, and a hall for dances and parties.

Over 7,000 trees were planted in the grounds representative of those found in the rain forests of Northern Queensland. In particular, the huge Kauri pine tree was a prominent specimen, and an avenue lined with these awesome giants formed an impressive entry into the Park. We were led along this avenue, guarded by these magnificent trees, to the swimming pool, sunken terrace, tennis courts and the falls over the creek. Here, one of the earliest hydroelectric generating plants in North Queensland had been built to supply power to the whole Park. Cyclones and wet-season floods at different times did much to devastate the Park and today, only parts of the original Castle remain Although no longer in the ownership of the Paronella family, it has gained National Trust listing and the current owners are dedicated to maintaining the Park as a place of beauty and to the memory of Jose and Margarita Paronella.

As I returned to my car, I was glad of the cool-box, and took a long, hard pull of a bottle of chilled water. I had no real plan in mind, but the guide had told me about a nearby beauty spot (regrettably, it wasn't on her rather lovely body), called the Josephine Falls.

These falls were about twenty kilometres north of Innisfail and it didn't take me very long to find them. Parking my car, it appeared that the falls were reached by following a winding path through the rain forest. It was really quite dim along this path, as the dense foliage cut out much of the light. It was also damp and humid, and really quite spooky, with no one else in view.

As I was walking carefully along, I heard a quite loud rustling in the brush to my left. My heart was beating really quickly now, and as I looked towards the source of the rustling, I witnessed a most incredible sight. About twenty metres away stood a large, ugly, and rather evil looking bird (quite a few of my girlfriends have been so described). It took me a few moments to register that this was the rarely seen, in the wild, Cassowary. Perhaps even more rare was the slightly smaller, but equally ugly, chick.

It was quite unconcerned and scratching away at the brush, looking for whatever it was that it ate.

Mother meanwhile was staring intently at me, probably thinking what a nice, fat, juicy grub I was. It was an electrifying moment, and how I wished that I had my video camera out of my backpack to record this event. I was almost afraid to move, for fear of scaring the pair into flight (not literally as they can't fly), so I just stood and stared. The mother's eye never left me, and after what seemed like ages, but in reality was only a few minutes, they turned and disappeared back into the thick forest foliage. I could hear scratching and rustling for a few more minutes but saw no further sign of them.

I was still stood staring intently into the forest with my camcorder ready some ten minutes or so later, when a couple approached from further up the pathway. In a whispered voice, that in hindsight must have seemed quite sinister, I said "There, twenty metres in, a Cassowary and its chick. The couple looked somewhat worried, but followed my pointed finger, then looked back at me warily. It turned out that they were German tourists and must have thought that some English nutter was on the loose. The lady spoke the better English, and eventually showed some recognition of my statement and explained it in her native tongue to her now visibly relieved companion.

We wished each other well and I left them staring into the forest, cameras in hand, whilst I continued on up to the falls. There were three swimming holes with huge, smooth boulders over which the water splashed. In the bottom hole were a couple of folk, splashing around in the seemingly cold water. Signs were clearly warning people of the danger caused by climbing on these boulders, as they would be slippery when wet. Picnic tables were set up nearby but no other people were about, so I left the pair to their frolicking and returned to my car.

I had the constant feeling that I was being watched all the way back down the trail, but saw or heard nothing. I half expected to be met by the police at the car park, as the German couple reported a strange man with a video camera wandering the trail. As it transpired, the car park was empty, which seemed a little strange, considering the couple swimming at the falls, but perhaps they had hiked there. A map on a board depicted a hiking trail to Mt. Bartle Frere, Queensland's highest peak at 1,657m. Mind you, I couldn't see where they could go from there. Another information board that I had missed on my first arrival gave information on local wildlife and in particular the Cassowary. Well, well, I had been lucky to see this elusive bird in the wild.

I took the route back to Mission Beach using the Bruce Highway as the light faded and the rain returned with a vengeance, making the use of headlights a necessity. It was completely dark when I got back to Wongaling Beach and absolutely pouring down. The rental office was closed for the night, but I had the car for 24 hours, so I just parked up and went into the hostel.

I had had a good day, and now I decided that I needed a good night prior to leaving tomorrow for Cairns. On one of my earlier walks I had seen an Italian Pizzeria just a short walk from the hostel, well actually, everything was just a short walk from the hostel. It was quite full inside and I had a reasonable wait before my pizza was presented at my table. By then a couple of beers had been consumed along with a green salad and garlic bread. I'd decided to have some wine, and let the waitress choose a local red that proved to be most agreeable with my pizza.

Upon leaving the restaurant, the weather had once again turned ugly and I sought shelter in the Mission Beach Lodge. It was Saturday, and was really busy with a mixture of locals and tourists. From what I had seen, there was not a lot of choice for the locals, and they were out to party in a big way. As usual, the television screens were being avidly watched, with Rugby League and AFL Footie the most popular. I found a place at the bar and was soon in conversation with a chap and his girlfriend who lived at Bingil Bay. He worked on the water taxi service to Dunk Island during the main season and for the Queensland Forestry Commission at other times. I never discovered what his girlfriend did, as she was incapable of stringing two sentences together, other than, "More drinks now, sport". A bit later I caught her in a rather loud conversation with a couple of the English girls, who she was accusing of trying to steal her bloke.

I discovered that the English Premier League football was being screened live in the bar, but due to the time difference, this would not start until about 1.30am. I thought that I might wait and watch some, but the beer got to me, and I eventually made my way rather unsteadily across to the hostel at about 12.45am. I think I was going to be sorry in the morning.

A Medical Setback As I Take A Dive.

Predictably, I felt jaded as I made my way to the bus stop to recommence the journey to Cairns. I slept most of the two-hour journey, and had a blinding headache by the time I was forced off the bus into the steady rainfall that greeted my arrival in the city of Cairns.

I shouldn't have been surprised that it was raining, as Cairns has an average of 154 days per year when it rains, and during the months of December through April, it is subject to cyclonic weather.

Today was the 14th April and fortunately, there were not any cyclone warnings that I was aware of. It was certainly humid, but in some ways, the rain was quite refreshing as I decided to walk to find my accommodation, the Belleview Hotel situated on the Esplanade.

I was warmly welcomed and shown to my en-suite, double-bedded room. I was very impressed, and the air conditioning and a ceiling fan would keep me nice and cool. The Belleview also had multi-bedded dormitory accommodation as a more economical option, and a laundry facility that I would need to utilise soon. It's little extra was a small indoor swimming pool, situated at the heart of the ground floor space, around which they had made a deck area complete with tables and chairs and some splendid potted plants.

When I had been speaking with the Belleview to make my reservation, I had asked them about the possibility of undertaking a PADI (Professional Associational of Dive Instructors) course. They had a tour desk and had recommended a company called 'Down Under Dive', which I had asked them to book for me.

My five day PADI course was to commence the next morning, but my immediate plans were to explore the area, find something to eat and possibly buy a new pair of swimmers for the diving course. I was told that there was an indoor night market with a food court a few hundred yards along the Esplanade from the hotel. There were also a number of cafes and a pub called 'The Rattle and Hum', so my choices seemed numerous.

I found the night market, and sure enough there was a food court with a variety of different culinary delights; pizza, Chinese meals, Indonesian and Thai cuisine, pies and salads and good old fish and chips. The great thing was that the prices were all really cheap, and in the end I opted for an Indonesian curry. It was reasonably spicy, I was told by the smiling lady, and she wasn't wrong. Her English for 'reasonably' was, I think, a little wayward, as after a few mouthfuls, my lips were tingling and, even with the air conditioning, I was getting quite hot. I finished my meal, washed down by nearly a litre of water, and I had to admit that my first experience of Indonesian food was pleasantly agreeable. I could see that I was going to be visiting this food court quite a bit during my week in Cairns.

I found a barber's shop further into the market and decided to have a haircut. The barber was not Australian and I wasn't sure what nationality he was, but he seemed popular, as a couple of lads were queuing in front of me. It transpired that he was Bulgarian and I immediately nicknamed him 'Uncle Bulgaria' after one of the Wombles (fictitious creatures who inhabited Wimbledon Common and cleared up people's rubbish). I wish I had never mentioned this to him, as I spent the entire haircut trying to explain what it meant!

Newly shorn, I wandered in search of some new swimmers. I found a little boutique selling clothing and started sorting through the racks. There were plenty of bikinis on show, how about some 'mankinis'! As if reading my mind, a diminutive oriental lady appeared at my elbow and held out a pale blue bikini. "Nice for your wife", she said. "No, I'm looking for me" I replied, immediately realising what I had said as she gave me a quizzical look. "Swimmers", I added quickly. "Ah, what size for you? Big, I think". I resisted the urge to punch her, smiled wanly, and nodded.

She disappeared, and returned a few minutes later with a couple of pairs of swimmers. "You try" she said. I didn't see a changing room so moved behind one of the crowded racks and dropped my shorts. The first pair didn't go beyond my thighs but the second were of some stretchy Lycra material and I pulled them up to fit snugly around my parts!

"Good for you, yes?" she said. Depends on your definition of good, I suppose. I agreed to the purchase out of a sense of desperation, and struggled out of them, narrowly avoiding falling over amongst the racks. "You come back sir, many good items for you". I smiled and nodded, and left with my stretchy swimmers tucked under my arm.

I was up at 7am and took a bacon and egg sandwich and a flat white coffee before reporting to the Down Under Dive shop nearby. Our group of aspiring divers, (sounds like an Argentinian football finishing class), was loaded into a minibus and transported to a venue across the city. This facility had a classroom where we would undertake theory lessons and a swimming pool for some practical sessions.

The group seemed quite a lively bunch, and our instructor, Nolan, was quite laid back and fun. It was explained to us that we would spend that morning on theory, the afternoon in the pool, half of the next morning on theory, followed by a test, which we would need to pass to allow further participation. Days three, four and five would be onboard a dive ship out on the Great Barrier Reef, where we would undertake a number of dives, including a night dive.

I couldn't wait, but first there was to be a medical assessment by a doctor that lunchtime. I had no fears, despite my weight, queued up and completed my questionnaire. When it was my turn, the doctor checked my pulse and blood pressure, and asked me how I felt in general. He read the answers to my medical questionnaire, and queried my use of blood pressure tablets. Whilst my blood pressure reading was good, he told me that the type of medication that I was on was, in his opinion, prohibitive to the type of activity that I was about to embark upon, and recommended an alternative medication to be taken for the duration of the course.

I was relieved to be able to continue and he gave me a prescription to obtain the alternative tablets from a pharmacy that evening. The afternoon pool session started by having to swim, float or basically stay in the water without putting your feet down for 15 minutes. This was to ensure that in an emergency situation, we would not drown before, hopefully, being rescued. Whilst not a strong swimmer and certainly not stylish, I was able to satisfy this requirement with a mixture of known and some unknown swimming strokes. It was very hot and the water in the pool was a fabulous temperature.

Next there was practice in the use of a regulator, and having an oxygen tank strapped to your back. In order to aid buoyancy, or perhaps to ensure that you stayed down to counter buoyancy, a weight belt was strapped around your waist. This I found incredibly uncomfortable, as it was chafing the skin where my new swimmers were rolling down slightly. The knack was to try and breathe normally with the regulator in your mouth and your face mask covering your nose. Having just about mastered this technique, we were then asked to practice another safety contingency, that of 'buddy' breathing. This is where you share your regulator with another person to simulate an emergency, as for example, a situation where you have run out of oxygen and need to share until you reach the surface. Tricky, this one, as you have to remember when not to breathe through your mouth, and only through your nose.

Before we knew it, the day was at an end, and we excitedly went on our way to complete our homework and revision for tomorrow's theory test. In my case, I called into a pharmacy and handed in my prescription. The pharmacist asked me if I was already on medication for blood pressure, and if so, what sort. I told him what I was taking, and he advised me that the new prescription had the opposite effect to my current medication. Whilst he doubted if they would cause me problems in the short term, he felt that I should consult my own doctor.

Being 12,000 miles away presented a major problem in that respect, especially with an eleven hour time difference. To be honest, it is virtually impossible to speak with my doctor when I'm in the UK, unless you have an appointment! I took the tablets and thanked him for his advice. That evening I crammed for my dive theory test the next morning, and also gave plenty of thought to those tablets.

By the morning, my mind was made up. I just couldn't afford to take the risk that something may go wrong, not just for me, but for the well-being of the group. I sought out Nolan and spoke with him, explaining my thoughts and concerns. He was great and thanked me for my consideration. He was happy to go with my decision, but was not happy with their doctor, especially as he had not flagged this for his attention. He suggested I take the theory test, and then make a final decision at lunchtime. I passed the test, but erred on the side of caution and pulled out of the rest of the course. Nolan arranged for me to receive a full refund of my course fees and said that I was welcome to participate in the afternoon practical session. I decided against this, and made my farewells to the group, wishing them well and promising to meet up with them at the Rattle and Hum for the after-course party.

I was very disappointed, and returned to the Belleview with a heavy heart. I went to the tour desk and the staff who were brilliant, suggested a number of tours and activities that I could take to fill my remaining time in Cairns. I had soon confirmed a white water rafting experience, a day's snorkelling on the Great Barrier Reef, and a couple of other tours taking in the area's scenery. Things didn't seem so bad now and I grabbed a couple of hour's siesta before preparing myself for the first of the trips the next morning.

Rapids, Waterfalls and Uncle Brian.

A strange chirping noise awoke me from my slumber at 5.30am. It wasn't an indigenous early morning bird or an insect of the night... but my bloody alarm clock ensuring I was up and ready for the 6am pick-up for my River Rafting day on the Tully River.

The side of the bus had the name "Raging Thunder" painted in a vivid red and yellow, and the legend 'to raft to live'. I certainly hoped so, and settled down to sleep away the two-hour drive to our starting point. A video was played on the bus that highlighted a few basic safety rules, and gave us an insight into what to expect throughout the day.

On arrival at the Tully River, we were allocated a raft number, helmet and life-vest. Our instructor was called Rheese and as he told us a bit later, he was a former member of the Australian White Water Rafting Team that had won the World Championships about fifteen years ago. This relaxed me for one, as I felt in expert hands now, and as he said encouragingly, "I haven't lost anyone yet".

Dressed in our life-vests and helmets and clutching a paddle each, we looked a motley crew, and by chance we were all English, except for one lad who was from the Orkney Islands of Scotland. Rheese allocated us each a position within the raft and made sure we knew that we were to perch on the edge, and not on the cross-sections. This sounded somewhat precarious to me, but we would see.

The first exercise when we were out on the river was to fall out of the raft, so as to experience what it would be like to be thrown out, and then how to turn so that your feet were pointing downstream. In this way you could use your feet to help protect yourself and bounce yourself away from danger! (Or, you could more easily see which boulder you were about to smash into!). As we were dragged back onto the raft, the first lesson had been learned...don't let yourself be thrown out. After further instructions about teamwork and movement within the raft, we paddled smoothly and as one body down the river. Around the first bend, we could hear the roar of faster flowing water, and before we could say "Arggh!" we came upon our first rapids, the aptly named 'Staircase' (a number of rapids following each other). Listening to Rheese's shouted instructions above the roar of the water, we negotiated our first rapids. "Shift left, shift right, paddles up, paddle forward left, both, back and hold tight." What a rush I felt, as Rheese told us to relax, and we watched as a raft full of Japanese was being pulled out of the water. This was to become an often-repeated occurrence, because as soon they saw a video or cameraman on the bank, they would all stand up, wave and take an early bath!

On we sped, through rapids with colourful names such as 'Wet and Moisty', 'The Corkscrew', 'Pipeline' and 'The Disappearing Falls'. As we paddled, Rheese also found time to tell us about the rapids and how the river had evolved over the years, and about the trees and fauna found along its banks. Three hours seemed to fly by, and soon we were pulling into the shallows and disembarking the raft to enjoy a sumptuous BBQ lunch and the much needed opportunity to stretch our legs.

After 45 minutes, it was back to the rafts and more rapids to survive. We successfully negotiated 'The Divine Rapid', 'Jabba the Hut', 'Shark's Tooth', 'Alarm Clock' and 'The Instructor's Revenge'. This last rapid is where the Instructor attempts to tip you out of the raft, but makes it look like an accident. We turned the tables and flipped ourselves out first, leaving Rheese with a rueful smile. Five hours of white water rafting without falling out, other than deliberately. What a great day and introduction to this exhilarating sport! On the way back to Cairns we stopped at a roadside restaurant and were able to watch a video compilation of the day's greatest hits (or capsizes), which featured many of our friends from the 'Land of the Rising Sun'.

Next morning was a lie-in until 6.30am, and a short walk to Pier 'A', where I boarded the rather sleek-looking 'SuperCat', a twin-hulled catamaran. It took us ninety minutes sailing time to reach Hastings Reef, where we were to have two to three hours to dive, snorkel or simply swim. Our vessel had a special pontoon, which is lowered at the stern to enable easy access to the ocean. The weather was absolutely glorious, with clear blue skies and an air temperature of 34C. The sea temperature was a delightful 29C, and water visibility was fifteen metres. Having applied copious amounts of factor 30, I donned my flippers, spat into my mask (a nasty habit but a requirement to clean it) and disappeared into the azure blue. All around the catamaran were fish of all shapes and colours, and looking down I could make out the shapes of divers swimming below me. With my flippers, I swam easily away from the vessel and then, 'wow!' the reef appeared below me and around me at a depth of about seven metres, or less in some places. The panorama that lay before me was breathtaking, with corals of blue, yellow, brown, green and white. It was indeed a wondrous garden, with some coral shaped like small tables, where you felt that you could sit and take afternoon tea. Other corals were bell shaped and some were just a weird, abstract clump. All about them, fish of varying sizes and colours were nibbling here and there, looking for scraps of food.

The silence, save for the steady rasping of my own breathing, was amazing, and only added to my feeling of serenity as I floated over this precious landscape. I am not much of an expert on reef life, but I did recognise the distinctive parrotfish, of which there are a number of different colours. Black and white Zebra fish were swimming in small shoals, and occasionally, a much larger fish, a Grubber I believe, would materialise. From a relatively shallow bottom, I suddenly swam over the edge of a deep gully, and for a moment felt rather small and insignificant in this underwater environment. The strong sunlight helped to illuminate this dark place and a myriad of fish could be seen. Oh how I wished at that moment that I could dive, and explore beyond the range of my eyesight.

I had been told that this was a great turtle viewing time as it was breeding season, but my luck was out today. (I guess they were busy complying with their duties of a reproductive nature, and having seen this act at first hand in the Galapagos Islands, it can go on for hours). I took a number of photographs with my 'Boots' underwater camera, which I hope will develop somewhat better than my efforts in the Galapagos, by all accounts. (I haven't seen them yet!).

After another delicious lunch on board the 'SeaCat', we left Hastings Reef and sailed to rendezvous with another of the dive ships, where we exchanged passengers who had been diving on the reef as part of their 'PADI' qualification.

We then had a further period for snorkelling on a reef known as 'Saxon', that was much shallower, but just as pretty. There didn't initially seem to be as many fish here, to my disappointment, and I was sort of drifting along with the occasional kick of my flippers, when I saw a turtle. It was about a metre and a half ahead of me, gliding silently along. It was quite a moment and I had stopped breathing, which is a stupid thing to do really, so I gasped in some good breaths and set off in pursuit, with thoughts of holding on to its shell and getting a tow through the water, (as I had seen on television once). With my little chubby legs pumping as hard as they could,

I seemed to be making not the slightest impression on the distance between us, and I started thinking how useless I would be, should I need to get away from a shark chasing me! My target was soon out of sight, and I realized that this burst of energy had made me feel quite tired, so I just floated a bit. I popped my head above the surface to orientate myself with the catamaran, which was someway off, and felt somewhat isolated in this huge ocean.

I returned to my marine garden, and the fish were back in large numbers to reward me with some more photographic opportunities. As I returned to the catamaran, I caught sight of something wondrous - a 'Bond Girl', just like a mermaid, heading right for me, blond hair trailing in the water. I made the universal signal for OK (not what you were thinking, eh?) and received the OK signal back and then the signal for "look". Following her pointed finger down, I saw a large Ray flapping its wings and floating majestically below us. It was too far below me for a photograph, unfortunately, but we continued to swim together silently for another fifteen minutes before re-boarding the catamaran. Once free of our masks and flippers, I discovered that my 'Bond Girl' was called Trine, and came from Denmark, and so the voyage back to Cairns was spent in rather pleasant company, as we chatted about our respective journeys.

The next day was a tour to Cape Tribulation and the Daintree River, led by an operator called 'Billy Tea Bush Safaris'. Using a 4WD vehicle, we headed for Mossman, a small town to the north of Cairns, and picked up provisions for our lunch. Following the coastline, we soon came to Daintree, a town famous for a blend of tea and also for locally made ice creams. After an opportunity to sample the tea, we boarded a flat-bottomed vessel for a cruise up the Daintree River with a guide. The weather was again superb, and we were advised to apply both sunscreen and insect repellent for our time on the river and for walking through the rainforest later in the day.

The river was quite serene in the sunlight, and the mangroves coming right down to the water's edge added degrees of shade and reflection, ideal for concealing wildlife of all sorts. We were fortunate to find a baby crocodile in the shallows, visible only by its two eyes protruding from the water. Later we saw a larger crocodile sunbathing on a sandy strip of riverbank. Our guide was eagle-eyed, and pointed out various species of kingfisher (there are four different types), butterflies, and a tree snake that, although he said it was harmless, you wouldn't fancy falling down your neck as you passed underneath.

The cruise left us at a car ferry crossing where we were reunited with our van and Wylie our driver/guide. Shortly after this, we stopped and indulged ourselves by trying the Daintree ice cream, which was both delicious and cooling as the temperature continued to rise. After this short break, we started to climb upwards into the Alexandra Range, where the rainforest reaches the ocean, or to be more accurate, the Coral Sea. The whole area is a dedicated World Heritage Conservation Site.

As we drove on, and our thoughts (well mine anyway) began to turn to lunch, the van suddenly lurched violently to the left, and we were treated to some 'off road' driving as Wylie drove up a small stream. He splashed along without a word for about half a kilometre, before pulling up at a small shaded creek called 'Emmagen'. This was to be our lunch spot, and beautiful it was. While Wylie prepared our BBQ lunch, we had the opportunity to swim in the crystal clear, but fairly cool waters of the creek. We were all ready for our lunch and Wylie had excelled himself with a range of exotic fruits and some super large steaks and fresh salads. This was washed down with a glass or two of white wine and a mug of 'Billy Tea', specially prepared in a 'Billy Can' and swung round in large circles to mix it well and truly - absolutely delicious. We were joined by a 'Goanna' (lizard), which was about half a metre in length, and was looking for scraps from our picnic.

Driving up the stream prior to lunch was just to get us used to the bumps and lumps to come, as we travelled up the 'Bloomfield Track' and beyond Cape Tribulation. Here we walked out onto a superb sandy beach, deserted save for us, and the temptation to throw oneself into the azure blue sea was almost overwhelming. It was then that you remembered the 'stinger' warnings, and realized why no one else was swimming. Wylie took us on an interesting tour of the rainforest, pointing out details of the different fauna and flora found within its humid and sticky environs. On the way back to Cairns, we stopped at a small sanctuary where orphaned kangaroos and wallabies were taken in. We were able to feed them milk from baby bottles and they were affectionate and cuddly, with the softest of fur. (Ahhhhhh)!

Saturday morning, and the last of my four consecutive days of excursions was under way when Uncle Brian's bus collected me for a tour of falls, forest and fun. It soon became clear that the emphasis was on the fun element, and our driver/guide 'Cousin Darren' made sure that everyone was introduced, and he passed back various logic puzzles for us to try and complete, to take our minds off the rather boring sugar cane scenery prevalent in this area.

We reached our first falls, the Babinda Boulders after about two hours and, following a guided walk to the said boulders and an explanation of their origin, we had the first swim of the day in the rock pool at the top of the falls. The water was again crystal clear, but rather refreshing in temperature, although warm spots were to be found.

We then journeyed on a short distance to the Josephine Falls (where I had been on my own the previous week), but this time, the weather was perfect, and we were able to swim in the rock pool here also. Great care was needed, as the rocks over which we had to clamber to enter the pool were as slippery as a 'slippery snake'. One such set of rocks was so smooth that they acted just like a natural water slide, which was great fun once you managed to get to the top of the slide! The water was a little clearer than at the Babinda and definitely more fun.

Lunch was taken at a small restaurant at Milla, before heading for the falls called 'Milla Milla' (presumably they named them twice because they are so good!), and they were absolutely beautiful!. Here you can actually sit behind the falls as the water tumbles down in front of you, forming a curtain of mist. It was at these falls that they made a 'Timotei' advertisement, shown in the UK some years ago. This proved to be the best and most exciting of our swims, but the water was without doubt the coldest.

Afterwards, we made our way back to the East Johnson River, by which time dusk was falling, and 'Cousin Darren' promised us that we could see the Duck Billed Platypus, one of Australia's shyest creatures. They spend only a few minutes on the surface before diving back under to catch more food and if disturbed, can stay submerged for ten minutes. Whether our attempt at stealth had scared them off, we didn't know, but as it would have been impossible to spot them in the darkness, we had to abandon our vigil. The sounds of the forest at night were incredible and this in some way compensated for our earlier disappointment.

The journey back to the Cairns was memorable for the unrestrained singing of rock and pop classics and it was with some regret that we realised that our tour was finished. Some of us continued the party by having dinner and a few drinks together at one of Cairns' many excellent restaurants.

Sunday, being the day of rest was just that, with no tours, but time to do my laundry, that loathsome task, ready for the next phase of my Australian adventure to the 'Top End' and the 'Red Centre'.

Top End Adventure.

Today I flew to Darwin from Cairns, leaving at 5.35pm.The flight back took two hours and arrived a few minutes early. I was quickly through the airport and, much to my amazement my backpack was one of the first to judder round the carousel. I had a reservation at the Gecko Lodge and used the free phone at the airport to call them up for a courtesy transfer, "Be with you soon mate", was the answer and fifteen minutes later, a battered Ford something pulled up and I was bundled in and driven away. The Gecko was somewhat further out of the centre of Darwin than I had imagined, and having checked in, I was left with a feeling of disappointment about the general standard of accommodation, which felt as though it needed refurbishment. Still, I was only there for one night, and then it was off on a tour for the next three days, with accommodation in tents. I double-checked that I had plenty of insect repellent for the expected onslaught and turned in for the night as I had a 6am start next morning.

All too soon the alarm was ringing, and after a cold shower (well, hardly cold!), I checked my main baggage into the Gecko's storage area pending my return on Thursday evening. The tour bus turned up on time and Dan, who was to be our driver/guide for the tour, welcomed me. We picked up other travellers who came from England, Holland, Germany, Switzerland, Israel, America, Japan and a first for me this trip, a lad from the Czech. Republic.

The drive to Litchfield National Park took about two hours, and most of the group soon fell asleep at this early hour. Mindful of this, Dan kept his information to a minimum until we were much nearer our first stop, and played us a collection of nondescript and never-before-heard tracks...that hopefully, will never be heard again!

We stopped, and were initially grateful to get out and stretch our cramped limbs, that is, until we were hit by the heat of a 'Top End' day. Copious amounts of sunscreen were applied, and hats were recommended to protect the head from the fierce rays of the sun. Dan took us only a short walk to where we were able to view some huge termite mounds. These colonies have in some cases been in use for 80 years or more, and these ones were about three metres high and a metre wide, and were as hard as rock. Millions of termites have lived in these mounds and are an important part of the ecology of the environment. We saw two different types of mounds, 'Cathedral' and 'Magnetic'. The latter are built so that the largest surface is facing south and therefore receives the warmth of the sun far earlier and for longer and can also, apparently, affect compass readings.

Even at this early hour (well it was for me!) the heat was scorching, so our next stop at the Buley Rock Holes was really welcome These are a series of very pretty waterfalls, forming small rock pools ideal for swimming in (or in my case wallowing!).

Litchfield covers 650 sq. km. and is mainly visited at the weekends, when it is a popular day out for the locals. The Wangi Falls (pronounced 'Wong-Gye') are probably Litchfield's most popular attraction. These beautiful falls flow all year round into a large swimming hole, but the Rangers had yet to declare it crocodile-free after the 'wet season'.

For your information, there are two types of croc in Australia, and both are found in the Northern Territory. The freshwater or 'freshie' and the saltwater or 'saltie' are the two in question. The saltie is by far the larger and more dangerous, and can be found in or near just about any body of water, fresh or salt. They are also found throughout S.E. Asia and parts of the Indian subcontinent. The freshie meanwhile is smaller, and is endemic to Australia, being found in freshwater rivers and billabongs (a waterhole cut off in the dry season by receding waters in the river.). It is still dangerous, nonetheless, and will give you a nasty fright when dangling your feet in that tempting water. Since 1964, crocodiles have been a protected species in the Northern Territory and are once again thriving.

Moving on to the Tolmer Falls, we were once again denied a dip in the temptingly cool waters, but further on at the Florence Falls, we were in luck. The drawback to swimming here was the hike involving 259 steps down to the swimming hole. The hike was well worth it, as you were rewarded with not one, but two waterfalls. The water was beautifully cool and clear, and we could have happily stayed there for considerably longer, but we still had a lot to see and a long drive to our campsite. The return hike was hot and sweaty, and the flies were a damn nuisance, getting into your eyes, mouth and ears. (I know why Aussies have those corks hanging from their hats now, and it's not in case they run short of toilet paper!)

Our overnight campsite was at Point Stuart Wilderness Lodge and it was pitch black when we arrived. As we unrolled our sleeping bags the first wave of 632 Mosquito Squadron made a sortie. We were frantically applying the repellent that the makers claim 'WILL STOP ALL INSECTS DEAD', but these little buggers had little gas masks, and could bite through cotton trousers and shirts such was their voracity and blood lust. "Cheer up" said Dan, "at least they are not malaria-carrying mozzies".

With that thought to reassure us, we trotted out into the sticky night air to witness an Aboriginal 'Corroboree' (welcome). Gathered around the campfire, we were entertained to a series of dances and chanting, all accompanied by the haunting, dulcet sounds of the didgeridoo. (As far as musical instruments go, it must be on a par with the bagpipes, in both the difficulty to play and the range of noises possible).

The campsite was now full of grazing wallabies (pity they don't eat mozzies) and they were quite unafraid of us as we carefully made our way back to our tents. Would the three mozzie coils that we had lit before leaving the tent give us any respite? As I swatted like a whirling dervish, I somehow doubted this, and resigned myself to a long, hot night.

6am arrived all too soon and we stumbled through the darkness to the shower block, where another mozzie ambush awaited us. (An early morning snack for them, I guess, before retiring for the day). We decamped and headed for the Mary River where we were to have a two-hour guided wildlife cruise. The sun was beginning to shine brightly as we boarded the boat and liberal amounts of 'factor 30' were applied over the red blotches where the mozzies had struck.

Wes, our river guide, was on top form, keeping us amused, as well as pointing out an endless stream of birds and insects. He also explained in some detail the way that the wetlands surrounding the river support the wildlife found here and vice-versa. Amongst the wildlife seen were Egrets, Herons, Cormorants, Kingfishers, Darters, Magpie Geese, Whistling Ducks, Jabirus (big storks, with a vicious-looking beak, that have been known to attack crocs), magnificent White-bellied Sea Eagles floating effortlessly across the river, and of course, a couple of salties. One very large one was quite undaunted by our presence. (Normally, a croc will disappear beneath the surface, but not this one).

The cruise over and back on board the bus, many of us took the opportunity to catch up on some sleep. Dan suddenly braked hard, and all but the really zonked were rudely awakened. Eagle-eyed Dan had spotted a 'Frilly-necked Lizard' basking underneath a tree and turned the bus around so that we might also see it. Stealthily approaching the tree, he grabbed for the lizard's tail, and secured it so that it couldn't sink its fangs into his hand or forearm. We took the opportunity to take pictures of this rarely seen creature with its 'choirboy ruffle' in all its glory. When Dan had set him down onto the ground, we had yet another surprise, as the lizard took to its hind legs and raced off Linford Christie-like and shot up the nearest tree.

Another lunch by the South Alligator River (no alligators here) and then it was on to the Bowali Visitor Centre (pronounced Vis-it-tor Cen-ter), well actually ('Bor-warl-ee'). Here you can view videos on Kakadu National Park, the largest National Park in Australia, covering 20,000 sq.km.The Park is home to a number of Aboriginal tribes, and is actually owned by them. The management of the Park is a cooperative between the Aborigines and the National Park Authority.

Many sites are sacred to the Aboriginal people and are closed to visitors. One site, which is open now, is at Ubirr (Oo-beerr) and has some of the finest and best-preserved cave artwork to be found anywhere. Beyond these marvels you can climb up to a flat plateau that provides stunning panoramic views of the Nardab floodplain and escarpment leading into Arnhem Land. This was a truly spectacular sight and was so peaceful, until a busload of American tourists clambered their way up to where we were sitting. We made a quick descent. I was lucky enough to see a Rock Wallaby, not usually viewed during the day. Then it was on to our next overnight campsite within the Park. Maybe it was my imagination, but there seemed to be fewer mozzies out here (we'll see!).

Another 6am start and it was still dark, but we had a long drive to Narlangie Rock where there were more Aboriginal paintings. We were excited to see a Blue-winged Kookaburra, but he had the last laugh, as he steadfastly refused to show us the aforementioned wings.

Jim Jim Falls, Kakadu's most famous and reputedly spectacular falls were still not open following the 'wet', but Dan took a chance, and drove us to Gunlom Falls. These Falls are only accessible by a 4WD vehicle at this time of year, and after a rather 'hairy' and bumpy journey, our bus got through. Gunlom has two pools, one by the campsite and another much better one, which involves a twenty-five minute climb over rough and rocky terrain. Boy! Was I ever glad to be able to immerse myself into that welcoming and cool water! You can swim right up to the edge of the pool, where the water was only trickling down some hundreds of feet to the lower pool, although in the 'wet', it would be more like a torrent. No one wanted to leave, but lunch beckoned at the bottom, so we made a very careful and, in my case slow, descent.

The drive back to Darwin was long and hot, punctuated by stops to stretch our aching limbs and take on some liquid refreshment. The group all met up back in Darwin for an evening meal at a local bar, and with it being Anzac Day a big party was in progress, which kept us up to the small wee hours.

After a glorious lie-in, I caught the shuttle bus into the centre of Darwin, and set about exploring the city. The museum was excellent, (free and air-conditioned), and had a large exhibit about 'Cyclone Tracy', which had quite literally destroyed Darwin on Christmas Eve, 1974. Miraculously, despite 90% of the buildings being destroyed, only 66 people lost their lives. The recordings of the sound of the Cyclone at its height were quite frightening and unlike anything I have ever heard before.

Reluctantly, I left the cool chambers of the museum, and made my way to Cullen Bay where I wandered along the piers and looked enviously at the sleek motor yachts moored there. I asked a fisherman from where I would be likely to get the best vantage point for the sunset. He directed me to a Mexican restaurant called 'Dos Amigos', whose patio looked right out over the ocean.

As I was walking to this place, a sign caught my eye: 'Barra and Chips with Giant Prawns' all for $8.50. This was my chance to sample Barramundi, and fresh at that. The piece of fish was huge, hanging over both ends of a large oval dish, and was piled high with crispy golden chips, two large battered prawns, and what looked like half a lemon! The meal was delicious, and having thanked my hosts, I made my way to the 'Dos Amigos'.

I had thought that I could just order a couple of beers, and take my photographs, but a large sign proclaimed that outside tables were for diners only (obviously had cheapskates like me in before!) and so I bluffed my way initially, taking time to read through their extensive menu. In the end I ordered a nacho starter and explained truthfully that my lunch had been taken rather late (well about thirty minutes ago actually!) and I would just take a dessert a little later. The young waitress believed my story, but the Manager obviously saw through me, and as if in punishment, he delivered to my table the largest portion of nachos and dip that I had ever seen. I got my sunset shots and splendid they were, but it was some time after dark when I eventually left the 'Dos Amigos', bloated and poorer.

For some strange reason I skipped both breakfast and lunch the following day, and it was soon time for my afternoon flight to Alice Springs. It was still light when we touched down at the Alice Springs Airport, and I was disappointed not to see any camels, or even a Flying Doctor's aircraft. It was still very warm, but somehow not as sticky as Darwin had felt. I checked into my hostel and immediately set the alarm for 4.30am, as I had a 5am departure the next morning for a two-day safari to see Australia's Red Centre.

What a killer that time of the morning is, and I found twenty fellow zombies littered around the departure area. Woody and Steve our guides for this trip arrived eventually at 5.55am, full of apologies and full of life. It was apparent that this trip was going to be lively, despite our current demeanour, but they kindly let us slumber for a good proportion of the five-hour drive to Watarrha (Kings Canyon). Topping up our water bottles (I've never drunk so much before...water that is!) we started the long climb to the top of Watarrha. This incline is known as 'Heart Attack Hill', but with frequent stops for explanation of the formation and history of the Watarrha from Woody and Steve, the climb wasn't too bad.

These guys really know their stuff, and Woody told me that, before being employed, he had to undergo various examinations and sit through classes on fauna and flora as well as geology and Aboriginal history and culture. The wildlife and general bush know-how are also essential ingredients to make a successful tour guide for the Red Centre, and of course, when dealing with so many people of different nationalities, so are a sense of humour and infinite patience. Woody summed it all up when he said simply "I just love this place and the job".

The views from the top were stunning. I don't know how many times I've used this phrase since I started travelling, but I know I'll be using it many more times before I return home to stunning Heathrow! I've been fortunate enough to visit the Grand Canyon in Nevada, USA, and Watarrha is not on the same scale of 'Wow' factor, but it is a beautiful view, and the rock strata, formed over thousands of years, change colour in the sunlight.

It was about now that I realised that my heels were on fire and as sore as hell. All this walking over rough terrain, I guess, and so it was a slow and painful descent to the bus. We had another long drive to 'Uluru' and 'Kata Tjuta' (Ayers Rock and The Olgas), which would take about five hours and get us there by sunset.

Some hours later, a large stone lump had appeared as we looked out to the left-hand side of the bus. Could this be it? Could this be 'The Rock' to which we were being drawn? An excited murmur was circulating the bus (considering our mix of nationalities, this was about all we normally got!) and sensing our state of heightened activity, Woody informed us that we were looking at Mount Connor. It is often mistaken for Uluru, but is actually the world's second largest tabletop mountain. The first obviously is 'Mount IKEA' (Joke...tabletop...IKEA. Get it?).

Steve told us to keep an eye out for the real thing that could be glimpsed from some distance away, as can Kata Tjuta, and with the latter, to see if we could visualise a famous person when looking at it! A little while later and shortly after a brief glimpse of Uluru, we saw Kata Tjuta for the first time. I instantly had a vision of 'Homer Simpson' lying on his back and almost involuntarily blurted it out. To my utter surprise, and that of everyone else, Steve advised me that I was correct and told me that my guess was a new record. (This shows my startling intellect, I guess!).

The icon that is Uluru was now larger, and you could see the red colour for which it is famous. When you consider that experts believe that about two-thirds is buried beneath the surface, you begin to realise what a huge bit of rock this baby really is. We were still well over an hour away, but it was still an impressive sight, and one I will always remember.

We reached our campsite about thirty minutes before sunset and made our way to the viewing platform to reserve our spots for... yes, for what exactly? The sun going down on a huge boulder! About 100 other pilgrims, anxious to snap, video, or simply gaze and say they had been there, joined us.

Through my binoculars, I could make out vertical stripes and contours that were once maybe rivers or waterfalls. As the sun's dying rays played upon its seemingly smooth surface, the red seemed to become darker, almost blood red. Over my shoulder, and not attracting nearly as much attention, was my old mate 'Homer', lying quietly as the evening sun set behind him. At the penultimate moment, the sun disappeared behind some very low-lying cloud, and the expected spectacle rather fizzled out.

It was only now that I began to realise just how red the soil actually was, and my socks and boots bore testament to this phenomenon as we made our way back to camp for a BBQ of Australian proportions, and a sing-a-long around the campfire. Later, this turned into a joke session and finally, to confessing your most embarrassing moments.

With seemingly only a few mozzies for company, many of us are encouraged to spend the night under the stars sleeping in a 'swag' or canvas-covered bedroll. It was a wonderful moment, watching a million stars shining so intensely, and the dying embers of the campfire adding a comforting glow to the scene. In the distance you could hear the occasional bark of a dingo (or at least I hope it was in the distance) and the gentle grunts of the people not used to sleeping in swags. Sweet dreams.

When I was awakened by Woody's melodic rendition of the old Rolf 'Didgeridoo' Harris classic "Sun Arise, Come in the Morning", the stars had all but disappeared under a blanket of cloud, and a brisk wind had materialised, lowering the temperature by quite a few degrees. It was 5am, and time for ablutions and breakfast, before heading for the magic of Uluru at sunrise.

The strong gusting wind had forced the closure of the Uluru climb (frowned upon by the Aborigines) and so we took the other option of the base walk, covering 11.9km. Wearing a fleece top and shorts, my 'chubby' little legs exposed to this sudden cold, we started out in darkness, with a large dark feature to our right. As the sun began to arc into the sky, Uluru took on a life of its own, as the colours began to change, and we just gazed in awe at this extraordinary sight.

My heels were so sore that it was a real struggle to keep going and soon the group had left me far behind, except for Eva, a kindly girl from Madrid, who kept me company and ensured that we arrived back at the rendezvous point within the two-hour time limit set by Woody.

Close up, the rock was actually pitted with small caves and gullies, and there were other parts which were sacred sites, where photography was banned. All the time, as the light improved, so the colours changed to different hues of red and brown. By the end of the walk, the track resembled the M25 such were the numbers upon it, with some going clockwise and others anti-clockwise.

I slumped into my seat on the bus and wished at that moment for a foot spa to soothe my burning heels. What had caused this discomfort was a mystery to me, but a mystery I'd have to get to the bottom of as soon as possible. The prospect of climbing Kata Tjuta shortly was one that I was dreading in my current state, but, I was here, and when might I ever get the chance again?

Uluru is three and a half kilometres long, and rises to a height of 348m, whereas Kata Tjuta's tallest rock stands at 546mt. This is Mt. Olga, and it tops a number of smaller monoliths that comprise the site. The Aborigines regard this site as amongst their most sacred and, as such, only a few areas are actually open to the public. It was at one of these that we were to visit, the aptly named (for today anyway) 'Valley of the Winds'. It is a seven kilometre return walk and I set off with great determination, which quickly evaporated after about one kilometre. I was about to give up when I met an elderly lady with a walking stick moving slowly in my direction. We spoke and she told me that her knees were killing her, but that the experience was one she would cherish. I decided to continue, and she was right, the experience was very worthwhile.

Our short but action packed safari was over, and I now had a whole host of memories, some of which I have shared with you in this update. I hope that the video film will do justice to the stunning landscapes I have been privileged to witness.

My flight back to Sydney was spent in the enjoyable company of a lovely couple from Clearwater, Florida, called Betty and Dick, who have kindly (if foolishly) offered me accommodation whenever I'm in their neck of the woods. That's the great thing about travelling, the people you meet, and of course the sights and sounds you experience.

Back home in Newcastle (well it feels like home to me) and it was time to plan the next phase of my journey.

Birthday Time.

After the excitement of the past month, arriving back in Adamstown was a little like returning home for me. The weather had become noticeably cooler in NSW, which was hardly surprising as Australia was now well into the autumn. That said, the temperature was reaching a daytime high of about 18/19 C, which compares very favourably with the UK in May.

I had been whingeing about my heels, and how sore they had become for some time, so I decided to do something about it, and went to see a podiatrist recommended to me by Neil. This chap looks after the feet of all the conquering 'Newcastle Knights' Rugby League Team, so I felt that my feet would be in good hands, so to speak.

He quickly diagnosed my problem, 'plantar fasciitis', or a tear at the attachment of the planter ligament on the calcaneus of both feet. This is, I was told, a common injury for hikers and camels and, as it affects the load-bearing part of the foot, it is very painful. (In my case the load is considerable; therefore it is very, very painful).

To treat this injury, a cast of both feet was taken, and from these, using a computer, a set of 'Kinetic Orthotics' (implants to you and me), was produced and designed exactly to my foot biomechanics. These were fitted into the shoes that I was wearing and, together with a series of stretching exercises, should ensure that the tear repaired itself. They would help me to walk more upright, which in turn would help to prevent back pain and arthritis.

Just as I was thinking that I would have to move to another continent to get some warmer weather, a trough of high pressure situated itself over NSW and the temperature rose appreciably. Blue skies and hot sunshine during the day, and clear, cool nights with heavy morning dew, became the norm. I took advantage of these lovely conditions and spent three to four hours a day at Nobbys Beach. What a life, and as a bonus, the exercise made me feel good.

Neil had cleared a few days from his schedule and we headed north to spend a few days in Queensland. The drive to his brother's home at a small town called Bangalow took about eight hours and we had followed the Pacific Highway for 400 miles. It was an interesting route, as we travelled through or past various towns, such as Nambucca Heads, Bellingen, Urunga and Coffs Harbour. From Coffs Harbour you pass through Woolgoolga, which has a large Indian Sikh population, and the imposing Guru Nanah Temple stands alongside the main road.

Sugar cane had now become the major crop, and the temperature had risen steadily, as we progressed further north. Over the Clarence River and past the town of Grafton, then on to Ballina, that sits at the mouth of the Richmond River. The largest and best known resort on this part of the coast is Bryon Bay, which has the distinction of being the most Easterly point on the Australian mainland.

Bangalow is a lovely town, consisting of one main street with a variety of antique, craft and clothing shops stretching along its length. The street is actually quite a steep hill and it is here that the infamous Bangalow 'Billy-cart Derby' takes place annually.

The countryside in this area is very green and rolling, not unlike the UK, with cattle dotted around, grazing happily. After a pleasant evening with Neil's brother and family, we continued north, taking the coast road rather than the Pacific Highway, from which the ocean was not visible!

We passed through some small and attractive resorts and stopped at one called Cabarita Beach. This resort had two marvellous beaches separated by a headland, which gave excellent views of both. The part of the coast we were travelling along now was called the 'Tweed Coast' and we continued until reaching the larger resort of Tweed Heads.

Following the street along led us into Queensland, to a resort known as Coolangatta, which marks the Southern end of the Gold Coast. We visited 'Point Danger' and the towering Captain Cook Memorial, which straddles the

NSW/QLD border. Cook named this point on the 17th May, 1770 and the date of our visit was a spooky 17th May, 2002. The lighthouse on top of the memorial has a laser beam light and is visible 35km out to sea.

From Coolangatta, the Gold Coast is a thirty five kilometre strip of beaches, which are the most popular and commercialised in Australia. Kirra, Billinga, Tugan, Palm Beach, Burleigh (Barmy Army, an Ipswich Football joke!) Heads, Miami, and Nobby's Beach all flashed by before we reached our next overnight stay at Broadbeach Waters, which sits on the Nerang River. Our hosts Laurie and Carolyn have a beautiful house with a rear river aspect, and we enjoyed the warm evening by having our meal outside on the patio.

After a walk along the beach next morning, we rewarded ourselves with a hearty breakfast at the Kuwarra Surf Club, overlooking the Ocean. We returned to Broadbeach to prepare ourselves for Sonja's 40th Birthday party, to which Neil had got me an invitation. I had been introduced to Sonja and her husband Michael earlier when they had been visiting Sonja's mother in Newcastle. The party was to take place on a yacht, which would sail up the coast on the inland stretch of water known as the Broadwater as far as South Stradbroke Island before returning. We met at the swanky Sheraton Hotel at Surfers Paradise before boarding our luxury yacht. The journey took place after sunset and the lights from the shore twinkled brightly as we sailed.

The next morning, at breakfast, Carolyn presented me with a muffin, into which a lighted candle had been placed in honour of my birthday. Having said our goodbyes for the time being (we should be staying with them again on our return south), we departed, and headed for Brisbane. Taking a slight detour, we were able to visit the City Of Ipswich, and take a few photos at the home of the Ipswich Knights Soccer Club. (It has some way to go before the stadium matches that of Portman Road).

My curiosity satisfied, we drove on to Brisbane, which by now was as busy as hell, and parking spaces were at a premium. We decided to go to one of the suburbs called Bulimba, which is a pleasant tree-lined area with cafés and curio shops. It is also possible to catch a ferry into the centre of Brisbane from Bulimba Wharf, and it was this strategy that we decided upon for the next day.

Sonja, the birthday girl, and Michael, her husband, had kindly offered us accommodation for the night at their home at Victoria Point. In heading there, another short detour took us to Logan City, and a chance to catch up with some old friends of mine from Ipswich. Barry and Jan emigrated some eleven years ago and I hadn't seen either of them since I sold them the airline ticket. (Wish I could have said the same for some of my more difficult customers over the years!). As we pulled into their street, Jan was busy in her front garden (apparently a tree had blown over that morning and had just been removed) but recognised me as soon as she looked up. We spent a pleasant hour or so catching up on the interim years. Unfortunately, Barry is working in Thailand at the moment, but I hope to catch up with him later on in my itinerary. Jan sent her regards to all who know her back home, especially Ian and Tricia.

And so to Victoria Point, which lies in a wind-protected area of small islands, known as Moreton Bay and is sheltered by North Stradbroke Island. We had a pleasant evening, capped when I was presented with a birthday cake and a beautifully framed painting of Nobbys Beach, Newcastle, dated 1886. This was a lovely memento and a lovely thought.

An early start the following morning enabled us to have a sumptuous breakfast in Bulimba, before catching the aforementioned CityCat from Bulimba Wharf, and we were soon speeding up the Brisbane River towards the city centre. We passed various parks and former industrial areas that have been transformed into trendy waterfront restaurants. Many old colonial buildings survive, and look quite majestic beside the river.

The CityCat stops at various points on its journey to collect or deposit passengers, and one such stop is at Captain Burke Park. The park is named, unsurprisingly, after a certain John Burke. What is interesting is that this Irish gentleman arrived in 1863, allegedly wearing only a barrel, and carrying a stick of tobacco, a bottle of rum and a sixpence! (Sounds like most backpackers to me). He went on to build a thriving shipping business, so there is hope for us all!

As we got closer to our destination, the river takes on two distinctive aspects on its opposing banks. On one side you have the City skyline beginning to take shape, with office blocks, and on the other bank, you have the sheer cliffs of Kangaroo Point. Our stop was the South Bank, and it was here that 'Expo 1988' was sited. It is now a hub for entertainment, dining and the arts.

We walked through this area of boulevards and water features and across the river over the Victoria Bridge. This leads into the heart of Brisbane and a mixture of old and new buildings and open squares. In King George Square, you find the City Hall and, within the same building, the Brisbane City Art Centre. This is a listed building and quite ornate both inside and out. From here you can walk down the Queen Street Mall, with a myriad of street entertainers, eateries and some 500 speciality shops. Brisbane has a population of some 1.6 million but still retains an air of spaciousness and comfort. We didn't have much time to explore its other attractions on this occasion, but I was hopeful of returning again sometime in June.

Back in Adamstown, and time to reflect on another football season completed, and my beloved Ipswich, relegated from the Premier League. We'll be back, but the question is, when? On a football theme, the 17th World Cup of Football had started in South Korea and Japan. Thanks to the favourable timings of matches, Australian TV had seen fit to screen all the matches and so I was able to enjoy a surfeit of my favourite sport. Couch potato? Me? You bet I am. To date, England had qualified for the last sixteen and France and Argentina were out. (Don't cry for me...da da da!)

I had managed to prove my convict past, and had my visa extension granted for a further three months, which gave me more time to plan the rest of my trip: Canberra and the Blue Mountains, Melbourne and Philip Island to see the Fairy Penguin Parade (yes, really!), along The Great Ocean Road to Adelaide, then on to Perth.

As of 9th June, I had been away from 'Blighty' for six months. (I can hear them cheering now). In many ways, it hardly seems any time at all, and in others it seems ages. I really miss my family and all my friends, but when I think back to the places I've been to and the people I've met in that time, it's really amazing: -

- Quito, Ecuador with its high attitude and so very persistent street traders.

- The Galapagos Islands, which were simply outstanding.

- Beautiful Banos and busy Cuenca. (Ecuador).

- Scary bus journeys, with overcrowding the norm rather than the exception.

- A dodgy rip-off incident at Huaquillas on the Ecuador/Peruvian border.

- Trujillo (Peru) at Christmas and its colourful, beautifully decorated Plaza de Armas.

- Michael, our 'Brummie' host and tourist guide extraordinaire, who showed us some of Peru's finest archaeological sites.

- Cusco, gateway to the Inca Trail and Machu Picchu, with its high attitude, quaint, twisting passageways and the numerous and young postcard and shoeshine vendors.

- The Inca Trail, the pain and ecstasy, and the glorious never-to-be-forgotten views.

- Puno and Lake Titicaca which, owing to 'The Inca's Revenge', I didn't get to see at all.

- A nightmare thirteen-hour overnight bus journey to Arequipa, where the on-board toilet was being used as a passenger seat.

- A cancelled flight back to Lima caused by the Airline's failure.

- A leg infection that laid me up for two weeks in Lima.

- Sophisticated Santiago, Chile and a cheating taxi driver called Gustavo.

- Quaint Valparaiso, with its buildings clinging to the side of the hills.

- Easter Island, a strange and wonderful place. Hundreds of stone heads (moai), lovely friendly people and a quiet serenity unlike anything I have experienced before. I stayed so long I had to forfeit my planned visits to Brazil and Argentina and flew straight to New Zealand.

- The 'Land of the Long White Cloud' didn't disappoint with magnificent scenery, especially around Queenstown and Wanaka on the South Island.

- Rotorua with its 'Geysers' and rotten egg smell.

- The beautiful Bay of Islands and the wild dolphins.

- Auckland, the 'City of Sails', with its huge harbour and plenitude of yachts.

Yes, I've been lucky so far, and can only look forward to the next 6 months.

To all my friends old and new... thank you for being just that.

Back To Business.

As soon as Ronaldo scored his second goal against Germany to win the World Cup for Brazil I realised how little I had done in the preceding month, other than watch football. True, I had travelled to Brisbane for a few days, but even here I had managed to watch England lose 2-1 to Brazil in the quarterfinals, along it would seem with the entire ex-pat population of Brisbane. The City was strangely quiet as kick off time approached, save for the clinking of beer glasses and a growing chant of "En-ger-land". Of course, the Brazilian fans, with their samba rhythm drumming out side by side with their English counterparts, made for a great spectacle and terrific atmosphere.

Anyway, that's enough about football. I know the World is a relatively small place, but the following is a real coincidence. Neil and I had arranged to watch the game with a friend of his. This guy brought along his flatmate, who happened to be a Pom, and on chatting with him, I discovered that not only was he from Suffolk, but that he was actually born in Ipswich, my home town. He then told me that he was born and lived in the next street to where I grew up, went to the same Primary and Secondary schools as I did, and his best friend was the son of a couple that I knew. Isn't life full of surprises?

Australia was now in the grip of winter, and the temperatures had dropped off a lot, especially at night. In Newcastle the days had been sunny and warm, about 18-20 C, with absolutely no rain for weeks. A state of drought was in force across NSW and farmers were being badly affected. As for me, I caught my first cold since leaving England last December. Some cough sweets and a few hot whisky and honey drinks soon saw it off.

I started researching the next phase of my journey, and as I looked through guides and maps and used the internet, I was glad of my years spent travel planning as a professional. Should you travel to Australia in the future, it is worth knowing that you can use the internet free in public libraries, although e-mail messages are not free.

The Newcastle area has some outstanding areas of natural beauty and together with Neil and his other housemate Ray, (Ray is a great bloke with a dry sense of humour and is a great listener... just as I am a good talker!), we spent one Saturday driving around the shores of Lake Macquarie. Lying just to the South of Newcastle, this salt-water lake is over twice the size of Sydney Harbour and is a Mecca for boats and water-based activities of all types. Despite driving many kilometres and seeing some spectacular views and properties, we covered only a fraction of the total shoreline.

As my departure day was drawing ever closer, I hired a car for a couple of days. In perfect weather, I headed south to the area known as Central Coast. My first stop was Gosford City, which sits on the beautiful Brisbane Water. At this point I was only 85 km from Sydney. Driving onwards, I came to the beach resort of Terrigal. The buildings were rather old fashioned and the main street ran alongside the beach, with many cafés and gift shops. Being school holidays in Australia, there were a number of families taking advantage of the 'winter weather' by sunbathing and even swimming.

Following along the coast, I came to a series of saltwater lakes, including Tuggerah Lake. Here at the mouth of the lake is the town simply named The Entrance. Famous for its boating, fishing and huge population of pelicans, The Entrance is an interesting township, and the point at which Lake Macquarie flows into the Tasman Sea. As the sun was setting, I was able to get some beautiful video footage of fisherman out on the lake.

The next day I headed into a small coastal resort north of Newcastle called Lemon Tree Passage. Whether there were any lemon trees or not I never found out, but it is known for its koala population. I had been told to look for eucalyptus and gum trees, especially those with lots of claw marks on the bark. Did I see a koala? Not one. I did spot the odd kookaburra and even these couldn't be bothered to laugh at me. Still I had a nice walk, and was pleased that I could distinguish some native trees, such as Melaleucas and the ghost gums, from telephone poles!

The second part of the day, I was to visit nearby Nelson Bay and go on a whale-watching cruise. The weather was perfect and the sea calm, with only a slight swell. We picked up two humpback whales almost as soon as we were into the open ocean and with skill born of years of practice our skipper eased us to within 100 metres of those magnificent creatures of the deep. Apparently, 100 metres is the closest that you are allowed to approach whales. If they choose to come closer to you, then that is fine.

The excitement was incredible when the 'blow' (waterspout plus other nasty bits forced out of the whale's blowhole.) signalled that the whale was surfacing, and cameras and camcorders were trained on the water. There they were, in perfect synchronisation as they broke surface gently and gracefully, and rode the waves for a few minutes. When they were ready, and again in total unison, they dived leaving you with the sight of their massive tails.

Our skipper told us that whales are creatures of habit, and tend to stay down between three and four4 minutes. (Whales can stay submerged for as long as forty five minutes if they need to, or are unnerved.). Letting the boat drift with the current, we waited patiently for the next blow. Again our skipper had manoeuvred our vessel into the right place, as the whales surfaced about seventy five metres off our starboard bow, (How nautical . . . the right to you and me). These beautiful mammals didn't do anything spectacular like breach (jump from the water), but they entranced us even so for about forty five minutes. Why nations still hunt whales is beyond me, other than of course for pure greed.

We did spot one other humpback, but it was fairly juvenile, according to our skipper, and didn't keep to any dive or directional pattern, making tracking it next to impossible. As we were heading back into the bay I was feeling a little disappointed at our lack of sightings, but this quickly turned to joy when a school of bottle-nosed dolphins was spotted feeding in a patch of disturbed water.

We edged in closer, and after a while the dolphins, ever the crowd pleasers, broke off from their tucker to perform for us. We were treated to a few leaps and a lot of playful nudging and chasing. They sped right up to our boat, going under the bow and appearing either side, giving excellent viewing. This made up for the whales as far as I was concerned.

When you are travelling, as I have been, you meet lots of people, and invitations to visit when in their area are extended. I met Helen and Geoff in Valparaiso, Chile, and they invited me to visit them at their home in the Sydney suburb of Fairlight. A weekend was arranged, and we had an excellent time finding out what we had been doing in the interim period. They had been invited by friends to attend the Rosehill Garden Race Course and managed to swing an extra invitation for me.

A slight problem with the invitation was that it was for the members' enclosure, so I had to borrow a pair of shoes, a jacket and a tie for the occasion. I looked a bit strange, but admittedly we had a splendid afternoon cheering home their friend's horse. I really got into the action, and at one point was $36 up, before finishing $40 down. Still it was fun and something I very rarely do, which is probably just as well.

It was great to catch up with Helen and Geoff and meet their family, and also be given another contact for possible accommodation in Adelaide. The next day I was travelling on to Katoomba in the Blue Mountains and was praying that the excellent winter weather would hold up for the next few days.

The Blue Mountains.

As I waved goodbye to Helen and Geoff, and boarded the ferry from Manly to Sydney Circular Quay, I couldn't help but think that there were more tedious ways of commuting to work each day. The journey takes 30 minutes and you pass some of the prettiest parts of Sydney Harbour. Craft of all shapes and sizes use the harbour and just recently, you may have heard on the news that three Southern Right Whales have also used the harbour. Breaking off from their migration to their breeding grounds in the cooler Southern Ocean, these three rascals entertained the people of Sydney by frolicking in the harbour, swimming right up under the Harbour Bridge. (I wish I'd been there to see them!).

My journey to the Blue Mountains began at Sydney Central Railway Station, and two hours later, I had reached my destination of Katoomba that lay 109km from Sydney, but is in reality a lifetime away. I had been warned that you could be sweltering in Sydney and yet find that it's very chilly in Katoomba, and it was definitely the case today. The weather was clear and sunny but because of the wind, it felt even colder when you were out of the sun.

My accommodation was to be at the Katoomba Hotel and it was only a few minutes' walk from the station. Described in the Lonely Planet guide as being "a smoky Aussie local with unglamorous but heated rooms, all with shared facilities", I entered the hotel with something approaching trepidation.

There was a raging log fire pumping out a welcome heat. The bar was as described, smoky, and I had a quick look for the kippers hanging from the ceilings! The two occupants of bar stools turned to stare at me as I lumbered in with my backpack and just as quickly resumed their conversation about the horse racing being shown on the bar T.V.

Behind the bar, my gaze fell upon the shapely denim-clad bottom of the barmaid/person who was stacking bottles on a low shelf. As she straightened up to face me, what I can only describe kindly as a hard, lived-in face (lived in by what, I'm not sure?) stared at me. In a voice that could crack cement she enquired of me "Whatchya want mate?"

Breathing apparatus immediately came to mind. "I have a reservation," I replied meekly. The lady located this in a large book and asked me if I wanted to see the room first. Not a bad idea, I thought, as she tossed the key with a huge metal weight attached. As if reading my mind (God, I hope she couldn't!) she said, "Stops the buggers wandering off with the key" - wandering off, that could well be an event in World's Strongest Man!

Considering that you had to leave a $20 key deposit, I began to wonder if it would be more advantageous to melt the weight down. The room was fine, and I checked that the heater did work before accepting. Let's face it, at $20 per night, I was hardly going to stay at the Hilton.

Walking into Katoomba High Street I quickly found a café near to where the Explorer Bus departed, and had lunch. The Explorer Bus is an old London Double-Decker and drives around a popular circuit of attractions. You are able to jump off and on at any point throughout the day. I persuaded the young lady at the tourist office to validate my ticket that afternoon and the following day for the same price.

On her advice, I went that afternoon to the Scenic Railway and Scenic Skyway. The railway runs to the foot of the Jamison Valley, and at an incline of 45 degrees, it is one of the steepest descents in the world. It was built in the 1880's to transport coal-miners to their daily toil. You virtually lie in your seat, with a large bar to hold you in position as you descend into the dark of a tunnel. The descent takes only a few minutes and you then have the choice of two walks.. One is to the Katoomba Falls and takes about 10 minutes, or there is the 'popular' six-hour walk to see the ruined castle rock formation.

Call me old fashioned, but I doubt if I would walk 6 hours to see a perfect castle, let alone a ruined one! The falls were very nice as falls go. The Scenic Skyway is a cable car that traverses the Katoomba Falls Gorge 200mt above the valley floor. This gives you absolutely excellent views of the area, and in particular of one of the Blue Mountains' most famous sights, the Three Sisters. (More on these later).

As I waited for the bus to return, the temperature dropped considerably, as the sun had disappeared behind the mountains, and a cool wind added to the sensation. I hoped it wouldn't be too long a wait and thought longingly of a hot chocolate and marshmallows waiting back in town.

To my amazement, Katoomba High Street, earlier a bustling and vibrant place, full of tourists, was now deserted and only a couple of cafés remained open. I suppose that being so close to Sydney, many tourists just visit for the day. So it was back to the pub with a takeaway hot chocolate, minus the marshmallows. The room was quite cold, so I put the heater on full and even though it was only 6.45pm, I climbed into bed to get warmer more quickly. The next thing I knew it was 10pm, so I cleaned my teeth and retired for the night, vowing to get up early and enjoy a full day in the mountains.

The alarm went at 7am and I snaked an arm out of my warm-as-toast bed to shut it off. The temperature overnight had dropped to −2C and there was evidence of ice as I made my way to Katoomba High Street for breakfast. A strong wind made it feel much cooler and I ducked into the first open café. After a hearty breakfast and an excellent flat white, I was set up for the day ahead.

The weather was sunny and bright, perfect sightseeing weather in the mountains. I made my way to a lookout known as Honeymoon Point, which gives you excellent views of the Jamison Valley and Kings Tableland. A cliff top walk extends from here to Echo Point, which is the popular lookout for the Three Sisters rock formation. It took me about 30 minutes to walk and I hardly saw a soul. The views were dramatic, and early morning mist was still lingering in the lower valley.

Here is a little Aborigine folklore for you concerning the Three Sisters. Three sisters called Meehni, Wilma and Gunnedoo lived on a mountain with their witchdoctor father, whose name was Tyawan. All was perfect except for an evil spirit called Bunyip, who dwelt in a large cave halfway down the mountain.

Whenever Tyawan was away doctoring, (well what else does a Witchdoctor do?) he would hide his daughters on a high ledge behind a big rock, safe from Bunyip. One day Meehni was bored and on seeing a large centipede, she started to throw rocks at it. Some of the rocks went over the ledge and rattled into Bunyip's cave. He was angry to be awoken and immediately looked for the culprits. He discovered the sisters on their ledge and closed in upon them.

Tyawan heard their screams and rushed back to protect his daughters. Bunyip was between him and the ledge and the only way he could save his daughters was to turn them into rock with his magic bone (no comments please). Bunyip was even more enraged by this, and chased after his old adversary Tyawan.

Tyawan was trapped, and to save himself, he turned into a Lyrebird and flew to safety. Unfortunately in so doing he dropped his magic bone onto the valley floor and was unable to find it again. This condemned the three sisters to be cast in rock forever, and is why you will often see the Lyrebird picking up sticks on the valley floor, looking for the elusive magic bone to bring the three sisters back to life!

After a surfeit of Three Sister shots, I made my way to the Leura Cascades (I wonder, if there had been naked people bathing there, would they be known as the Lurid Cascades?) and after walking down through the rain forest I continued along a much more strenuous track to reach the Gordon Falls. The views were magnificent, especially from Tarpeian Rock. I sat here in the silence for some time, just in awe of the view and the virtual silence. It seemed an appropriate time to say a few prayers for my mother, family and friends, and wish they could all be here with me to share the moment.

Feeling somewhat tired after my walks and the bracing air, I headed back to town. Once again the centre was deserted and once again I returned to my room with a coffee, packet of peanuts and a Mars bar. It had been a fabulous day, and I had many happy memories of my stay in the Blue Mountains.

The next morning I caught the 7.35am train back to Sydney Central and spent a few hours tramping around the harbour area. Soon, I would be leaving New South Wales for good and heading to the ACT (Australian Capital Territories), to continue my Australian odyssey.

Farewell Cobbers.

I had spent the last four months in Newcastle, and being able to have a base from which to travel around Australia was a real bonus. It certainly became my home from home, and whilst I have been in Australia I have met some lovely folk.

To celebrate my last week in Newcastle, Neil had agreed to host a small party where we could invite those people who had made me so welcome. Mara, a lovely lady who keeps Neil's house and office ship-shape, was unable to make the Saturday party, so Neil, Ray and I arranged to meet her and her husband Ralph at the local pub. The beers flowed and all had a great night, an excellent start to the weekend.

Saturday morning, I was feeling surprisingly ok. I was still last up, needless to say, and I found Neil and Ray busy clearing out the spare room. Tables and chairs were discovered in the depths and dusted down ready for use. We borrowed Gerry's gas BBQ from next door and Ray's son Troy arrived in his capacity of 'Chef extraordinaire' or should that be 'extraordinary'? Now Troy is a top bloke, albeit a sad Newcastle United fan, and is a chef by profession. Looking resplendent in his Newcastle shirt and chef's trousers, we left him and Ray in control of the food preparation, whilst Neil and I swanned around like a couple of tarts!

The weather was excellent, with bright warm sunshine and we were able to sit in the garden. Not bad for the middle of winter, eh! Everyone who could, turned up to say goodbye, or was it to make sure I left? Either way I was genuinely touched. There was Drago, of Slovenian stock and a Newcastle Knights and Leeds United fanatic. Janet and George (Janet works for Neil and hails from Hartlepool), Bobby (A West Country lad supporting Spurs) and his wife Sonya, more English migrants, Stephen, Trudy and son Tyler, Mark Wilson and his partner Stephanie, Peter (Neil's dad) and Lynn, Peter from Nelson Bay (still talking about Neil's off-road driving escapades), Mark, Shauna, Glen, and Babe, Gerry and Natasha from next door. The only folk missing were Laurie and Carolyn, Michael and Sonja, Karen and Gabriel, Stephen and Michelle (Neil's brother and sister-in-law), Karin and Steve (Neil's sister and brother-in-law), and of course, dear old Ray, our regular lunch partner. All these people showed me true friendship and hospitality in the best of Australian traditions... thank you so much.

Above all my special thanks to Neil, who allowed me to blunder into his life and has been and will remain a true friend.

On my first day in Australia we had breakfast at the 'Bogie Hole' café near to the beach in Newcastle, and it was to become my favourite stop. On that morning I was introduced to Stephen and Trudy and was immediately invited to their Easter BBQ party. It seemed fitting, therefore, that on my last Sunday, we should breakfast at the Bogie Hole, and they joined Neil, Ray and I for the occasion. Now, as on that first morning, it was marvellous to be able to eat outside, and whilst it was a few degrees cooler, the weather was as bright and sunny as it had been on that first morning.

Ray and I took a last walk along to Nobbys Beach and back along the foreshore, whilst Neil was officiating at some local football matches. That evening the three of us went for a quiet meal and recalled the fun we had had over the last few months.

Time to close this chapter of the trip and move on to the next phase of my Australian adventure, which would see me travelling to the Australian Capital Territory, Victoria and Tasmania.

A Capital Time.

It was time to leave Newcastle and the many friends I had made over the last few months. I hate goodbyes, but in this case I knew I would be returning sometime in the future, so I wasn't so sad. I caught the train to Sydney Central, which passes through the scenic Central Coast en route. On arrival, I placed my backpack in a left luggage locker and purchased a day rover pass on the Sydney transport systems. My first stop was at the McCafferty's coach office. Here I purchased a ticket to Melbourne, which allowed me to make a stopover at Canberra for a couple of nights.

As this would be my last day in Sydney, I was keen to see as much of it as possible before leaving. Sydney is dominated by its harbour and it was to here that I headed, having decided to take the RiverCat ferry to Parramatta. The journey takes about an hour from Circular Quay, passing Sydney's waterfront homes and on into the tranquil Parramatta River. The Aboriginal name for Parramatta is 'place of eels' and explains the nickname of the local rugby league side.

From the Parramatta landing, I followed the yellow brick road, well, the pink concrete path that follows the river to the Parramatta Heritage Centre. Aboriginal artwork on the path depicts the history and culture of the area and has been completed by the Burramatta people. Local school children have been encouraged to exhibit paintings depicting Parramatta's history in the Heritage Centre here. The Old Government House, built between 1799 and 1818, was the seat of Government in the formative years of the young colony. Nowadays it is home to the finest collection of colonial furniture in Australia. Nearby, within the grounds of Parramatta Park, is the Old Dairy Cottage, with its sunken milk room and the stone steps used to separate the milk from the cream.

Speeding back to Circular Quay with the wind slapping me in the face, I couldn't help but video the Harbour Bridge and the Opera House one more time. Whichever way you look at it, they dominate the harbour vista.

Back at Central Station, I sought out my left luggage locker. I always feel relieved when the door clicks open, and my luggage is still there. I had previously packed an overnight bag, which I now took from the locker, before putting a further six dollars into the slot and leaving the bulk of my luggage locked away. I made my way back to Circular Quay to catch the Manly ferry, to spend the night as a guest of Geoff and Helen. That evening, Helen cooked us a superb Indian meal, washed down with some agreeable wine.

Geoff drove me to the ferry terminal the next morning and I was soon crossing the harbour for the last time on this trip. I didn't have far to carry my backpack from the left luggage area, as the coach station is immediately underneath Central Station. The journey to Canberra takes about four hours and is somewhat scenically challenged! Seated next to me for the journey was a young Irish lad, who was actually travelling onward to Melbourne.

He had a copy of the Daily Express newspaper and I was able to catch up on the news back home. Strangely there was not a lot of difference to that which I had read in the Sydney Morning Herald. Saddam and his efforts to block UN weapon inspectors; Bush, Howard and Blair repeating threats to attack Iraq; Israel retaliating after the latest suicide bomb outrage, severe flooding in Europe; and Prince Charles and Camilla given Royal nod of approval. With the exception of that last headline, what a sad and sick world we live in. Come to think of it, that last headline is pretty sad too!

The Australian Capital Territory (ACT) is in fact surrounded by New South Wales, and lies roughly between Sydney and Melbourne. When the separate colonies of Australia became states in 1901, a decision to build a national capital was included in the constitution. Sydney and Melbourne were the major cities, but it was decided to site the capital between the two. They organised an international competition to design the city, and an American architect, Walter Burley Griffin, was the winner. In 1911, the Commonwealth Government purchased land from New South Wales, calling it ACT. The name for the new capital was not decided upon until 1913. Canberra, believed to be an Aboriginal term for 'meeting place' was chosen.

As our coach pulled into Canberra, I was immediately struck by its ordered, grid-like nature. The city was set out and developed around Lake Burley Griffin, a man-made lake formed by the damming of the Molonglo River in 1964. Development of Canberra was really slow until the mid 1950s, since when, it has been quite spectacular. I checked into a budget hotel in the city centre and after inspecting my room on the 5th floor, I set off on foot to explore its pedestrianised malls. That evening I found a small Peruvian restaurant, and enjoyed my meal, whilst taking the opportunity to reminisce with the owner and his lovely daughter about my time in his homeland.

The next day, I booked up for a half-day tour of the city and its must-see attractions. The weather in Canberra was decidedly cooler than I had previously experienced anywhere in Australia, and a strong wind made it feel cooler than the actual 12 C. We first made our way around Lake Burley Griffin, which we were told had three places of interest; the Carillon on Aspen Island, a three-column bell tower that was a gift from the British Government to mark Canberra's jubilee; the Captain Cook Memorial, a 150m water jet and terrestrial globe on the foreshore; and the National Capital Exhibition at Regatta Point, which has a pavilion with exhibits showing Canberra's development.

From here, we headed for Parliament House on Capital Hill, where we had a guided tour of this ultra-modern building. It houses one of only four known originals of the Magna Carta, but my favourite part was a room with a montage of every Australian Prime Minister through to the present incumbent, John Howard.

In front of this is the Old Parliament House, completed in 1927, which houses the National Art Gallery and retains the original furniture in the debating chambers. Being the capital, Canberra is also home to some 60 Embassies and High Commissions. We drove through the area where they are located, and some are quite interesting structures. The US Embassy is a copy of a Southern mansion in the style of those found in Williamsburg, Virginia. The Thai Embassy, with its pointed orange-tiled roof, is in a style similar to that of Bangkok temples.

There are a number of lookouts in the surrounding hills, and we went to the one atop Mount Ainslie. This gave fine views of central Canberra and Lake Burley Griffin. We drove along Anzac Parade, with its plaques commemorating various battles and campaigns. At the end of Anzac Parade stands the Australian War Memorial Museum. You need far longer than the hour that we were allowed to take in the galleries and exhibits here. The tomb of the unknown Australian soldier, returned from a World War One battlefield in 1993, is found here and at the close of each day, a piper or bugler performs a poignant rendition of the 'last post'.

I had spent some time wandering around with a young woman from Syria, who was now living in Sweden, (she was impressed by my Swedish, learnt back in 1981...well not really, as being able to say fluently," how much are a kilo of potatoes" is a bit of a conversation killer!), so we took a coffee before she headed home to her sister's at Wagga Wagga. (So good they named it twice!). She had the most beautiful almond eyes and... dinner alone again tonight.

I was not sorry to be leaving Canberra, although there were many places I hadn't visited, but it just didn't do anything for me. Perhaps the weather influenced my thoughts, but many Australians whom I have spoken with seem to share my opinion. My bus departed for Melbourne at 12.15pm the following day and would take about nine hours, passing through some pretty nondescript land.

As the on board video played 'Father of the bride 2' starring Steve Martin, I managed to get some sleep and eventually, at 9.30pm, we pulled into Melbourne. I checked into a hotel called 'Toad Hall' in the next street to the bus station and gratefully crashed out, as I was very tired from the hours on the bus. The next day would see me travelling to Tasmania and I will tell you about my time on the island state in the following chapter.

In Search Of A Little Devil.

Friday 26th July, and once the people who were tramping up and down the corridor outside of my room got tired, I had managed a reasonable night's sleep. I went in search of a hearty breakfast and noticed that a café across the road from the hotel seemed busy, always a good sign, so I went to study the breakfast options. Cereals, muesli, fruit and continental breakfasts were all on offer but no, I was looking for a good old-fashioned, cholesterol-damaging fry-up. I opted for the 'Aussie Outback' (not the dunny, although that was quite a real possibility) consisting of steak, bacon, sausage, eggs, mushrooms, beans and toast. I dropped the steak and beans, and with fresh orange juice and a large flat white to finish, felt brilliantly set up for the day ahead.

After checking out of 'Toad Hall' I waited outside for the airport shuttle bus I had booked the previous evening. My flight to Launceston, Tasmania was scheduled for an 11.40am departure, and I arrived at Melbourne's Tullamarine airport at about 10.30am.

Qantas check-in was as usual crowded, and it never ceases to amaze me why there are two economy desks and four business class desks, when the latter are virtually unused most of the time.

Having checked-in and proceeded air-side, I shuffled around the little shops and boutiques that you find in nearly every airport, selling everything from tourist gifts and memorabilia, to perfume and after-shave lotions. I freshened up by using sample bottles of after-shave, and smelling 'lovely', went to my check-in gate. My designer aroma worked, and I soon had a row of seats to myself.

The boarding procedure for an aircraft is another source of great amusement to me. It seems that people lose their hearing at the point that the first announcement is made, telling passengers that boarding will commence in row order, starting with rows 1 to 12 and those passengers with young children. This is the signal for a mad rush to queue, as three quarters of the passengers seem to be seated in these rows. Children become separated from their panic-stricken parents in the general melee to get on board and claim their seat. Personally, I am quite pleased, as it would appear that I and about 15 others have the rest of the aircraft to ourselves!

I always request an aisle seat so that I may get up easily without disturbing my fellow passengers. The downside of this being that the aircrew can bash your elbow, shoulder and any other protruding body part as they pass by with the refreshment trolley. On this occasion, I had a row to myself (the after-shave is still working) and I moved into the window seat for a view of Melbourne from the air.

Being of generous proportions, I often have trouble with the seat-back tray table. This tends to lodge somewhere between my chest and stomach, usually at an angle of 45 degrees. This makes eating and drinking an art form as you try to balance it without it sliding off and onto your legs. On this flight I had either lost weight or the seat pitch was greater than on most aircraft, as the table sat in its intended position. What bliss, but as it turned out, our cold sandwich didn't really warrant a table at all!

It was pretty overcast on arrival in Launceston and the puddles on the tarmac told their own story. Still, the outside temperature was 16C and a weak sun was trying its best to break through the grey. I had pre-arranged a hire car for my period on the island and was required to call the company on arrival so that they could collect me. Their rate was considerably cheaper than those of the major car hire companies and, when my chap pulled up in my Nissan Pulsar, I began to understand why.

Brand new it wasn't, shiny paintwork it hadn't, but it didn't stand out as a hire car and this could be an advantage if a thief thought about breaking into it. The engine sounded fine (as if I would know?) and the interior was clean, in a well-used sort of way. Having sorted out the necessary paperwork, I headed off along the Midland Highway towards Hobart. I had only gone a few kilometres when I noticed that the odeometer wasn't registering. I wonder how many miles my little car had actually done?

I remembered reading that the first European to set foot on this island was a Dutchman named Abel Tasman. This was in 1642, and he decided to name this place Van Diemen's Land, after the governor of the Dutch East Indies. He, like all of the early explorers, thought that Van Diemen's Land was a part of the Australian mainland, and it was not until 1798 that Lieutenant Matthew Flinders proved it to be an island. He named the rough stretch of sea between the island and the mainland Bass Strait, after his ship's surgeon, George Bass.

Now this rather inhospitable island would make an ideal penal colony. In 1803, at Risden Cove, on the Derwent River, Australia's second convict colony was established, and for the next thirty years Van Diemen's Land was the most feared destination for British convicts. It was not until 1856 that transportation to this colony was abolished and, in an effort to forget its dreadful past reputation, Van Diemen's Land officially became known as Tasmania, after its first European visitor.

I had driven for about an hour from Launceston when I came upon a roadside sign proclaiming 'Ross, Tasmania's Finest Heritage Village'. I am all for heritage, especially of the fine variety, so I turned off the Highway and was soon driving along a pleasant elm tree-lined street. How did I know they were elms, I hear my good friends asking, knowingly? Because it said so in the leaflet I had picked up on Ross at the airport. (Who do you think I am? David Bellamy?)

Colonial style buildings were on either side of the street and a crossroads ahead had a signpost indicating that the tourist information office was 20 metres away.

This building shared its space with the Tasmanian Wool Centre, complete with a life-size and life-like merino ram standing at the entrance. My Scottish Mum, Maisie, would have had a field day in a place like this. I picked up a few leaflets on the village, and inquired about accommodation. I was directed to the Man O' Ross Hotel on one corner of the crossroads and decided that as it was getting late, it would be better to explore the village properly the next morning in daylight.

I inquired of the Innkeeper if he had any rooms for the evening and he led me upstairs, apologizing as we went, as they were in the midst of refurbishing the rooms, and he immediately offered me a discounted rate. The room was superb, virginal in so much as the bed was brand new and had yet to be slept in. The smell of freshly built wooden furniture filled my nostrils, a not unpleasant smell, and I was well pleased with my accommodation. The toilet and shower rooms were also newly refurbished, and a large room at the end of the corridor had been turned into a guest lounge and TV room, complete with fridge, kettle, and tea and coffee facilities, albeit without any tea or coffee. I had a relaxing shower and then rested on my 'new' bed whilst, I read up on the history of Ross.

One interesting fact about Ross is that it sits on the 42nd parallel of latitude. This parallel is 29,827km in length and in the Southern Hemisphere, only 4.2% of this covers land, and most of that terrain is inaccessible. So, in Ross you can cross the 42nd parallel, and I did. That's something else I can chalk up as unusual in my life, 'wow'!

The crossroads have a significant role in Ross's history quite apart from being the geographical centre of the village. Known locally as the four corners (something that Ipswich fails to gain in most matches!), each was given a name according to the building that sat upon it. **Temptation** represented by the Man O' Ross Hotel; **Salvation**, the Roman Catholic Church; **Damnation**, the Old Town Gaol, and **Recreation**, the Town Hall. (Personally, I'm not too sure about the last one, judging by most Town Halls in my experience).

So, I'm sitting in a place of temptation and frankly, I'm weak, and give in to the lovely smells of cooking wafting up the stairs. That evening I enjoyed the most delicious meal of lamb shanks imaginable. The meat literally fell off the bone, and was as tender as my heels had been after walking around Ayers Rock. Accompanied by a fine South Australian Red (the wine was good as well!) I was completely sated, and retired for some more reading. This proved to be about two minutes worth before my new bed and 'dunna' (Australian slang for a duvet) had me fast asleep.

The overnight rain had disappeared, and the morning was a mixture of sunshine and dark clouds. I first walked to the Old Ross Bridge, another result of convict labour. In this instance, two fine stonemasons, Daniel Herbert and James Colbeck, put in three years of literally hard labour to complete their work. They carved some 186 stones depicting Celtic symbols, interspersed with images of notable persons and carvings of animals. For their efforts, both men received pardons and became free men.

From the bridge can be seen a fine looking church, standing on the hill. This is the Uniting Church, formerly the Methodist Church, and dates from 1885. Local stone from Beaufort quarries was used in its construction, and the beautiful interior includes black wood pews and a ceiling of Oregon pine, two fine stained glass windows and the carved heads of eight cherubim on the font. They may have been convicts, but there was a multitude of fine tradesmen amongst them.

Following a path from the Uniting Church, I came to the 'Female Factory' that between 1848 and 1854 housed the female convicts and their babies. Here, the women would be trained in the art of domestic services and hired out to surrounding estates. Children were looked after in a form of crèche, but on the evidence of the bare-looking rooms of the 'Factory', this must have been a pretty dismal place for a child to grow up, and life expectancy was not great, as you can witness in the Old Convict Burial Ground at the rear of the Factory. I was impressed by some of the elaborately decorated gravestones and discovered, in talking to two local ladies out walking their dogs, that most were the handiwork of Herbert and Colbeck. They showed me Herbert's own gravestone, beautifully crafted by him, and originally for his own son, who died in infancy in 1846.

Walking back to the village via Church Street and past the Man O' Ross, I came to the Old Ross Post Office built in 1896. The cast iron columns supporting the roof overhang were particularly impressive and an old stone mounting block, that would have enabled riders to mount their horses more easily, stood on the road. Across the road are the Old Ross General Store and Tea Rooms. The interior was suitably decorated for that period long ago and, as I sat by a roaring log fire, I wondered if the cream tea I had ordered would be of the vintage variety. I need not have worried, as the scones (pronounce them as you wish) were light and fluffy, and the homemade strawberry jam was delicious.

It was time to leave Ross and continue my journey southwards. At a steady speed, it took me only two hours to drive the 120km to reach the outskirts of Hobart. Not only is it the State Capital, but it is also Australia's second oldest city after Sydney. It straddles the mouth of the Derwent River, and is overshadowed by the towering Mt. Wellington.

As I mentioned earlier, the convict colony was established in 1803 at Risden Cove, but about a year later, it was moved some 10km below Risden and to the opposite shore. This was Hobart's humble beginning, with a population of 262, of whom 178 were convicts. (Sounds like the current day percentages of many of our towns and cities!) . Being a natural deep-water harbour, commerce boomed, and the city grew in both size and prosperity.

I had noticed quite a few motels; only five to ten minutes from the city centre, and the tourist office were able to confirm a reservation for me at one such establishment called the Tower Hotel. Guess what? That's right, it's got a tower, and guests are welcome to climb it and have views over the north of Hobart and the motorway. The price included breakfast and the room was spacious and comfortable. Feeling pleased with my choice, I decided to drive up to the top of Mt. Wellington and make the most of the clear, sunny afternoon.

Standing at 1270m, the road up to the summit twisted and climbed affording some pretty dramatic views. Road signs warned of icy conditions as I neared the top, and indeed after parking, the remains of a recent snowfall could be evidenced in a sheltered spot. The temperature had been 18C at sea level, but up here, it was literally freezing and the wind chill alone was amazing. I was wearing a sweat-top and shorts and my legs felt the full force of the wind as it tore at my body. A hat flew past and my decision not to wear mine was fully vindicated, although my hair must have resembled that of one of those Norwegian Trolls!

The views down to the Tasman Bridge and Derwent River were fabulous and through the video camera, I could magnify the view. Despite the marvels of such cameras, and I will hopefully have some amazing footage and memories, you should not underestimate your eyesight. It is without doubt the most marvellous gift, and long may mine serve me well.

Having breakfast included in the room rate was great, but to have it delivered to your room was brilliant. This was the arrangement at The Tower and it set me up nicely for the day ahead. My decision to visit Mt. Wellington the previous afternoon seemed a good one as dark, heavy clouds were obscuring the peak from the city today.

I parked on the quayside, and walked to a nearby area known as Salamanca Place that has, reputedly, the finest row of early merchant warehouses in Australia. These warehouses have been converted to house art galleries, restaurants and even a Puppet Theatre. Each Saturday, an open-air market is held there, selling all types of art and craft goods.

Wedged between two of the warehouses are Kelly's Steps and these lead you into the heart of an area called Battery Point. Formerly a Mariners' Village, it has retained much of its 19th century character. Quaint cottages and tearooms and a number of restaurants are found here. Walking ever upwards from the quay, I was surprised to find a circle of Georgian-style houses clustered around a small village green. The sign proclaimed it to be called Arthur's Circus.

Once back in Salamanca Place, I visited a cash machine. To my annoyance, the transaction was declined. I tried another machine and then a third, all with the same result, transaction declined. As I had very few dollars left, I was rather concerned and headed back to The Tower, where I telephoned the Barclays Bank 24 hour help line.

A very polite lady told me that I could have a replacement card issued, but not until I returned the existing card. "Could I arrange a cash transfer?" I asked. "Oh yes" she replied brightly, "but not until the banks open at 9.30am the following day". With the time difference it would be some time before I could get this arrangement underway. No cash, what was I to do for dinner? In the bedside table, I found some menus for an Italian and a Chinese restaurant, and ordered a pizza to be delivered to the room, paying by credit card.

Next morning, as I waited outside a bank for it to open, I thought I would try the card in a machine one more time. The receptionist at The Tower had advised me to rub the metallic strip against a stone or similar, and this I did before entering the card. To my surprise and relief, the transaction was accepted, and I was once again solvent.

The big excitement around Hobart that morning, other than my cash card dilemma, was the arrival of the twin super ferries, 'Spirit of Tasmania 1 & 2. These impressive ships would be operating between Devonport and Melbourne across the Bass Strait, providing a daily service. This was the official launch of the service, and the media and other interested parties were much in evidence. I dare say dignitaries and other invited guests would be going aboard for a reception. This reminded me of my past as a travel agent, when I was often one of those invited to such launches in the UK.

Hobart is a relatively compact city with many fine buildings, 90 of which have a National Trust classification. There is a rather splendid and interesting statue of Abel Tasman and his ships, commemorating his being the first European to set foot on Tasmania. The serious shopper is not forgotten in Hobart with the fine Elizabeth Street Mall and the Cat and Fiddle Arcade. At the latter, there is a fountain and an animated mural that performs on the hour.

I had hoped to visit historic Port Arthur, but I just didn't have time, so crossed the Tasman Bridge and headed for the East Coast, following the Tasman Highway. I stopped at a small resort called Triabunna and took some refreshment in a quaint little teashop filled with knick-knacks and memorabilia. Refreshed, I drove on through the Freycinet Peninsular and passed Coles Bay, which is dominated by large granite outcrops known as the Hazards. There were beautiful views over Great Oyster Bay on the coast side and lush, thick forests on the landside.

I stopped at another of Tasmania's convict-built monuments, called Spiky Bridge. No one knows why the bridge ramparts had these crude spikes attached. Perhaps it was for defence or maybe, just for decoration? To me it looked as though they had some spare bits of rock, and just scattered them along the ramparts. Still, it was an unusual photo opportunity not to be missed. The last part of my day's journey took me through Swansea and onto Bicheno, my overnight stop.

Bicheno, a small fishing port and holiday destination, was named after a former Colonial Secretary of Van Diemen's Land. Only a few fishing boats now work out of Bicheno and so tourism has become its major source of income and employment. I went to the Bicheno Holiday Park that, despite it being out of season, was open. The owner seemed delighted to see me (or anyone!) and said I could have a one-bedroom villa with lounge and kitchen at a knockdown rate. On inspection it was great, and I even had a little carport. All around were old wagon wheels and plough parts, to add to the rural atmosphere. The villas were set amongst trees and grassy areas that would be great for families.

The owner advised me that one of Bicheno's big tourist attractions were the fairy penguins that waddle ashore each evening. Just before dusk I made my way to the bit of beach where I had been told I would see the penguins. I was slightly surprised that there were no other people to witness the parade, but put this down to the time of year. It became darker and darker and then dark! I flashed my torch around, but could see nothing. No penguins, just the odd bat flitting around my head and a plenitude of moths and other flying beasties. I was beginning to feel quite unnerved here in the dark and silence, save for the sound of the incoming tide in the distance and some rather weird-sounding creature. Feeling rather cheated, I walked back to my villa and set about cooking dinner.

The following morning was glorious, and I took some video footage on Bicheno's lovely beach. A lady out walking her dog told me that you often sight whales from this beach and that the fairy penguins had started coming ashore further around the headland from where I had been standing. Typical I thought, I could have stood there all of the previous night and still seen 'Sweet Fanny Adams'.

Leaving Bicheno, I rejoined the Tasman Highway and stopped at various points in order to capture a particularly nice bay or vista on film. I passed through Four Mile Creek and stopped for lunch at Scamander, where I ate my sandwich in the warm sunshine, overlooking the ocean.

I reached the resort of St.Helens early in the afternoon and checked into a motel with a marvellous bay view. After a short rest, I went for a drive, and came to a small resort with the quirky name of Bingalong Bay. I was most amused with the resort sign that incorporated an image of a rather buxom young lady in a blue bikini. That would be the colour of your skin, were you to be tempted into the sea today, despite the pleasant sunshine.

From here I headed towards the Bay of Fires, so called because passing ships spotted the fires of the Aborigines on the beach. (Must have been having a 'barbie'?). The weather was so good, I reckoned I would be able to see a spectacular sunset, so followed a sign to a lookout point known as Humbug Point. It was quite a way from the coast amongst a fairly dense forested area and, as the sun faded, it became dark and spooky with no one about.

I was really pleased when I emerged off the track leading to this remote place and back into Bingalong Bay and then onwards to St.Helens and the motel. I went in search of a meal in the adjacent hotel complex, but food had already stopped being served, so I made do with some crisps and a couple of tinnies to take back to the room. That evening, I watched some of the Commonwealth Games action from Manchester. Judging by the torrential rainfall there, Australian winter was winning hands down over British summer.

My last day on Tasmania had arrived, and I had a long journey ahead to reach Launceston from St. Helens, so I left early the next morning in bright sunshine. Following the A3, I was making good time, so I decided to make a slight detour to take in the St. Columba Falls. These are supposedly the highest in Tasmania at 90m high. I parked the car and a notice told me it was a gentle 10-minute walk to the foot of the falls. Having been duped by these claims before, I set off rather sceptically, but to my surprise, they were right. They were not the most impressive falls I have seen, but were nonetheless worth the detour.

Back on the road, and it soon started to climb and twist as I entered the Bass Forest. The highest point through the forest was a point called Weldborough Pass and I was lucky enough to get a break in the rain clouds, which had now begun to dominate the sky, to be able to get some great views down into the valley below. I arrived in an old tin mining town called Derby and found a small café on the main street. A nice man called Tony served me (a very nice man, if you get my drift!) but his flat white really hit the spot. The caffeine surged through my bloodstream, giving me renewed vigour to complete the drive through Scotsdale and eventually into Launceston. I found the car hire garage first time and they dropped me off in time for my flight back to Melbourne.

So Tasmania, a great place to visit and I feel that I only scratched the surface. I didn't see a Tasmanian devil or the supposedly extinct 'Thylacine' (Tasmanian tiger). Having said that, no one has seen a Thylacine since the one that died in the zoo in 1936. However, with swathes of virgin forests as yet unexplored, who can really rule out the possibility of one or more roaming free? If you are planning to visit Tasmania, allow yourself ten days minimum to do it real justice. There is still much I would like to see here and hopefully I will be able to return at some time in the future.

Melbourne And The Great Ocean Road.

Here I am, back in Melbourne, the State Capital of Victoria. My accommodation for this stay is the Duke of Wellington Hotel, situated near the main railway station and commercial district. This hotel is the oldest continuing inn/hotel in Melbourne, and has been in existence since 1835. Unsurprisingly, there are many pictures of the Duke and his many military campaigns. More surprisingly, the walls are also adorned with AFL 'footy' memorabilia (Australian Football League), as the owner, a huge, bear-like man, was apparently a former professional player.

Melbourne has one of the largest tram and light-rail networks in the world. One of these, the City Circle, does just as it suggests, and is free! As you approach each stop, the driver gives you advice on any significant tourist attractions in the vicinity. After I had completed one full circle, I was more decided as to where to get on and off to see most of the sights. I had also purchased a cheap day pass on all trains and buses, a very economical way of travelling within the city's environs.

Being sports mad, I took the tram out to one of Australia's sporting Meccas, the MCG (Melbourne Cricket Ground), also known simply as the 'G'. This magnificent stadium was beginning extensive rebuilding to be ready for the 2006 Commonwealth Games that the city would be hosting. As well as being an International Test Match venue for the all-conquering Aussie cricketers, the 'G' is home (I think) to the Collingwood AFL team. I joined a guided tour that was very informative and interesting and conducted to a background of shouts and grunts, as the aforementioned Collingwood players went through their paces in preparation for that evening's big game. The changing rooms were really quite small, especially the visitors' and you could imagine the stars sitting there practising their 'slating' techniques. Oops, I mean concentrating on how to win fairly!

From here we moved on to the excellent cricket museum, with pictures and memorabilia from the 1890s to the current day. The Cricket Hall of Honour features many famous Australians who have inflicted pain on their English counterparts over a period of years, with Sir Donald Bradman being probably the most famous of them all. Next to the cricket museum was a special exhibition tracing the history of the Olympic Games from Greece to the last games held in Sydney in 2000. The Olympics were to return to their Greek spiritual home in 2004, when Athens would act as host city.

I then took the bus out to Melbourne's trendy beachside suburb of St. Kilda. Obviously, in high season, this would be a very busy resort area, to which its 'Cappuccino Strip' bore testament. Some of Melbourne's finest 'eateries' were to be located here according to the guidebooks. I had a hot dog and a flat white in one such establishment, sitting alone outside on the café's pavement terrace. Quite a few people who were walking past stopped and took a seat, and I thought the proprietor might give me a discount for helping to attract custom. Wrong, they were all ordering mouth-watering lunches and bottles of chilled wine. When my hot dog arrived, it was greasy and the onions were cold and slimy. As for my flat white, it was well...flat. I left my money on the table, as he didn't want to be bothered with me at all and strolled off along the seafront. The sun was shining but it was not particularly warm that day, so the exercise kept the chill at bay.

Melbourne was really hopping that evening, with footy fans heading for the MCG and the big AFL clash. The opposing team was the Brisbane Lions, and their fans, having travelled down from Queensland, were out in force enjoying themselves. Added to these were the good folk of Melbourne, out to celebrate the start of the weekend. I enjoyed a meal on a busy thoroughfare and a few beers in a couple of hostelries that were heaving with people. This atmosphere was the nearest to that found in England that I had yet experienced in Australia.

I found a cheap Internet café and caught up with friends near and far, before returning to the Duke of Wellington where I had a nightcap prior to retiring to my room and watching live coverage of the Commonwealth Games from 'sunny' Manchester.

The next morning I had a brilliantly cheap breakfast at a little café near to Flinders Street Railway Station, before returning to the hotel to finalise my packing. I was leaving Melbourne for a four-day tour, taking in the Great Ocean Road (GOR). The tour would take me through to Adelaide, and was booked with a company called 'Wayward Bus'!

I had enjoyed my stay in Melbourne, a city with many fantastic old buildings nestling side by side with modern high-rise office blocks. Work had already commenced on sprucing up the city in time for the expected influx of foreign visitors for the Commonwealth Games, and I wondered what impact this would have on its delicate infrastructure.

I joined my fellow travellers for the GOR tour, and a cosmopolitan bunch we were too. There were representatives from Ireland, France, Belgium, New Zealand, Germany, Czech Republic, and England. The Australian representative was Dan, our laid-back driver/guide. We set off in driving rain and prayed for fine weather as we progressed. From what fellow travellers had told me, the GOR could turn out to be one of the highlights of my entire trip to date.

Dan was anything but 'wayward' and soon he had outlined the tour for us, displaying a dry sense of humour. Our first stop was at Bell's Beach, a famous surf spot that featured in the movie 'Point Break' starring Keanu Reeves. It didn't look that glamorous in the current misty and soggy conditions. Next came the picturesque resort of Lorne, where we headed straight down to the beach, and had a slice of gorgeous chocolate cake and steaming mugs of hot chocolate (yes it really was that chilly), whilst we became better acquainted with each other.

The road really began to climb and twist dramatically after Lorne and from one bend in the road, Dan pointed out the distant lights of Apollo Bay, our overnight stop. As we drove along the esplanade, it soon became apparent that much of Apollo Bay was being affected by a power cut. Candlelight flickered in shop and restaurant windows adding to the 'olde world' nature of the resort. Fortunately our hostel accommodation was not affected by the shortage and we were able to check into our rooms and make up our beds under electric lighting.

Whilst breakfast was included in the tour price, dinner was not, so a group of us made our way back to the esplanade and located a restaurant that had not actually closed due to the power cut. They offered various 'fast foods' and most of us opted for fish and chips, served in newspaper. This was marvellous for me, and took me back to my childhood, but seemed to be of great amusement to my new colleagues.

Suitably sated, we made our way to one of the two pubs in Apollo Bay. Both seemed quite packed, being a Saturday night, and having settled on one, we enjoyed a few good beers, while our initial inhibitions melted away with the alcohol. In my case this just meant that the jokes started to flow, and we were having a grand time. To add to this convivial atmosphere, a live telecast of the Australia and New Zealand rugby union game was being shown. Edna, our Kiwi, was in her element and I was surprised by the depth of knowledge that Marie, a bubbly French girl, had on the sport. Well the French do have a reasonably competent rugby team, I suppose. The All Blacks (New Zealand) lost with the last kick of the game and the resident Wallaby (Australian) supporters were in jubilant mood. We eventually staggered back to the hostel, having created a great bond of comradeship that boded well for the remainder of the tour.

The next morning, there were a few throbbing heads and bleary eyes as we sat unusually quietly over breakfast. Breakfast was a self-made affair and afterwards we had to wash up and leave the kitchen area as spotless as we had found it. This is standard procedure in hostels, the only difference being that on this occasion, 'Wayward Bus' had provided the food items. Danielle, from the Czech Republic, promised to make us typical breakfast waffles the next morning.

Having loaded the bus, we left Apollo Bay and headed for the Otway Ranges. We drove through the town of Marengo, supposedly named after Napoleon Bonaparte's warhorse (there, I bet you didn't know that?) and Castle Cove, before stopping at Melba Gully for our morning constitutional. Here we had a pleasant stroll through the rainforest and marvelled at the fern gullies, Mountain Ash and Soft Fern trees that thrive in this environment. Dan gave us a lot of information regarding the fauna to be found in this gully. Additional information can be found on plaques at varying points along the path.

Leaving the Otway Ranges, we headed back down to the coast, and were now travelling through the Port Campbell National Park. The spectacular sheer cliffs of this coastline are where you will find one of Australia's, and perhaps the worlds, most beautiful and natural wonders.

The huge limestone stacks known as the 'Twelve Apostles' sit like sentries in the surf and are an awe-inspiring sight. The weather was kind to us and already mesmerising viewing was enhanced by the brilliant sunshine that was so kind to us. Despite their name, there are actually only nine and a bit Apostles left standing nowadays, due to the ravages of wind and water. Close by are Gibson's Steps, natural steps cut into the cliffs by weathering, which leads unsurprisingly to Gibson's Beach. From this beach you are given yet another aspect from which to view the Apostles.

The whole area has a number of gorges, blowholes and natural rock arches. The most famous of these is nearby Loch Ard Gorge. Adjacent to the gorge is a jagged-topped rock known as the 'Razorback'. Loch Ard was the name of an iron-hulled clipper that was driven onto these rocks during a tremendous storm in 1878. Only two of the 55 passengers and crew survived. Her fellow survivor, Tom Pearce, rescued Eva Carmichael. Both were 18 years of age and speculation of a romance between the two tragic youngsters was rife. Unlike good fairy tales and the seeming keenness of Tom, Eva spurned his advances, and returned to her home in Ireland. Tom went on to become a successful Victorian businessman in the shipping line. This beautiful, but treacherous, stretch of Victorian coastline claimed as many as 80 ships in a 40-year period from 1880.

After lunch, we arrived at the nearby landmarks of 'The Arch' and 'London Bridge'. Here a natural rock platform used to link the stack to the mainland but, in 1990, it suddenly collapsed, leaving two very startled tourists stranded on the seaward side. A helicopter was summoned, and television viewers worldwide witnessed their rescue, much to the surprise of their respective spouses!

Moving further on, we passed through Martyrs Bay where many small stacks sit in the surf, and then to Logan Bay. Here we were able to spend some time whale watching, as two Southern Right whales were spotted frolicking in the breakers. Apparently, this is a popular bay for the Southern Right whales as they make their way to their feeding grounds in the cold waters of the Southern Ocean.

This had already been a magical day, and our last treat was a visit to the Tower Hill State Park, where we were able to view emus, red kangaroos and koalas in their natural habitat. This was my first sighting of a koala in the wild since arriving in Australia. (You may recall my earlier unsuccessful mission to Lemon Tree Passage in New South Wales). Even here, the koalas were virtually in a state of suspended animation, being as they were wedged in the fork of a tree, but occasionally one would reach out a tiny paw for a tasty leaf. When all is said and done, it's what they do, 'eat roots, shoots and leaves'. Never mind!

It was dark by the time we pulled into Port Fairey, a small seaside township founded in 1835 by whalers and seal hunters. Our hostel, a splendid example of colonial style architecture, had once been the home of the wealthiest merchant in town. Once again we found ourselves in a local pub, enjoying delicious, yet simple home-cooked food, washed down with some equally excellent Victorian red wine. Everyone had a favourite moment from a staggering day on the Great Ocean Road, and we discussed these late into the evening.

Next day we journeyed onwards to Portland, Victoria's first settled township. These first settlers were the Henty family, who arrived from Van Diemen's Land (Tasmania) in 1834. One of our group Edna, our Kiwi, was actually a descendant of the Hentys, and we were able to make an impromptu stop at Burswood Homestead, built in 1850. Edna was able to establish that the current owners were not directly descended from the Henty family, but were able to provide some information that Edna could follow up at a later date.

From Portland, we travelled on to Nelson, stopping to visit the Terragal Caves. These caves provided refuge for Aborigine travellers and animals alike. It was an easy amble from the road to the caves, that are still home to eagles, as was witnessed by the bones and remains of their prey, (unless they were from the nearest 'KFC').

We took our lunch at Nelson and not from KFC either. Our lunch was included in the tour price and we utilised the facilities of one of the many public picnic areas to be found in Australia. We were all involved in the preparation of the meal, clearing up and re-packing the food and utensils etc. onto the bus. It would be great to have this sort of facility in the UK, but I doubt they would remain usable for long, let alone be cleaned and left ready for the next party.

Nelson is a small village that sits at the mouth of the Glenelg River, and not far away is the long dead (we trusted) volcano, Mount Schank. It was quite an effort to climb the large number of steps up to the rim of the volcano, but it was worth it for the panoramic views of the surrounding area. At 600mt it was extremely blustery, and a number of us lay down to minimise its effect, and to watch the clouds scudding across the sky. For my part it was because I was exhausted from the climb!

As we neared Beachport, our overnight stop, the weather had really closed in and made the scenic walk along the cliff top a miserable non-event. The strong winds and steadily increasing rain that stung our faces caused us to curtail this activity and return to the shelter of our tour bus. We were a rather bedraggled bunch when we arrived at our hostel, the imaginatively named 'Bompars'. Adjacent to the coast, this really pleasant and welcoming establishment would have been even better on a fine, bright evening. As it was, after freshening up, we had a celebratory dinner in honour of Edna's birthday. As it was also the last night of the tour, we cracked open a few extra bottles of wine as we reminisced about our shared experiences on the Great Ocean Road.

Although we had now officially completed the Great Ocean Road, we still had a long day's drive into South Australia and on to Adelaide, its State Capital. We passed through Robe and then Kingston where guess what we found? Another of Australia's larger than life phenomena, namely 'Larry the Lobster'. I've seen the 'Big Banana' at Coffs Harbour added to which there is a 'Two-Tonne Trout' at Adaminaby, and a huge bull at Nambour. Right about now, I would have been grateful for a 'larger than life' glass of beer.

Our lunch stop promised to be somewhat different, and so it proved. We were at the Coorong Wilderness Lodge, where the Ngarrindjeri Aborigine people have built up a thriving business venture. Currently, they have a restaurant and camping area, and are gradually replanting the land on this peninsula. The Coorong is a 100km saltwater lagoon, separated from the Southern Ocean by huge sand dunes. Over 200 species of birds are found on the Coorong, with the most populous being the pelicans. We were able to witness the young pelicans being given flying lessons by the adult birds, which led them in some quite intricate patterns for such large birds.

After a lovely home cooked lunch including kangaroo burgers and 'damper' scones, a gentleman called Cyril took us on a bush walk. He showed us various plants that the Aborigines has used for generations as medicine and for food and drink. There is an ongoing education programme in operation for young Aborigines and other children alike, to ensure that the Aborigine culture is not lost. As Cyril said, "It is rewarding to be able to teach the old ways to a new generation of people".

We took our leave of the Coorong and headed towards Adelaide. At Wellington we had to cross the mighty Murray River and this was accomplished using an old chain ferry. We eventually arrived in Adelaide at 9.30pm, and it was with much sadness that we said our final goodbyes to each other, and expressed our gratitude to Dan and the flagrant 'Wayward Bus'.

I had been going to stay with a friend of a friend whilst in Adelaide, but the best made plans often come apart, and I ended up booking into the centrally situated Adelaide YHA. This is an ultramodern and superbly appointed hostel, that would shame many three or even four star hotels that I have stayed in, and I quickly decided that this would make an excellent base from which to explore the city in the coming days.

Fine Wine And Great Company.

Some of our group was travelling on with Wayward Bus to Alice Springs, and a few of us were resting up in Adelaide for a few days. Tina, Edna and I met up and arranged to go on a day's wine tasting tour of the Barossa Valley. Travelling by mini bus, we drove out of Adelaide and headed into the Torrens Gorge.

People from Prussia and Silesia settled the Barossa Valley in 1842, having arrived in South Australia to practise their religion free from persecution. They obviously liked a tipple and brought their skills with them, to create the Barossa Valley of today, probably Australia's finest wine growing area.

As we journeyed into the valley, we stopped at the small village of Gumeracha, famous for its toy factory and perhaps more famously, the biggest 'Rocking Horse' in the world (equal to six-storeys high). What is it with these Aussies and their fascination with oversized objects?

We visited one winery prior to lunch and they were generous with their samples, which gave us the taste for a nice bottle of Cabernet Sauvignon with our meal. The venue for our lunch was Barossa Junction, where they have converted a 1920s Australian train carriage into a restaurant. The meal was excellent (kangaroo steak for me), all washed down with the aforementioned wine. We were even more in the mood now, and sampled fine wines and liqueurs at the next two wineries before visiting the Menglers Hill Lookout for a panoramic view over the vineyards. Our last stop was at the Yalanda Estate, which is housed in a magnificent chateau, with wonderful gardens. It was interesting to see how these wineries were developed as plush homes for their owners. This particular winery is now owned by the McMillan family, which also has a large wine business in the Hunter Valley in New South Wales.

Our return journey took us to a reservoir, not exciting in itself, but the dam wall here acts as a microphone. If you stand on one side and talk normally, or whisper, you can be heard clearly on the far side. A whispering dam... what next?

I had discovered that Adelaide was hosting an under-20 football festival, featuring teams from England, Scotland, Germany, Italy, Holland, Brazil, China and Australia. That evening, matches were taking place at the Hindmarch Stadium, so I caught a bus, which took me fairly close, then followed the floodlights to the stadium. I saw the youngsters of Bayern Munich beat those of Ajax Amsterdam 3-0 and then Newcastle United (UK) triumph over the Australs (Australian national squad) 2-0. It was strange to watch a football game alongside many locals, to whom this King of Sports is alien. As a matter of record, Glasgow Rangers (Scotland) went on to win the trophy by defeating the Australs in the final. (Sorry Semi! He's an avid Glasgow Celtic fan.)

Double-U-Ay!

During the three-hour flight to Perth from Adelaide, I did some research on Western Australia (more commonly known as W.A. or 'double-u-ay'). It is Australia's largest state and it was not until 1826 that a British party from Sydney landed at King George Sound, Albany, and claimed it formally, for fear of French colonisation. Three years later, Captain James Stirling founded the first non-convict settlement in Australia at what is now Perth. The area was so isolated and rugged that it was deemed a natural prison, and convicts were transported here in 1850. As settlers spread out into the southwest, many convicts went as their labour force. Development was very slow and it was not until gold was discovered at Coolgardie in 1892 that the economy boomed. Today, W.A.'s economic wealth is based largely on its immensely rich mineral deposits.

My second cousin Bill and his daughter Pam, who live in the small beach resort of Coogee, met me at Perth. Coogee is about a forty-minute drive south from Perth.

The plan was for me to stay with Bill for a couple of days, while I finalised my itinerary for visiting as much of W.A. as possible.

The following day, we went into nearby Fremantle or 'Freo' as the locals know it. Situated at the foot of the Swan River on the shores of the Indian Ocean, Freo lies about eleven kilometres north of Coogee and nineteen kilometres from Perth. Freo was founded in 1829 when HMS Challenger, captained by Charles Fremantle, first dropped anchor here. It is probably most well-known for the unsuccessful defence of the America's Cup yachting trophy in 1987. This event transformed Freo into a more modern, colourful and expansive city, as preparations were made for the influx of tourists associated with the competition.

The colonial-style buildings in the city struck me first, and as we walked from the car park to the centre, there were many vibrant and colourful street cafes too. Along one street, South Terrace, the cafes blend into one another and the area has become known as the 'Cappuccino Strip'. We were headed for a splendid old 'Australian' pub called Rosie O'Gradys, This building has been completely renovated in the style of an Irish pub, complete with Guinness and other Irish ales and also, reputedly, wonderful meals. After a sumptuous meal and a couple of pints of McCaffreys Irish ale, I can whole-heartedly recommend it. On the way back to the car, I dropped into the tourist office and picked up various maps and leaflets to immerse myself in later. It was another short-sleeved winter's day, and I took myself off for a walk down to the beach close to Bill's home.

I negotiated an excellent deal with a local car hire firm and was now ready to head south and west to see as much of the state as I could, with the intention of doing a big loop and returning to Perth before heading for Singapore on the 30th of August. I had also remembered that I still needed to apply for an Indian visa, and the only option open to me was to make a postal application to the Indian High Commission in Sydney. I made inquiries and was assured that a postal application could be completed within eight working days. I gathered the necessary documentation and purchased a postal order to cover the fee ($20 extra for not being an Australian citizen!) and gave Bill's address for its safe return. No problems, I thought... more on this later.

With everything in hand, or so I thought, I left Bill and Coogee and headed south with the intention of hugging the coastline as far as possible. My first stop was about an hour's drive away at Rockingham. This popular beach resort is, surprisingly, W.A.'s second largest city in terms of population. Just off the coast lies Penguin Island, home to the largest colony of blue fairy penguins in Australia and a major tourist attraction. Unfortunately for me, I was unable to visit the island at this time, as it was in the middle of the breeding season. I was left to try and glimpse a fairy penguin through my binoculars (breeding or otherwise!).

Not much further along the coast is the resort of Mandurah. It was built around the calm waters of the Peel Inlet and Harvey Estuary, creating one of the largest inland waterways in Australia. I booked onto a sightseeing cruise with the promise of dolphin sightings. The weather was warm and the sun sparkled off the water, which might prove to be a problem with any dolphin sightings. Just before we embarked (very nautical, eh?), a party of schoolchildren had swept aboard. Being like any fourteen or so year-olds, they were more interested in their drinks and snacks than in the various wildlife being pointed out to us. However, at the first sighting of a dolphin, any semblance of rational behaviour disappeared altogether. Their shrieks and 'oohs' and 'aahs' and, more irritatingly, their bodies, ensured that not only could you not hear the commentary, but neither could you see the dolphins. Fortunately I had a window seat (or at least I would have had, had there been a window in place), and the dolphins later obliged me by swimming along my side of the boat. The cruise over, I grabbed a burger and a flat white before driving on to Bunbury.

Mandurah to Bunbury took me a leisurely two hours' drive in the warm afternoon sunshine. The city is uniquely situated on a peninsula of land surrounded by water. I went to the tourist office and they found me a single room at the Chateau La Mer motel. For you non-French speakers, this means I was situated right on the coast, and about a five-minute drive from the city centre. A strong wind had developed and the sun had disappeared behind the clouds, which had the effect of lowering the temperature considerably.

Bunbury is a neat, compact city and has many nice colonial-style buildings with a mixture of restaurants and retail outlets. The best viewing point in Bunbury is the Marlston Hill Lookout. From here, I had an uninterrupted view across the city. I made out Koombana Bay and the

Dolphin Discovery Centre, where I was to make my way later. This lookout was actually higher than the lighthouse nearby, and was the original lighthouse site.

The Dolphin Discovery Centre is famous because the dolphins swim right up to the sandy beach of Koombana Bay. This gives you the opportunity to have a unique experience with wild dolphins. Although the dolphins visit on most days, they are wild, and the centre staff in no way induces them to visit. The dolphins are monitored carefully and have been named by the centre. On my particular visit I was unlucky, as no dolphins had visited the bay that morning, or in the period whilst I was there. The centre has a dolphin adoption scheme, allowing you to choose a dolphin from the regulars that visit the bay and follow its fortunes via a website. I decided to buy an adoption pack for my nieces and my friend's daughter, Rebecca. These subsequently provided great excitement in two households.

Busselton is a further forty kilometres from Bunbury and is located on the shores of Geographe Bay. The wind was really blowing here, and as I walked towards Busselton's famous timber jetty, it was straight into my face. At a length of two kilometres, it is the longest timber jetty in the southern hemisphere. A few hardy souls could be seen in the distance, walking on the jetty, but I for one wasn't about to join them on this occasion.

As I drove out of Busselton, I noticed a number of motels advertising vacancies at reasonable rates. This somewhat surprised me, as the local tourist office had warned me that accommodation was not cheap in this area. About fifteen kilometres from Busselton is the small town of Dunsborough, the gateway to Cape Naturaliste and some of the most spectacular coastal scenery in Australia. I drove the thirteen kilometres to the Cape Naturaliste lighthouse. There are a number of walking trails starting here, ranging from twenty minutes to seven days' duration (guess which one I opted for?). I walked around the cliff top and to a lookout point overlooking Geographe Bay. The weather was blustery and the waves were crashing in on the rocks below. It was somehow very peaceful though, and I sat for some thirty minutes, taking in the view, but failed to spy any whales. Accommodation in Dunsborough was at a premium and also at premium rates, so I decided to return to Busselton, where I found a motel at a much more reasonable rate. I had just checked into my room when a torrential rainstorm hit Busselton, so I opted for a bowl of cornflakes and an early night.

The following day, I planned to drive to Augusta, but first decided to visit Yallingup (the Aboriginal word meaning 'place of love'). My guidebook also told me that Yallingup has three world famous surf breaks.' The Three Bears', 'Yallingup' and 'Smith's Beach' breaks are known all over the world (apparently).

I had come to see another of Yallingup's claims to fame, Ngilgi Cave. The whole coast between Cape Naturaliste and Augusta is dotted with these natural caves. At the meeting point for the 10am tour, a chap called Andy informed me that I *was* the 10am tour (I should have gone back and asked for a group rate!) and walked me to the entrance for my underground adventure. You descend into the depths on your own, and follow a trail. I immediately noticed the atmosphere within the cave, which was quite humid, and the handrails were wet to the touch. The trail leads to a large cavern where another guide is on hand to answer questions and show you a number of limestone crystal formations.

You continue your stroll through the cave until you reach the exit, which is in fact the entrance. Clever use of lighting gives you some pretty spectacular views of various stalactites and stalagmites. Now which is the one that grows down, and which grows up? I have always remembered it by the following phrase: 'As mites go up to bed, so tights come down.' Slightly risqué I suppose, but as good a way of remembering as any. You can let your imagination run wild in these caves and picture various animals and objects in the strange shapes formed over the centuries. One in particular is a stunning formation known as 'The Arab's Tent', which is a colourful, banded shawl of limestone. The largest stalactite in the cave weighs in at two tonnes. The cave was first explored in 1899 but dates back some forty thousand years. Carbon dating of fossils from the cave confirms these estimates. The last fact about the cave relates to the growth rate of the stalactites and stalagmites, which grow twenty five millimetres every hundred years.

It was nice to return to the surface and feel the sun on my face and the wind in my hair (what the hell is this turning into, a Mills and Boon novel? I do apologise for such flowery prose). Now, where was the handsome hero?

On my way again south, I was driving past many signs for caves and increasingly, wineries, as I got closer to Margaret River. This small, almost 'bijou' township is approximately eight kilometres from the coast. Everyone had told me how lovely Margaret River was and yes, I agree, it is pretty to look at, with its arts and crafts galleries and smart restaurants and hotel. However, I found it rather soulless and pretentious, and decided to stay only as long as it took me to eat lunch and use the Internet. The former was quite quick and the latter was somewhat slower, such are my typing skills.

I drove on towards Augusta and the scenery changed yet again, this time to thick forest. Augusta is a small holiday resort with a couple of hotels, a couple of motels and a YHA backpackers' hostel. I checked with the tourist office and the rather prim lady there offered me a reservation at one of the hotels and one of the motels, but neither was very cheap. Even the YHA was expensive, so I wandered across to the other motel that the tourist office didn't represent and was offered a room at a very agreeable rate (a further point to remember when travelling – always check out all your options). The room was comfortable with a separate lounge, and I went across to the local store and got in supplies, as I decided to stay for a few days and have a bit of a rest.

I had found out that there was a daily whale-watching cruise that departed at 10.30am, so I walked to the booking office after breakfast to see if that morning's cruise was to take place. The wind was out of the west, and although it was likely to be a bit choppy, the cruise was on, so I joined my fellow watchers at the Flinders Bay jetty. Even here the swell was high, so the transfer by dinghy to our twin-hulled vessel was in itself quite exciting, and I got a wet bum into the bargain, as the water washed over the side.

As soon as we were underway, the swell took immediate effect and, further convinced by a loose seat that bounced and swayed in opposite movement to the boat, I decided that on-deck in the fresh air would be the best option. I swayed and 'disco danced' my way to the bow (front for non-nautical types), where by clinging to the rail, I was able to enjoy the ride. As we plunged into huge troughs, the deck seemed to drop very suddenly, having the effect of leaving your feet in mid-air, and then banging you down hard as the deck rose up on the next swell. All in all, it was quite exhilarating, and I found that by bending my knees on the downward plunge, I was able to counter the drop. I know this makes it sound like we were out in a major storm, but for people like me it was fairly rough.

It wasn't long before we sighted our first whales a small pod of humpbacks. Holding onto the rail with one hand and videoing with the other was quite challenging. Keeping whales in view in the ocean is difficult enough normally, but these conditions made it doubly so, and. I was therefore really pleased that the footage I took that morning was amongst the best whale footage that I took on the whole trip. We made our way back to Flinders Bay and disembarked via the dinghy once more. This time, as we approached the jetty, we had to time our lunge onto the steps most carefully, as the swell ensured a tricky last few moments. Safely back on terra firma, frozen stiff and somewhat wet, I made my way back into town and huddled in a café clutching a large flat white.

Just five kilometres from Augusta is Cape Leeuwin, the most southwesterly point in Australia. It also marks the point where the Indian and Southern Oceans converge. This is one of the reasons that whale watching is so good off Augusta, as the whales are making their way to and from their breeding grounds in Antarctica. It was now late afternoon and the sun had broken through. With the promise of a fine sunset, I drove to Cape Leeuwin. Here, the lighthouse, built in 1895, dominates the landscape. Alongside this can be seen an old water wheel, which originally provided the power for the lighthouse. I took some wonderful footage of the rocky coastline here, with the sun shining brightly as the surf pounded in. On my way back to the motel, I noticed a sign for 'Skippy Rock', and, amused by the name, I detoured to find it. Driving up an unmade road with large potholes, I arrived at a small car park. A track led along the cliffs, and I was presented with four or five large rocks sitting in the ocean. Now, which one was the aforementioned 'Skippy', was open to debate. With no one about to ask, and with none of them resembling a kangaroo (Skippy), I decided to rename it 'Andy's Rock', and leave it at that.

I had found the local launderette and put a load through. The owner of the motel said that I could use her rotary line in the paddock at the rear of the motel, and as it was a warm day with a slight breeze, I hoped my clothes would dry ok. I drove a few kilometres out of Augusta to nearby Hamlin Bay. Although quite pretty, with a large curve of fine sand, there was precious little to see save for the few fishing boats, pulled up on the beach by the small jetty. I decided to walk along the beach and could imagine this was a very popular swimming beach in the summer months, judging by the huge car park, in which my car was the only one.

The sun was warm and the water was not too cold, as it lapped around my ankles. It was about now that I wished I'd taken my trainers off first! Listening to my personal mini-disc player as I strolled, I completely lost all track of time, and suddenly realised I had been walking for nearly an hour and a half. I had still not reached the end of the bay, but turned around and retraced my footsteps (well, not all of them, as my trainers had about dried out now, and I wanted to keep it that way!).

Back at the motel, my clothes were doing fine and, after collecting them in and carefully folding them (who am I kidding?), I went for a cream tea at the Augusta bakery. Here I enjoyed my scone and strawberry jam, whilst taking in the view of the River Blackwater in the distance.

Fascinated by sunsets, I visited the Augusta Hill lookout. From here, one can get a splendid view of Augusta's nine-hole golf course as well as of the coast. I hadn't expected to find a golf course on the top of a hill, and would imagine that it is a nice course to play on - as long as you have plenty of balls! The sunset shots I was hoping for were made almost impossible by the rather overgrown nature of the local flora (this was something I had experienced at a number of Australian lookouts – obviously Australian gardeners suffer from vertigo!).

Back at the motel, I watched the start of the English Premier League Football season live on Australian television. The featured game was Leeds United versus Manchester City, a game Leeds won easily 3-0. Due to time differences between England and Australia, the match didn't finish until 1am.

The next day I had a rare lie-in, and eventually roused myself at noon. The weather was glorious and I felt quite guilty for my sloth, so I strolled over to the aptly named 'Cozy Corner' café and partook of a delicious brunch of focaccias (easy for me to say) and… oh, a flat white. Suitably fortified and full of energy, I headed back to bed! Well, actually, I headed for a good long walk, of which there are a number in and around Augusta. Setting off along the shore of the Blackwater River, I headed towards the ocean. After a while, the riverbank gave way to semi-scrub dunes, but if you kept close to the river, you eventually came to the ocean. As the tide was out, a wide expanse of sandbank was visible and, being quite firm, I walked across it.. In doing so I added quite a distance to my walk, and suddenly hoped that the tide wasn't about to rush in again quickly, leaving me stranded. Certainly the wading birds were taking advantage of the tide for some rich pickings.

Listening to Freddie Mercury and Queen's 'Greatest Hits' and scanning the ocean for any signs of whales cavorting along the coast, I completely lost any sense of time. The realisation that Cape Leeuwin was only a short distance further on came as quite a surprise, and looking back over my shoulder, Augusta was but a speck in the distance. I calculated I had walked about eight kilometres and decided to retrace my footsteps before the sun set, and it got dark.

As I reached the outskirts of Augusta, the little café that I'd passed on my outward journey was still open, and I gratefully sat down on their patio and took in the idyllic scene set out before me. The sun glinting off the water, wading birds feeding, and the occasional small boat chugging by, made my tea and scone all the sweeter. The owner and her daughter joined me on the patio, relaxing after a busy afternoon, and we were soon chatting (who me?) about my journey and the parts of Australia that I had visited, but they had not. It was at times like these that I felt extremely lucky, and pleased that I had made that decision to travel, all those months ago.

I completed my walk and phoned England, where it was 10am on Sunday morning. My good buddy Carlton disguised his annoyance at being woken on his day off to talk with me, as I just felt I had to share my positive feelings on such a lovely day. I had also cheekily reverse-charged the call that Carlton had accepted. - Cheers, mate!

I had worked up quite an appetite (what a surprise), and, after showering, I walked to the Augusta Hotel to take dinner. It was only 7.15pm, but the bar area was already closed, and the lounge/dining room, whilst open, was populated by fewer than fifteen people. I ordered a Thai coconut curry and had my bottle of Jacobs Creek red with me (BYO is all the rage in Australia, even on licensed premises). By the time my meal arrived at the table, there was just a handful of folk left, and by the time I was into my third glass of wine, it was just me and the bar staff.

When I inquired as to where everyone was, I was told that it was just Sunday night, the quietest night in Augusta. As I bade my hosts' farewell at 8.15pm, the lights went out, and the doors were bolted behind me. (For some of you, this will come as no surprise, as this has happened to me before, notably at the 'Piano Bar' at the Messonghi Beach complex, Corfu). Strange, how when you fancy a night out, you often as not end up in front of the TV, or reading a book.

Well, more soon on Western Australia, as I visit huge Karri trees, walk in the tree tops, drive for hours without seeing another vehicle, surf an inland wave, and upset the local darts champion.

Whales, Waves And Darts!

I left Augusta behind, and headed south towards Walpole. The route led me to Pemberton, a small township, famous for its timber industry. The tourist centre also houses a small museum depicting Pemberton's history. Situated in the midst of Warren National Park with its magnificent Karri trees, the museum has many photographs and accounts of the construction of the world famous Gloucester Tree – a tree, used as a lookout for bush fires, that was named after the Duke of Gloucester (then Governor General of Australia), who visited the tree during construction of the lookout in 1946. There are one hundred and fifty three rungs which spiral up the tree to the platform, sixty-one metres above, giving 360-degree views for some one thousand kilometres. The tree is reputedly the tallest fire lookout tree in the world, and is open to the public to climb. It is, however, not for the faint-hearted or the dietary challenged!

As has happened a few times on my journey, I bumped into someone I had met previously. Judith had been on my Great Ocean Road tour, and was now doing a whistle-stop tour of South Western Australia. She was headed for another must-visit attraction; the Valley of the Giants. This valley was situated near Walpole, and was such a popular attraction that it was being visited to death. In order to save and protect the trees and forest floor, an innovative and stunning treetop walk was designed and built. You walk literally across the treetops, some forty metres above the forest floor, along six hundred metres of steel walkways. These huge Karri trees are ramrod straight, some are up to four hundred years old, and they have been known to grow to eighty metres in height. The roots of these trees, some distorted with lumps and eye-like scars, seem to take on the appearance of an aged human face.

Driving ever southwards, the towering Karri forests gave way to farmlands before reaching Denmark. The Wilson Inlet, which links the Denmark River with the Southern Ocean, has some rare evidence of Aboriginal settlement – three-thousand-year-old fish traps. (I hoped that the meal I was about to have didn't include any three thousand year-old fish!) The Wilson Inlet has another strange phenomenon; it is the tannins from the leaves that drop into it that are the cause the brownish colour of the water, the tannins wash out of the leaves much like a teabag in a teapot.

After lunch I drove the final leg to Albany, which took about an hour and a half. I had picked up a leaflet on a motel in Albany whilst in Walpole, and after inspecting rooms at a couple of city centre pubs, I made my way to Middleton Beach to view the motel. The room was more expensive, but far nicer than those I had viewed earlier and my mind was made up.

The coastal road from the city to Middleton Beach has excellent views over King George Sound. Another higher lookout is found on Mount Adelaide, where, in 1893, the Princess Royal Fortress was established to protect the natural harbour of King George Sound. It was perceived that the harbour was vulnerable to attack, and therefore to the security of Australia. This old fort is well worth a visit. You are able to view the barracks, the guardhouse complete with cells, the underground shell magazine, the original gun emplacements and the north and south lookouts. Up until its closure as a defensive fort in 1956, the guns over King George Sound were never fired in anger. For me, one of the most interesting displays was that of the garrison cookhouse and pantry, with some familiar and not-so-familiar products on view. Were you a 'Bisto Kid'?

The other notable lookout is found on nearby Mount Clarence. Here, after climbing a number of steps from the car park (my favourites!), you come to a memorial to the Desert Mounted Corps. This was originally erected in Port Said, Egypt, as a memorial to the events at Gallipoli. It was moved here when the Suez crisis in 1956 made colonial reminders less than popular in Egypt.

On the outskirts of Albany lies Frenchman Bay, a stunning stretch of coastline. The guidebooks advise you to visit the 'Gap' and 'Natural Bridge', two spectacular rock formations side by side. Having not seen any of my friends from 'The Land of The Rising Sun', I was joined at the 'Gap' (no pun intended) by a coach party of Japanese tourists. As we crowded onto the observation platform to view the seething mass of foam, spray and crashing surf thirty metres below, I was again amazed at how inappropriately dressed these elegant oriental ladies were for the weather and the venue. I drove to the nearby 'Blowholes' where, as I had guessed, the coach didn't follow. Here you have a fifteen-minute walk along the cliffs to an area where, especially when there is a heavy sea, the air is blown with great force through fissures in the rock – where were my Marilyn Monroe-look-alike Japanese ladies now?

Albany is steeped in whaling history, and, at Frenchman Bay, the Whale World Museum is situated on Cheynes Beach (pronounced 'Chains'). This was the original whaling station. Remarkably, this station only ceased operations in 1978, following the banning of commercial whaling. Whilst the tour describes the gory day-to-day running of a whaling station, it is nevertheless an interesting insight into the lives of those who depended on whaling for a living. Much of the current-day knowledge of whales and their conservation ironically comes from ex-whalers and stations like this one.

As befits its history, Albany has many old buildings, such as the Patrick Taylor Cottage and the Old Gaol. I'll be perfectly honest, and tell you that I couldn't take any more tramping around museums or buildings, so satisfied myself with some light window-shopping around the centre. The weather was pretty foul and you could imagine the scene a couple of hundred years ago, with a howling gale blowing in off the bay.

I had intended originally to drive along the coast to Esperance and then swing north to the gold mining town of Kalgoolie. From here, I would head west to Hyden and the infamous Wave Rock. However, I decided to miss out Esperance and Kalgoolie and make the journey directly to Wave Rock. As I was leaving Albany, I passed Dog Rock, a huge granite outcrop, so named because of its likeness to a bloodhound sniffing the air.

The road to Hyden heads through the Stirling Ranges, providing some good photo opportunities. As usual, the road was deserted and ramrod straight, and I passed through Borden and Pingrup. I stopped in this one-horse town for a cold drink, before driving on past Lake Grace, a huge salt lake. I encountered the occasional road-train, but other than that, little else. These elongated goods vehicles are now legally limited to four trailers in length, but are nonetheless impressive sights as they thunder along at one hundred kilometres per hour, creating a huge dust cloud in their wake.

The last stretch took me through Pingaring and then Kalgarin before Hyden was in sight. The weather was definitely warmer than it had been on leaving Albany, and the sun was now getting lower in the sky at the end of a glorious afternoon. The tourist isn't spoilt for choice in Hyden when it comes to accommodation, so I checked into the Hyden motel. The room was comfortable, and I enjoyed a few cold beers in the large bar before dinner.

Dinner was an exciting event, as they operated a 'cook your own' BBQ. You choose and pay for your choice of main course, then take it to the BBQ to cook as you wish, and a superb selection of salads, soups and hot vegetables are available to accompany your meal. After finishing with the BBQ you are requested to clean the hotplate for your fellow guests to use after you.

I ate well, and joined the locals for a few beers back in the bar, where the main excitement seemed to be watching 'The Price Is Right'. The sporting Aussies were gambling on who was closest to the price of each item. I declined an offer to participate in this game, but did accept the challenge of a game of darts from a young woman, who was knocking back beers like they had gone out of fashion.

We were to play 501, best of three games for a jug of beer. I won the first game convincingly, but had to take over the scoring from my somewhat arithmetically challenged opponent. My win didn't sit very well with Ronnie (probably short for Ronnie Biggs) and she decided to take the game more seriously by removing her Harley Riders jacket, revealing the Harley Riders tattoos on her forearms. The previously uninterested 'Price Is Right' crew was now lending its vocal support to Ronnie.

I hit my double to start second dart, and sensed Ronnie's growing annoyance, as she hurled her last dart at the board, embedding it so hard that I needed both hands to remove it. Should I throw the game in the interest of Australian/English relationships (or in case she wanted to arm wrestle afterwards as a double or quits clause), or go for a 2-0 win?

With a double sixteen finish, I went for the latter. I thought of some celebratory dance, but erred on the side of humility, claiming the win was a fluke, as I had not played darts for at least ten years. This actually made it worse, as Ronnie apparently plays every day, and hadn't lost for months. I offered to share my jug with her but she declined, and I last saw her tearing across the car park on her bicycle – perhaps it was a Harley brand?

Wave Rock is four kilometres from Hyden, and, despite a lack of visitors, the large car park was a 'pay and display' type. It is only a short walk to the Wave, and it is certainly a unique sight. Wave Rock is in fact a fifteen-metre high granite cliff that stretches for one hundred and ten metres. Carbon dating has recorded it as being 2700 million years old, amongst the oldest rocks in Australia. Many people adopt a surfing pose for photographs on the Wave, and I was no different. However, you don't see many surfers wearing trousers and a fleece jacket, but it was a cold morning. The Wave's unusual colours are a result of water from the springs running down the rock and dissolving minerals.

To the east of Hyden there is a fence; not just any old fence, but the State Barrier Fence, previously known as the Rabbit Proof Fence. Spanning a distance of 1.827km (1135 miles), it was constructed between 1901 and 1907, and is located between Starvation Bay, west of Esperance on the south coast, and Ninety Mile Beach, east of Port Hedland. The fence's original aim was to hold back the hordes of invading rabbits that were spreading across Australia from their place of introduction near Geelong, Victoria. A bigger threat to Australian agriculture currently would appear to be herds of hungry emus that are crossing state boundaries in search of food, due to drought conditions in NSW and Victoria.

I left Hyden and followed the signs for Perth, passing through Kondinin, Corrigin and then Brockton before I reached my overnight destination of York. A classified town under the National Trust, York is like an early 1900s English town, with its beautiful old buildings, red telephone boxes and, of course, the River Avon which flows through it.

One of the finest buildings is the old town hall, which now houses the tourist office. I was given excellent advice here and made my way to the Castle Hotel to check availability for the night. This hotel claims to be the oldest inland hotel in W.A. and dates back to coaching days. It is a very photogenic building, as befits its age, but modern motel style rooms have been added, and a drive-through bottle shop gives it a seal of Australianism.

I took a large single room in the main hotel above the main bar area. My hosts advised me that they had a big event on in the bar that evening and hoped I wouldn't be disturbed by any noise. I sleep pretty soundly, and with my snoring affliction, it could be the bar regulars who have to put up with the noise!

It was a beautifully warm afternoon and I went for a short stroll along the main street. York is the oldest inland town in W.A., having been settled in 1831.Fine buildings abound, the old police station, gaol and the settlers' house being excellent examples. There were the usual bistros and small curio shops and, more unusually, a veteran car museum.

Back at the Castle Hotel, I had showered and rested a while before making my way down to the restaurant for dinner. The bar was already quite full with an excited crowd, waiting for that evening's live event. Apparently, there was a special guest appearance by a panelist from the popular TV programme 'The Footy Show'. This show is devoted to 'Australian Rules Football' and is a big rating programme. Being a Friday evening, the bar television was broadcasting a live AFL (Australian Football League) game, and was being watched avidly. Much cheering and other associated banter was in evidence, and the in-house tote was doing a roaring trade (the 'tote' allows gamblers to place bets on most sporting fixtures, and would be a bookmaker in the UK). Not much different to us sad souls, who gather in pubs in the UK to watch our highly paid prima donnas kick a ball around for ninety minutes or so.

I found a table in the dining room, which was fairly well patronised, and perused the menu. I gathered by the way the waitresses were fawning over two chaps at an adjacent table, and how one had a mobile phone almost permanently attached to his ear, that they were the aforementioned 'special guests'. I was completely under-whelmed at being in the presence of such famous people. Each to their own, though, and after a delicious pepper steak with mushroom sauce (the celebrity ordered the same meal, so he did have some taste!), I went for a short stroll to let my food settle.

I had a half-empty (or half-full) bottle of Western Australian Cabernet Sauvignon, and retired to my room where, after fiddling with the TV tuner, I was able to watch Star Wars Episode V. The noise from the bar area was minimal, although the revellers making their way home much later were fairly high-spirited, outside in the main street.

As the sun rose, I wandered along the street to one of the small bistros for breakfast. Sitting on the pavement (well, not literally!) outside in the bright sunshine, all was well with the world. I was opposite the York Veteran Car Museum and decided to visit it. The museum did indeed house a wonderful collection of vintage, classic and racing cars, and it was explained that many of these get an outing during the annual 'Flying 50s' Vintage and Veteran car race that takes place every August, and also at 'Rally Australia' in November. Perhaps the most famous vehicle in the museum was the Saudi Williams Formula One racing car driven by former World Champion, and Australian, Alan Jones. I wandered around, and before I had realised it, two hours had elapsed.

It was time to take my leave of the lovely town of York and head for my next destination at Cervantes, two hundred and fifty-seven kilometres north of Perth. Here in the Nambung National Park, amid the flat sandy desert, is found another of Australia's natural wonders, 'The Pinnacles'. The journey from York had been made in gloriously sunny and warm conditions for the vast majority of the way, but as I neared Cervantes, it had clouded over. Minutes after checking into my motel room, the heavens opened and a fierce thunderstorm struck. It wasn't a short deluge, so any thoughts of exploring Cervantes and its small port were abandoned in favour of fiddling with the TV tuner, to try and get a reasonable picture on the SBS channel in readiness for the live UK Premier League football match being shown later that evening..

The following morning was overcast and somewhat cooler as I drove the eighteen kilometres or so into the Nambung National Park, to the entrance to the Pinnacles desert. The Pinnacles are actually thousands of limestone pillars, some as high as four metres. There is a one-way loop track that leads through the desert with a purpose-built viewing lookout. There are small clusters of pillars, large clusters, and solitary pillars guarding their own piece of desert like a sentry on duty. They vary from a regular cone shape to bizarre abstract formations. I found it quite amusing, trying to imagine what certain ones or groups reminded me of. I visualised a church, Darth Vader (of Star Wars fame), and a mother and child amongst others. The sun shone brightly and cast a different light in which to view these strange but mesmerising objects, growing in such a desolate place.

So, onwards to Perth, and it had been my intention to find a reasonably-priced motel on the outskirts of the city, but either I missed them, or there were not any on my approach route. I drove through the centre of Perth, which was crowded with Sunday visitors, and, finding nowhere to park, continued out of the city and picked up the Stirling highway towards Fremantle. I ended up booking into a rather elegant hotel that was by far the most expensive of my entire trip to date. That evening, as

I luxuriated in my junior suite (all they had left) and read the local paper, I noticed a good deal on accommodation at the Coogee Holiday Park. The next morning, I called in there and negotiated a few days in a self-contained static caravan. This would allow me to sightsee in both Perth and Fremantle and be close at hand to visit my relatives.

Do you remember me mentioning that I had applied by post for an Indian visa? Well it is now the 26th August and I was due to leave Australia for Singapore on the 30th. I tried in vain to get through to the Indian High Commission, but did not succeed until the following day. They were able to confirm that my passport was at their offices and would be processed and dispatched that day. Needless to say, the passport did not arrive the next day, and I began to consider putting my flight to Singapore back a few days, or weeks, or months!

Worth A Fortune.

Perth is a lovely city situated on the Swan River and has a feeling of openness and space, with lots of green parkland. It is claimed to be the sunniest state capital in Australia and is the most isolated capital city in the world. Founded in 1829 as the Swan River Settlement, it was not until convict labour was brought in around 1850 that the city's growth accelerated and many of its fine buildings, such as Government House and Perth Town Hall, were built, using convict labour. The one single factor that led to a spectacular interest in Perth was the discovery of gold in the 1890s, which resulted in a big population increase.

As with many Australian cities, Perth has a free bus service that will take you around the city. Called the CAT (City Area Transit), there are two routes, which both commence from the railway station on Wellington Street. Looking at the routes over a coffee, I was able to plan a route that would take me to the sites I particularly wanted to see. Being sports mad, I went first to the WACA

(Western Australia Cricket Association), Perth's famous cricket test stadium.

Unfortunately, guided tours had been suspended whilst building work was ongoing, in preparation for that winter's England Ashes tour. I was, however, able to visit the small museum, which was beautifully kept and contained some wonderful exhibitions and photographs of the greats of the game. I was talking to the museum curator and his wife and discovered that he came originally from Romford, Essex. After chatting about the forthcoming Ashes series, he handed me a hard hat, and asked me to follow him. I was now on an unofficial tour of the member's area of the WACA. In the member's lounge, they have a unique collection of stumps for every test match ever played at the WACA. These stumps have been cut in half and each of the players in the respective teams has signed them. I was privileged to see this collection, and thanked my hosts profusely before catching the CAT and heading for my next scheduled stop, the Perth Mint.

For those of you not au fait with the game of cricket, I would advise that there is a long history of matches between England and Australia. The first took place in March 1887 in Melbourne, and Australia was victorious by forty-five runs. Five years later in 1882 the Australians were again victorious, but on English soil. This prompted the Sporting Times newspaper to carry a mock obituary for English cricket, which read as follows: -

IN AFFECTIONATE REMEMBRANCE

Of

ENGLISH CRICKET

Which died at the Oval on the 29th August 1882.

Deeply lamented by a large circle of sorrowing friends and acquaintances.

R.I.P.

N.B. The body will be cremated and the ashes taken to Australia.

In the following year, the English cricket team regained their pride by defeating the Australians on their soil. Whilst playing in Melbourne, the English party was staying at Rupertwood, the country home in Sunbury of William Clarke. It was here, when playing a game against a local team on the Clarke estate, that the Ashes became reality in the physical sense. There is some doubt as to whether the actual Ashes were the remains of the ball used in that game or the bails (the little pieces of wood that sit upon the three wickets). The Ashes were placed in a small inscribed urn, presented to the English captain and returned to England. To this day the Ashes reside in the Memorial Gallery at the Lord's cricket ground in London.

Anyway, back to my tour of the Perth Mint. Opened in June 1899, as a branch of Britain's Royal Mint, the Perth Mint continued under British control until 1970, when it moved to the control of the Government of the state of Western Australia. Originally, the Mint was used to refine gold being produced by Western Australia's gold fields, and to turn it into British sovereigns and half-sovereigns. In April 1987, the Perth Mint commenced Australia's precious metal coin programme. Up to the end of June 1996, the Mint's coins had consumed more than one hundred and eleven tonnes of gold, two hundred tonnes of silver and fifteen tonnes of platinum. In December 1996, the Perth Mint was appointed, together with the Royal Australian Mint, to produce the commemorative coins for the Sydney 2000 Olympic Games.

The Perth Mint has very high security and visitors can see work in progress only through bullet and bombproof glass. I made my way to the Melting House, where a gold pour demonstration was to take place. I had witnessed a gold pour once before at Gold Reef City, Johannesburg, South Africa and that occasion could be filmed quite openly. Afterwards you could actually hold the gold ingot, albeit under the close control of two massive, armed guards. At this Melting House, photography of any kind was strictly prohibited.

With the gold pour over, I went to the original storage vault, where they have a range of natural nuggets. They also have a four hundred ounce gold bar worth in excess of $200,000, and you have the opportunity to try and pick it up. The difficult part is that it is contained within a case and there is only enough room to place your hand and wrist into the aperture. Still, at least I had a fortune within my grasp for a few short moments.

One of the advantages of being a large lad is that when you hear the phrase *'worth their weight in gold'* you know you are onto a good thing. My weight in gold is a cool $2,723,787 or approximately £990,468, a fact that I had inscribed on a souvenir medallion. I always knew I was a little treasure, but I hope I don't have to be buried to realise it!

Perth being a fairly compact city, it is easy to walk around the centre, with the main shopping areas being found along the Hay Street and Murray Street malls and the arcades that run between them.

Back at my caravan on Coogee Beach, I checked with my cousin Bill, whose address I had used for the return of my passport. Still nothing, so I decided to put my flight to Singapore back. My Australian visa was due to expire on the 15th of September, so I rearranged my flight for that date. In the meantime, I resolved to research Malaysia, Thailand and India and to see a bit more of Western Australia. I checked out some prices for travelling to Broome in the north of the state, and decided that a week there would be an excellent idea. I would be able to see some fantastic scenery, as well as to relax in some warm sunshine and acclimatise to the temperatures that I would find in Asia.

I wanted to meet my relatives before leaving Australia, and I was invited to my Cousin Pam's house, where a family get-together was to take place for Father's Day. We had an excellent afternoon, and I was able to meet the majority of the family members and, importantly, take some video footage for the folks back home to view.

Broome-Time.

My flight to Broome was scheduled to depart at 10.30am from Perth's domestic terminal and everything was going well, until a combination of poor road signs (come on Australia, you can do better than this!), my own arrogance for not bothering to use a map, and severe stomach cramps, caused me to miss my flight. That awful feeling when you know you need a toilet stop urgently, and you cannot find one, hit me as I sat in a long tailback of traffic. How could I get out of this traffic and find my salvation? As the traffic started moving, I annoyed countless drivers by cutting in and out of the lanes, in a desperate attempt to find a junction where I could turn off. I found one eventually and immediately sought a McDonalds, Burger King or similar which would have toilet facilities. After ten minutes of frantic driving through industrial and housing estates I happened upon a garage. As if sensing my predicament (quick, short steps with buttocks firmly clenched), the cashier pointed to the rear of the shop area. For a brief moment, all I could see was a large trash bin (well, in an emergency...) but there behind the bin was a customer toilet. Relieved (no pun intended), I then tried to orientate myself, and find the route for the airport again.

It was now 9.30am and I should have been checking in, ideally, yet there I was, somewhere in greater Perth, I guess. I eventually got back onto the right road, but into the wrong lane. This one was taking me to the International Airport rather than the Domestic one that I needed. Until I got to the airport junction, there was nowhere to turn around, so by the time I did pull into the Domestic Airport, it was 10.07am. I still had to deposit the car keys at the car park kiosk that is on the far side of the terminal, and realising that the flight would have closed, I didn't bother to rush (in my current state this was probably a good idea!). I presented myself at the Qantas Ticket Desk and explained my late arrival. Technically, the flight was non-changeable or refundable, but the ticket agent looked at his computer and advised me that he could get me on a flight at 5.10pm that afternoon. I had no option other than to accept, and checked-in my main bag there and then, so as not to be unnecessarily encumbered.

Perth's Domestic Airport has no café facilities until you go airside, so that is where I had to go. A spattering of the usual shops that you find at airports is found here, including a bookshop and a shop selling tourist tat. A small unit was selling W.A. wine and sun block products - an interesting combination (perhaps the idea is to slap on the sun block, and then, when you fall into a stupor drinking the wine, you don't get sunburn).

I found a comfortable seat in a quiet area and settled down to wait. The time passed fairly quickly and I was soon boarding the flight for Broome. The flight takes about three hours and covers some 2, 921 km (1,815 mi) of W.A. On arrival in Broome, you could instantly feel the warmer, humid air and I had broken into a sweat by the time I had carried my backpack from the luggage carousel to the courtesy bus that would take me to the Broometime Lodge, my budget accommodation in Broome.

I was greeted by the manageress, Ronnie, and was immediately struck by the atmosphere of 'bonhomie'. I thought, I'm going to enjoy my stay at Broometime. I turned on the air-conditioning in my room and took advantage of the complimentary tea/coffee and milk to make a welcome drink. I joined some of my fellow guests in the breezeway (covered patio area) and a quick look around showed me a TV and games lounge, a large and well-appointed kitchen/dining room and a swimming pool and patio area.

I slept very well in my nice cool room, and felt somewhat better than I had the previous day. This was just as well, as I had pre-booked a two-day tour visiting the Windjana and Geiki Gorges. I was picked up from Broometime at 7.00am and we picked up a further eight passengers from various locations in and around Broome.

The air-conditioned 4WD coach was extremely comfortable, and our driver/guide Paul gave us plenty of information relating to the tour and to the areas we would be passing through. The journey to Windjana Gorge would take about four and a half hours, and we had a scheduled stop at a famous landmark near to the township of Derby, called the Boab Prison Tree. The boab is a deciduous tree found on the sandy plains between Broome and Derby.

The Prison boab has a girth of fourteen metres, a hollow trunk and is said to be over a thousand years old. Fugitives were supposedly locked up in the tree as they were being transported to nearby Derby gaol. These prisoners had more often than not been walked to the Prison Tree from various parts of the Kimberley, one of Australia's last great frontiers.

The whole area of north W.A. is a rugged, and still little travelled area of outstanding natural beauty and magnificent scenery. Needless to say, the Prison Boab Tree is a recognised Aboriginal Heritage Site and visitors are asked not to enter its interior or climb upon it. Next to the Prison Tree is another remnant of the area's history, namely Myall's Bore and cattle trough. The cattle in these remote areas seem to wander completely free, unlike on the huge ranches found in North America. However, they do belong to someone, and instead of a ranch, the area is known as a 'station'.

These stations can stretch for thousands of kilometres and it was imperative that there were places where the cattle could be watered. As with much of the Australian outback/desert, there are underground rivers and water sources here, and a certain Alfred Duckworth Myall (I just had to tell you his middle name) sank the first bore here in the early 1890s. This original well was enlarged and dug deeper in 1910, and a huge concrete trough, measuring one hundred and twenty metres, was constructed and was able to handle five hundred bullocks at any one time (I know what you're thinking... that's a lot of bullocks? Well, it's not, it's the truth, and the guidebook says so!).

After tea and fruit cake provided by Paul, we headed on to Windjana Gorge. This gorge was formed by the Lennard River that gushes through it during the wet season of October to May. The whole area was once part of a western coral 'barrier reef' in the Devonian era 350 million years ago. The walls of the gorge rise some ninety metres above the river, and at this time of year, there are just relatively small pools. Within and around these pools, we were able to see many 'freshies' (freshwater crocodiles). Despite the intense heat of the sun, the gorge provided plenty of cool, welcoming shade. The limestone walls have been worn into incredible shapes by the river in flood, and by the ravages of wind and rain.

We moved on, after a delicious lunch again prepared by Paul, to another beautiful National Park called Tunnel Creek. This is reached by travelling up the infamous Gibb River Road. Known as the 'back road', at 667 km (414 mi) in length, it is more direct by several hundred kilometres than taking the Fitzroy Crossing to Halls Creek when travelling between Derby and Kununurta. The big drawback is that the road is almost all dirt and, during the wet, is impassable.

There is very little traffic and it is therefore not recommended for hitchhikers. One of the biggest hazards for drivers in the Kimberley is that the cattle tend to be light coloured, and wander onto the roads at will, taking the unwary driver by surprise, especially if he hasn't seen another vehicle for hours.

I digress as usual. Anyway, back to Tunnel Creek. This is a 750 mt long passage that has been cut through the Napier Range. We were going to walk (and wade) all the way along its length. It is advisable to wear swimming shorts, and you need a pair of shoes of some description to avoid cuts from sharp rocks and stones. I wore a pair of sandals, and whilst these were satisfactory, silt and small pebbles lodged themselves inside and caused a certain amount of discomfort.

Paul led the way and the water was cool and soothing after the hot sun outside. By torchlight, you could see flood debris still lodged in the cave from when the chambers were completely flooded during the wet season. There are several Aboriginal wall paintings and several different exits from the tunnel along its length. It was here, and at Windjana that the legendary exploits of the outlaw and Aboriginal tracker Jandamarra, took place (more on this later).

Our overnight accommodation was at the Fitzroy Crossing Lodge in safari cabins with en-suite facilities and air-conditioning. This lodge is owned by the local Aborigines, and brings much needed revenue for the small township of Fitzroy Crossing. These people began their community here after been thrown off the rich pastoral land around the crossing. This crossing was the only place to ford the Fitzroy River and the township is situated just out of reach of the floodwaters. That evening we enjoyed a few tinnies, and a BBQ meal of gargantuan proportions. Sitting around in the warm night air, we got to know one another a little better, as we discussed our travels.

I was amused by a notice in the cabin telling the occupier about one of the local inhabitants, namely, the Green Frog. These frogs are numerous and sometimes appear in your toilet basin (here's looking at you, Froggy!). I didn't give it another thought, until one of our female travellers came screaming from her cabin, shouting about a monster in her loo. All I could think of was to pity any poor frog that decided to visit my toilet the next morning!

A cup of tea and a couple of slices of toast and honey, and I was ready to depart the Fitzroy Crossing Lodge by 7am the following morning. Today we were headed for the Geiki Gorge about eighteen kilometres from the Fitzroy Crossing. At Geiki we were to have a guided river cruise with a young Aborigine boy called Rene, and he started immediately with some jokes at our expense.

As we proceeded along the Fitzroy River, the gorge rose up alongside us, and the discolouration showed how high the water actually reaches when in flood. In flood the Fitzroy River is second only to the Amazon in the area it covers, which is something to speculate about. Rene pointed out various outcrops that resembled either animals, or in one memorable case, the former United States President, Richard Nixon. Rene brought our vessel to a halt alongside a small jetty, and told us it was time for some exercise.

Although it was only 8.45am, the temperature had risen dramatically, and Rene ensured that we all had some water with us. We were going to climb up the rock face via an uneven and quite steep track, from where Rene had promised us a stupendous view across the gorge. This climb proved to be not too strenuous and soon we were all taking in that wonderful view. This lookout is known as Bunburra, and Rene showed us how the Aborigines use the plants, bushes and trees to survive in such an inhospitable environment.

I found one of the Aboriginal customs rather interesting, which is the use of punishment spears. If a person had perpetrated a major crime, then he had the option of 'trial by spear'. The alleged guilty person would stand still while three of his accusers would throw their spears at him. He was only able to move his upper body to try and avoid the spears and, with luck, he might get away with only a slight wound and walk free (perhaps this is where the term 'three strikes and you're out' originates?).

Once we were at the foot of the escarpment we headed for the shade of a lone tree, where Rene gave us a display of making a campfire without the aid of matches. This was a fascinating and impressive display, and would help to keep you alive in the event of being lost in the outback. We completed our cruise, and marvelled at the sheer enormity of the landscape. It's hard to believe that the sandbank area we were walking on would be completely submerged during the wet season.

The cruise was over, and we were due to have lunch before a leisurely drive back to Broome, arriving at about 5pm. We would have been, if another of the company's vehicles hadn't broken down further into the Kimberley. Our vehicle was needed to rescue its passengers. We were therefore left here at Geiki Gorge with our lunch and plenty of water, to wait until another vehicle on a one-day tour to the gorge arrived to take us to Broome. Fortunately the wait was only a couple of hours, and there was plenty of shade from the scorching sun. On the return journey we stopped at a typical Australian Roadhouse. These pubs/restaurants/garages/inns are the lifeblood of the outback and are frequented by the road trains and travellers alike. We enjoyed a few cold tinnies of Emu Bitter, and the obligatory BBQ feast, before completing our trip to Broome, arriving shortly after midnight.

The next morning, I allowed myself a lie-in and then had a cooling dip in the pool. As part of my two-day tour, I qualified for a free half-day tour of Broome. Malcolm, our relief driver from yesterday, collected me from Broometime and, together with a retired couple from Queensland, this comprised our group. We started off by visiting Streeter's Jetty, the original jetty for the pearling luggers that plied their trade from Broome. This jetty is situated on Dampier Crescent, and named after the first European to visit the area in 1688. It was almost two hundred years later, in 1833, that Broome was recognised as a town, and named after the then-General Governor of W.A., Sir Frederick Napier Broome.

In the waters off Broome, the pearlers found the Pinctada Maxima oyster, and it was harvested for its shell value. The shells, known as Mother of Pearl (MOP), were used mainly to make buttons and jewellery, and in the early twentieth century, 80% of the world's MOP came from Broome. Whilst pearling was a lucrative business, it was often fatal for the many divers who were subject to drowning, shark attack and the bends. Many of these early divers were Japanese, and over nine hundred pearl divers have their final resting place within the Japanese Cemetery on Port Drive. In the 1950s, with the discovery of plastic, the bottom fell out of the MOP industry.

Something I had never realised was that for a pearl to grow in an oyster shell, something has to get into the oyster and irritate it. If the oyster is unable to flush out this irritant then it will coat the offending article in layers of nacre (a form of calcium carbonate) to reduce that irritation. The Japanese had been experimenting with different procedures to introduce an artificial irritant to oysters, and succeeded in producing cream coloured pearls up to ten millimetres in diameter. By introducing this irritant to the Pinctada Maxima oyster, the Australian Cultured Pearl industry began, and currently grosses over $200,000,000 per annum. People from all over the world purchase Broome pearls, but for the time being, not me.

All Good Things Come To An End.

From finding out all about the Broome pearling industry, we visited probably the world's oldest operating outdoor picture garden, the Sun Picture House. Officially opened in 1916, this splendid building also houses various movie memorabilia in a small museum within the foyer. Movies are shown every night and the current offering was the film 'Signs' starring Mel Gibson.

We visited the previously mentioned Japanese Cemetery, and drove on to Town Beach. An ideal picnic and swimming point now, but during World War Two it was the scene of one of the greatest tragedies for Broome and Australia. Civilians being evacuated using Flying Boats were waiting on board the planes for the tide to come in, thereby allowing take-off. A Japanese patrol struck Broome, with orders to attack only military targets. The Flying Boats fitted this description, but they had no idea that the planes were filled with civilian evacuees. Over one hundred people perished in the attack.

Our next stop was Gantheaume Point, situated approximately 8km from Broome. This scruffy-looking cliff area is famous for the dinosaur footprints found here. These historic prints are visible at a very low tide that takes place only about four times a year. To avoid incidences of drowning of historians and tourists alike, casts of the footprints have been placed on the edge of the cliffs. They are life size and very impressive, and I must admit, a little exciting. And so, from dinosaur footprints to camel tracks, and the wonderful Cable Beach. This beach, named as one of the top five beaches in the world, stretches for twenty two kilometres and vehicles are allowed to drive along the wide, flat expanses of sand. One of Cable Beach's claims to fame is to ride along the sands on top of a camel, whilst marvelling at the brilliant sunset over the Indian Ocean.

Yes, you've guessed it, Andy of Arabia and England! I found a sturdy young camel called Marcum to carry me along the beach for an hour. I had once previously mounted a camel (I'll rephrase that – taken a camel ride) in Morocco, and I had been terrified by the bad-tempered nature and unpleasant odour of my camel. By contrast these camels were in superb condition and Marcum certainly had a sweet nature. The view from a camel is great, and once I had fallen in with the rolling rhythm, I was able to relax and take some different video footage. The camel behind me didn't have a rider, and as a consequence, its head was soon nuzzling my left thigh. Now, camels are somewhat prone to slobber, and this one was in a particularly slobbering state. Call me old fashioned, but I think I'll stick to Amber Solar to rub into my legs! The sunset was spectacular and provided yet more footage of sunsets worldwide. I should think I have enough footage to produce a video on sunsets alone.

It was Saturday morning, although here it was 'Broometime' and one day was very much like another. After eating a healthy breakfast of cereal and a banana on the patio by the swimming pool, I decided to walk into the town centre. This took me a leisurely half an hour, and my first stop was the Broome Market. This market only takes place on a Saturday morning and the whole area was packed with people. As well as the usual t-shirt stalls there were also all manner of craft and food stalls. Adding to the feeling of gaiety and fun, were a number of different entertainers. The sun was baking hot, and I enjoyed a deliciously cooling fresh pineapple drink before heading for Chinatown and the historic Johnny Chi Lane, a narrow walkway housing a number of small, specialist shops.

Everything from jewellery to fortune telling is available in Chinatown. A lot of the shops closed down in the afternoon, and most people had taken a siesta. I decided to join them, and returned to Broometime to relax in and around the swimming pool. After dinner, I joined some of my fellow guests in the breezeway for a meaningful chat and a few tinnies. As more tinnies were consumed, so the chat became less meaningful!

The next morning brought more of the same hot sun and clear blue skies. I walked the short distance to the Broome Historical Society Museum, which is located in the old Customs House. This small, cosy museum is fascinating, and completely unlike a conventional museum. I was glad of the air-conditioning, however, as I made my way slowly around the cases and exhibits. First task was reading a number of folders that contained newspaper clippings, articles, and copies of various documents relating to Broome's history. The history of the pearling industry, shell collections, communications history, Aboriginal artifacts and early household furniture and war exhibits are all to be found here. Many of the exhibits are on loan from local residents and as such, the museum fulfills its role as a local history society.

That evening, my last in Broome, I celebrated with Antor, an Irish butcher, now living in London. We walked to Murphy's Bar, situated within the Mecure Inn, where we downed a number of pints (yes, pints) of Kilkenny Irish Ale. At $6.80 per pint (£2.50) this was about the same price as in good old England. To our horror, the bar staff advised us at 9pm that if we wanted another pint we should order it now, as they were closing at 10pm. We couldn't believe it. Not that they were closing at 10pm, but that they wouldn't serve us another drink after 9pm. It wasn't as if they were busy. What a way to conduct business. However, with no nearby alternative, it was back to Broometime for some tinnies in the breezeway.

Earlier, I told you that I would tell you more about the exploits of an Aboriginal tracker called Jandamarra, who became infamous around the Windjana and Geiki Gorge areas. Jandamarra, nicknamed 'Pigeon', was a member of the local Bunuba tribe. He had a job on the Lennard River Station as a stockman, but was offered good money to work as an armed tracker with the local police to capture Aborigines who were spearing sheep.

He became very successful, and a hated figure among his own people. However, having captured members of his own tribe, his loyalty to them got the better of him, and he killed his police colleague, freed the captured tribesmen and escaped into the Napier Ranges, where he led a band of dissident Bunuba people for almost three years. Pigeon's legend was enhanced when, about a month after running from the police, he was seriously wounded in a shootout at Windjana Gorge. He survived, and to the Aborigines, he was immortal, and had special powers.

His raids on the stations became more audacious, and he killed a further four white men, each time disappearing into his hideout at Tunnel Creek. As I saw myself, Tunnel Creek has a number of exits, which Pigeon knew intimately, and this aided his seemingly miraculous escapes from the clutches of the police. Eventually, an Aboriginal tracker from Queensland was brought in to help capture Pigeon, and it was he who used 'magic' to trap and then kill him near his hideout. Pigeon's story and his legend continue to be told to this day.

Once back in Fremantle, the full story of my Indian Visa saga was revealed. I had missed out on one vital part of my Cousin's address and the post office had returned the passport to the Indian Embassy in Sydney. My Cousin sorted it out with them, and sent a new self-addressed envelope for them to return the passport in.

I booked a day trip to Rottnest Island for the following day and then decided to take the catamaran from Fremantle to Perth. This forty-minute journey takes you up the Swan River, arriving in Perth at the Barrack Square

Jetty. A futuristic tower, known as the Swan Bells Tower, dominates the jetty, and houses the original Bells of St. Martin in the Field, London. I can only assume that the bells were given to Perth as some form of gift by London.

I wandered through the pedestrianised Hay Street Mall with its cafes, stylish shops and tourist rip-off joints. Perhaps the nicest, and certainly the most stylish, arcade is the Elizabethan-style London Court. It runs from Hay Street Mall to St. George's Terrace, and at the Hay Street entrance, four knights on horseback joust every fifteen minutes above a replica of Big Ben. Meanwhile, over the St. George's Terrace entrance, St. George and the Dragon do battle above the clock.

I called home, and the news that I had been dreading was given to me. My mother was doing badly, and the doctor had told the family to basically keep her as comfortable as possible. There was no doubt in my mind; I would return home by the first available flight. My odyssey was over for now, but I had some wonderful memories, and had met some lovely people.

Postscript

I arrived home on the 15th of September, 2002. Mother recovered somewhat, and was cared for by the family, until passing away at home in April, 2006. Rest in Peace Mum.